MC Flux

Dirty

THE CONFESSIONS OF A REFORMED DRUG ADDICT AND SOCCER HOOLIGAN WHO MADE IT BIG ON THE DANCE SCENE

MC Flux

Dirty

THE CONFESSIONS OF
A REFORMED DRUG ADDICT
AND SOCCER HOOLIGAN WHO
MADE IT BIG ON THE DANCE SCENE

MEMOIRS

Cirencester

Published by Mereo

Mereo Books

1A The Wool Market Dyer Street Cirencester Gloucestershire GL7 2PR
An imprint of Memoirs Publishing www.mereobooks.com

Dirty: 978-1-86151-355-7

First published in Great Britain in 2015
by Mereo Books, an imprint of Memoirs Publishing

Copyright ©2015

The address for Memoirs Publishing Group Limited can be found at
www.memoirspublishing.com

The Memoirs Publishing Group Ltd Reg. No. 7834348

The Memoirs Publishing Group supports both The Forest Stewardship Council® (FSC®) and the
PEFC® leading international forest-certification organisations. Our books carrying both the
FSC label and the PEFC® and are printed on FSC®-certified paper. FSC® is the only
forest-certification scheme supported by the leading environmental organisations including
Greenpeace. Our paper procurement policy can be found at
www.memoirspublishing.com/environment

Typeset in 10/15pt Franklin
by Wiltshire Associates Publisher Services Ltd. Printed and bound in Great Britain by
Printondemand-Worldwide, Peterborough PE2 6XD

CONTENTS

Foreword

Acknowledgements

What They Say

The Intro

FOREWORD

By Pete Nice

Once upon a time there was a little black boy named Rodney who grabbed a microphone, had fights and had issues with drugs.

The End

Oh sorry, did you want more details? OK!

Now some people may look on and think "Who the fuck wants to read a book about MC Flux?" Well, who indeed? My answer would be, who the fuck wants to read a book about an orphan who couldn't read and write but against all the odds became a multi billionaire, robbing Africa of diamonds and leaving its people to starve? Actually, I would, bad example, OK, who the fuck wants to read about a big-breasted glamour model from the south coast that shagged everyone, including a has-been pop star, to get a TV series? Exactly.

People like a story and I believe we have one to tell, so what makes MC Flux's story any different than the above? Well there isn't much difference, because this story has big tits and shagging in it as well. Many would also argue that I would be wasting my time writing a book and autobiography for Flux due to the nature of the topic this book is based on. Everyone who knows him knows he's hard work, but in my opinion his story had to be told and that's what made me determined to do it.

Now I am no author, not in respect of exceptional literature, so don't expect a Harry Potter turnout (or Beatrix Potter for that matter). However I do know how to talk to people and it is by talking to people that most of the stories came about from most of the conversations I had with Flux and other contributors - by listening and telling it back on paper.

I wanted it to read like we are sitting in a pub telling you the story. Whether it ends up that way we will just have to see. For the most part it is based on real events but also adapted in some cases to protect the innocent, the paranoid and the guilty.

Since our schooldays, more or less, I have known Flux, aka Rodders, aka the Goldfish, or Carl Rodney Thomas to give him his full name or rather, how he is addressed by the Old Bill and by a certain voluptuous female that we know. And I have been with him through many of the stories over the years, from growing up in Croydon as boys, through teenage kicks 'spitting bars' as ragamuffin lyrical dons to acid house parties dancing in fields, from having it all weekend long raving with the crew to cold winter afternoons in Grimsby for football. But as years went on and I got older, I took the secure and mundane career path in communications and the normal lifestyle of girlfriends, then getting married, having kids and being kept under the proverbial thumb. You know how it is, still part of the crew but not heavily involved in all the shenanigans.

Meanwhile he toured the world as an international entertainer, ran with football hooligans, became addicted to heroin and served time at Her Majesty's pleasure. Most people tend to think that just about sums Rodney up, but people tend to forget that underneath all that, he ran a largely successful and popular sound system, organised parties and raves, was one of the original pioneers of a generation of crowd entertainers on the UK dance music scene and also was involved in some heavy incidents that make it a miracle that he is still alive to tell the story.

Think what you want of him and judge him as most people do and will continue to do once they read the book. All I would say is remember this - much as he has been a pain in the arse, he has had a lot of struggles and issues to cope with and he may still continue to make the same mistakes. To me he is one of the most stand up people you could ever meet and if shit was going down, he's definitely someone you would want in your corner. He's also a very funny guy and I'm proud to have him as a friend. It has been great recollecting many of the memories of how we used to be. He'll always be the same old Flux in my eyes, full of ups and downs and dramas, but more than this, he'll always be my brother. This is his story.

Pete Nice

RIP

Roslyn Ellis; Barry Rhodes; Tracey Meade; Murray Beetson, Dreamscape;
Mensa, Interdance; Mickey Lynas, Amnesia House;
Garfield 'Beaver' Samuels; Garry Allen; DJ Kemistry; MC Charlie Brown;
Sean MC Sparks; DJ HMS; Stevie Hyper D; Peter 'La Cosa Nostra' Oduwole;
Paul Wright; Robbie Kennett.

ACKNOWLEDGEMENTS

Love to my mum and dad, Christine and Cecil Thomas. My sisters and brother Alison, Sonia and Howard. My nieces and nephews April, Summer, Andre, Tayla, Dayne and my sister in law Geneve Thomas.

Massive thanks to the boys and our brothers, Face and Killa. All the Inta Natty Crew - DJ Grooverider and Fabio also Paul 'Juicy' Johnson, Danny B and DJ Bailey. The Under 5s - Nifty, Dee, Inch high, Tony Roots, Wayne, Mendez, Jay. All the Palace main boys Nifty 50, Dirty 30 and the Yoof, Also thanks to Nikki Thorpe, Amanda Carr and Zoe Allaway

Shouts also to Goldie @Metalheadz, MC Cool & Deadly, Mickey Finn, Jumping Jack Frost, Brian Gee, Andy C @Ram Records and Darren Jay. MC Fats, GQ, MC Det. The 1st Lady-DJ Storm, Colin Dale, Danny Bukem, Cleveland Watkiss, DJ Friction, Caroline Kakoo and Sonia @Unique Artist, Michael Eastwood @Mastermind PR, Alex MC Energy @Fantasia, Sarah Sandy @Groove Connection, Rob Playford @Movin Shadow, big up Sean and Simon 2 Bad Mice. Funky @Innovation, Jay @AWOL and World Dance, Mick and Phil @Desire, actor and film director Terry (Turbo) Stone @One nation, Rolling with the Nines and Gateway Films for the experience of working for or alongside you all, it's been a pleasure. Also Julie Richards and Chris and Laura Deller, and editor Chris Newton of Memoirs Publishing.

Thanks to William Barnet @HMP Channings Wood for saving my life. To all the girls and boys from the manor - Croydon, South Norwood & Thornton Heath, and anyone else who I have missed out. Thank you to everyone who has either worked with me, been around me, watched my back or shared a joke with me along the way.

MC Flux

Very special thanks to Frazer, Georgia Verapen, Daniel Lehane, Sherry Morrison, Darren Andrews, Heidi Leybourne, Gary Pitcher, Nikki Stoy, Danny Harman, Martin Brobbey, Natalie Ellis, Robbie Bloomfield, Danny Rhodes, Susie Akehurst, Andy Powell, Nadine King, Cass Pennant. The cheeky Chelsea chap and author of From Ronnie's to Ravers - Stuart Deabill. Also Nicole Hajimichael from Hurricane Films for all the advice, contribution and feedback throughout the process no matter how little - it all counts, you have my upmost respect.

Love to my wife Ashley and our beautiful babies Millie and Elliot. To my mum Ednie and my sisters Wendy and Paulette. My niece and nephew Tianna and Ricardo. Also Kelly, Calan, Sandy, Carol, Roland, Kimmy and all the family.

Pete Nice

WHAT THEY SAY

I first met MC Flux at one of our One Nation events and being part of the 'Inta-Inta' crew, we always had loads of banter and lots of fun and Fluxy baby (as I used to call him) became a One Nation resident pretty soon after. Not many nights went by without him appearing on our legendary line ups. I've not seen him since we sold One Nation in 2003 but I hear he is still rabbiting on about dancing to the music and feeling the bassline and all the girlies in the place winding up their waists etc. Well done with your book Flux, may it sell many copies!

Terry Stone, actor and director, Bonded by Blood, Gateway Films

Have very fond memories of the time when MC Flux was my personal MC in the 90s at what I'd class as the high point of my career so far. It was a very busy time, so we were up and down the countries at the weekend sometimes doing 2-3 clubs a night. Carl was always the consummate professional who really knew how to work a crowd and would always be coming up with these catchy phrases, "Colin Dale, he's not stale, he'll put your body into a spell". As well as working together we were close friends and I hold Carl in high esteem. Luckily after not seeing him for a while we've manage to hook up again lately. Fantastic to see he's still as busy as ever and still coming up with those wonderful vocal hooks. One of the best MC's in the UK, period.

DJ Colin Dale, Abstrakt Dance/Wildlife AM

Flux is one of the main characters on the scene from way back in the day and I've known him for 30-odd years, not just as an MC but as a friend as well. I would always bump into him and his boys who I have known since the early 80s. As time went on there are always people who you meet that leave a big impression on you, and Flux is definitely one of those people.

Career wise, like many participants who were getting involved in the beginning, before it turned from an underground movement into this massive UK dance music industry we have today, working with Flux in the early days I wasn't too keen on MCs over my set to begin with and was ready to haul him off but like MC Cool & Deadly, he showed the raw passion and professionalism. He knew when to vibe the crowd and when to shut the fuck up. And like many of us who were negotiating our way through, he loved his work and you could feel the vibe from him through his response on the mic.

Like me Flux is from the tough streets of South London, full of traps and wrong turns, so I understand how difficult life can get. I know he's had his troubles and has overcome them. What more can I say, he's a great MC, one of the most pioneering to grace the mic on the jungle and drum and bass movement. I have been rolling with him for years, a great friend who is always by my side.

DJ Grooverider, The Godfather/Prototype records

My lasting memory of Flux is Brighton Centre in the mid-90s. All the lads were there, and I was getting pestered by some drunk who started to get abusive. I knew Carl but not enough to expect him to have my back - he was the first to react to the ensuing drama. I was on the deck, but this fool was persisting in causing a scene, Flux walks over and calmly says "Is there a problem?" in that passive aggressive way the police are masters of. "Fuck off" was the reply. Carl's "terrace" instinct kicked in. What followed was similar to a bar room brawl you see in old westerns. Carl drew the battle lines. Coming from the streets that meant so much, I feel indebted to him for life. He is a warrior, a true friend that will stand by you when the waters get rocky. That in itself is the biggest compliment a man can make.

DJ Fabio Creative Source/Swerve

When all the great names are mentioned in D&B, Flux is right up there with the best of them, originator and pioneer of the mic when D&B 1st broke out.

DJ LTJ Bukem Good Looking Records

Flux: A man who's been a huge inspiration to me over the years. Not just for being one of the leading MCs in Jungle/Drum & Bass music but for actually taking the time out to show an interest in my career in my early days and encourage me to keep DJing. Haven't forgotten you picking up the mic and jumping on my set more than once back then mate!

DJ Friction Radio 1/Radio 1 extra

MC Flux is one of the innovators of the rave culture MCs. I've always found him to be sincere and on the cutting edge of the business. I spent some time in Belfast with him during the times of political unrest and he brought joy and pleasure to a community that needed to dance.

DJ Jumping Jack Frost V Recordings/Team Frost

Legend in the game and very interesting character one of the originals, who compliments a DJs set properly.

MC Det Kool FM/Jungle Fever

Kemistry and I met Flux many years ago via Grooverider, who was part of the Inta Crew that consisted of Pete Nice, Killa, Face, Paul, Inch High, Bailey, Danny B and Flux. They were such a lovely group of guy's who came from South London. I have to say he was the charmer of the Crew and as an MC he knew how to chat. We sealed a close bond with the crew DJ'ing at a night they were running called Club Extreme in Croydon and of course Flux was on the mic.

Flux had a unique style on the mic and a fantastic voice that had some bass to it. Flux became part of Goldie's Metalheadz family working all over the UK and Europe, Kemistry and I worked alongside him frequently especially for an organisation called Hard:Edged in Berlin and he also worked alongside us for Radio 1's One in the Jungle. He was the last MC to record with us for our K7 album, " live from the living room" at Kemistry's flat before she passed away. His personality was infectious, his time keeping a little bit dodgy ha ha but on the whole a great performer.

DJ Storm The 1st Lady Metalheadz

I've had MC Flux on my set a few times over the years and he's good at it. As a person he's a nice guy, ain't got nothing dodgy to say about him.

DJ Kenny Ken

I see MC Flux as a pioneer in this music, been there from day one as well as doing events he got his own style which stands him out from the rest. Legend. He's from the Skool of hard knocks.

DJ Brockie

MC Flux... Wicked mc, been a good friend for a number of years.. from the Inta Natty Squad. Been Canada and a lot of places with this man and he always delivers big man up in this...

MC Fearless

True veteran on the scene, I first heard him working with the Moving shadow crew back in the 90's, he's an entertainer with his own flavor, his own original sound that's what this game is about finding your own individual thing and Flux has got it. Big respect.

Cleveland Watkiss Jazz Vocalist

THE INTRO

Who knew life would ever turn out like this? December 4th 2008 and tomorrow some cunting judge is going to give me more bird than I would get if I'd fiddled a 12-year-old's bum hole. My solicitor was already confident it would be custodial, since the guilty verdict and an extra slap on the wrist added for drawing this saga out, 9 Crystal Palace Hooligans already convicted for violent disorder, with the sentences ranging from 6-48 months, they went guilty 9 months ago and have already learned their fate. The panic at this moment is relentless and the cramps that are about to double me up are getting me anxious. I peer out of my curtains cursing, "Iz where dis bloodclaart bwoy deh king?"

The cunt, I called him an hour ago and now finally after 67 and a half minutes he turns up. I fling him the 30 pounds and fuck him off back out the door and have the brew cooked up in what seems like seconds and appreciate the relief. My hunger for whatever in life I was searching for has finally caught up with me. In 24hrs time I'll be looking at a 6ft by 8ft cell. Fuck my life, heroin helps me forget. I can't really explain the buzz or feeling I get on heroin but imagine falling asleep after 4 days of insomnia and then waking up to a beautiful woman, massaging you and then sucking your cock, then gets you so aroused when she eases her wet juicy crotch up and down your shaft until the force of the ejaculation twists and curl your toes 90 degrees. You then switch on the 62 inch TV set, just as Dougie Freedman scores the last minute winner and Palace wins the Champions League.

Well this feels fuck all like that. There is still a somewhat elated feeling, I have a respite now from the constant panic of my pending incarceration, carried on my shoulders during and since the trial and pretty much ever since the day they nicked me, just when I was about to tuck into a bit of jerk chicken early one Monday morning back in April. I had done well considering, having received all the calls on my mobile following raids on Palace hooligans as the Sky sports cameras followed CPFC football intelligence and British Transport Police on dawn raids across various addresses in South East London, Kent and Sussex.

I had laid low (mainly due to circumstance) and avoided capture since then, which was almost for 6 months. At an England v Croatia game at Wembley, one of the Palace Youth had warned me that I was definitely on the list of suspects. I guess the BTP had the wrong address and took them a while, for them to do their homework and surveillance me coming out of a drum and bass do I was working at, Herbal in Shoreditch. Following me through the night, they patiently waited, then made their move, until I was handcuffed in front of hungry revellers inside the Brixton Jamaican jerk chicken shop. It was weird because as they entered the shop I knew they were Old Bill, but thought it was unusual - they didn't look the type to come in for a plate of chicken with rice and peas. It was soon clear that the only thing that clucked that they wanted was me.

Fuck my life, fuck my life, my mind wanders away from jerk chicken and handcuffs as I catch a glimpse at the eyes drooping, head nodding, dishevelled, sorry looking, heroin-induced look of a broken man staring right back at me. I'm right down in the pits, even the barrel has been totally scraped clean and only the court room judge has the answer for what the future holds for Carl Rodney Thomas, the heroin addict. I thought it was only in films when you watch the end at the beginning because I literally started thinking back to times when things were a lot less fucked up.

CHAPTER 1

DRESSERS

Wet looks and Paisley shirts, gold rope chains, belchers and Janet Street Porter bins (glasses). 'The freaks come out at night, the freaks come out at night' (Whodini 1984). The sounds of a soulful 1984 were belting around Norwood Halls and the crowd and a makeup of us lot and other clans were sliding two foot (cutting a rug) on the dance floor. Looking back at us, we thought we were the bollocks, with our wet looks, suede and leather patchwork tops and Lois cords. Many of us 15-17 year olds had adopted the terrace look and tweaked it.

Sitting on a grease-filled Jheri curl activator barnet, courtesy of Jenny Cooper's hair salon for fuck sake, depending on your taste, was a pair of bins, Specsaver designer spectacles with the clear lenses because most of the time these were chored from the shop display. Armani or Yves Saint Lauren ones still had the designer display sticker visible on the lens, while some others would just don specs with mad colours, like bright red or yellow, that wouldn't have been misplaced on Janet Street Porter's or Christopher Biggins' boat race.

Girls who were looking for it were looking on, girls we would have met after weeks spent infiltrating youth clubs and parties in East Grinstead, Warlingham, Coulsdon and as far out as Westerham, when we were out on the pussy hunt. And now they came to us. They were coming on the bus from their Surrey suburbs to nab themselves a ghetto youth. That was the standard urban protocol and it must have been a wonder how some of the ugliest dudes would be strutting through Croydon town centre with the fittest sorts on their arms. Considering that it must have been all about the chat and the way we were all carrying ourselves, believe me, we were full of it but I bet their parents would not have been happy.

Streatham lads wore the standard Burberry scarves and matching jackets. Croydon faces dressed in Aquascutum or double-breasted jackets, Gabicci or Pringle jumpers and bleached Lois Jeans, this being a time when the clobber we wore and sought after was to get that refined London casual look. It was imperative that your wardrobe consisted of Pringle, Fila, Ellesse, Armani, Lacoste, Tacchini, Kappa, L'Alpina and Best Company and the even more sought-after desired footwear, Nike Wimbledons, Adidas Gazelles, Forest Hills, Trim Trabbs and the holy grail, Diadora Borg elites.

Much footwear was acquired from the Olympus sportswear store, which surprisingly used to have both left and right foot on display. This was irresistible for many a light-fingered youth at the time, who used this strategy to acquire all the labels that had sprung up on the football terraces.

Not everyone I knew had pledged allegiance to any of the football teams we supported during our boyhood days. Days were spent watching the big match on ITV, where back at school, everyone talked about Liverpool and Nottingham Forest with stars like Kevin Keegan, John Toshack, Woodcock and Francis, with black lads like myself lording up Crystal Palace flying winger Vince Hilaire and West Bromwich Albion's Cyril Regis and Laurie Cunningham.

Our local team, Crystal Palace, was the easiest to get to and bunk into. It was not much of a surprise that many Croydon boys would have gone to Palace to get their dose of live Football. As they grew older, they would start to attend their supported team home grounds, which surprisingly was Chelsea for many of the local lads I knew. I say surprisingly, when it was no real surprise because Croydon and surrounding areas like Mitcham, Sutton, Wallington, Cheam and other similar areas represented a strong Chelsea following over the years but it was also a time most lads represented for the manor. South Croydon, West Croydon, Thornton Heath, Norwood and Penge, with the exception of the Whitehorse Estate which crossed Thornton Heath and West Croydon borders who were classified as 'Whitehorse boys'. It was faces from there who I knew were heavily rumoured to be involved with football firms in 1984 and it was a breeding ground for game lads who also looked the part. Many attended the Saturday catwalk to get that insatiable buzz for violent young casuals in days when you couldn't avoid the violence.

It was not uncommon to hear about them travelling with either Arsenal, Palace or Spurs and even Leyton Orient all dressed up for a style war, landing on unknown territories to let anyone who wanted it known that they were representing and looking the bollocks, typified by the representation by some of our local casuals at the Luton v Millwall riot in 1985.

Crystal Palace is unknown as a centre of football hooliganism, if you have read most books over the years (I will touch on this later). But some games would often bring a mixture of lads together. We had main lads off the Whitehorse Estate that were involved with Tottenham and Chelsea mobs who were regulars at Palace and classed as Palace top boys. Over the years, you have had teams spouting off about Palace never showing anything. Which is unbelievable in my eyes and just proves the point that too many keyboard warriors know fuck all, because whenever there was a chance of mass public disorder, pubs like the Goat House, the Jolly Sailor, Wilton Arms, the Whitehorse and the Gloucester would be filled to the rafters with lads.

Some of us never went to Chelsea knowing their National Front links but we did hear of lads we knew who were 'fronted up' over there when they first attended but were soon able to make their mark and prove they were good heads. As it was back then, as young lads you had to grow up quickly in the world of the 80s Casual. It was no good

3

looking pretty if you were not prepared to get your threads dirty, but you could also understand the conflict of interest when you had forked out for or stole up to 80 quids' worth of clobber to see it ruined in a punch up. I was not heavy into the dressing side of football, being a little too young at the time. Apart from a few pieces of Armani, Ball and Best Company, I could not really afford many of the labels on parade. Co-writer Pete Nice, he was a keen observer of this period and an avid collector of 80s attire and reminds me that putting on a smart piece of clobber to go to a football match was all part of the buzz and the one-upmanship for many firms up and down the country at the time.

Thinking back I'm also reminded how you could easily become unstuck. On one occasion we were pottering about at London Bridge one Saturday afternoon, mob spotting during the school holidays. I was around 14 at the time and for the most part, mates of mine were fascinated with the football casuals. Nevertheless, like many 14 year olds, we did not have the money for clobber and bullied out of following main boys about to football. So the next best thing was to mob watch on the London transport network and then exaggerate what we had seen when we got back to school, like how we saw 100 top ICF boys bowling with flick hairdos and the smartest pieces of clobber you could imagine.

Victoria or Kings Cross on some Saturdays during the early eighties was like London Fashion week. You could always witness some teams come down and get terrorised, taxed and drapsed of their jewellery. I remember some poor cunt taking a severe beating at Kings Cross one afternoon. I later learned that it was QPR giving out the slaps on a small group of novices where some escaped by skipping over the live tracks, leaving the unfortunate individual ending up a Tacchini track suit top and a gold ring lighter when he came to.

Meanwhile back at London Bridge, as I said, it wouldn't take long before being made out as me and 3 pals stood about looking confident in our cheap excuse for casual wear one day when a menacing looking Millwall grizzly quietly told us that unless us kids were here looking for our pretty garments to get ruined, "I suggest You'z fuck off now as 70 Millwall will be landing here any minute". Because we always listened to our elders back then, we took up the advice and returned to the safety of Thornton Heath train station.

From then on, fanny spotting up in Croydon Whitgift Centre became more of our thing following that, as we hung about with and chatted up girls in pleated skirts and fur coats. Some girls were dropping Farah slacks and Gabicci and it was a pleasure to look at these finely-rounded arses donning many of the labels that the chaps wore. There are probably many lads up and down the country in their late 40s who after reading this are now imagining birds of their youth in these slacks that were pulling off the Farahs better than the boys, that was for certain. Of course Pete Nice confesses about his "Girls in Farah's" fetish back in the 80s and would often reel off a fit list from his schoolboy days, like Judy Hayes, Bev Jasper, Kim Ions, Christine Gray and Sian Carter... in fact the list was quite a long one, of those he considered had top Farah arses back then.

You could also imagine the queen of ass, Jennifer Lopez, would probably absolutely smash it in a pair of hopsacks, but we digress, this kind of impression on us was everlasting and was also personified by a local group of casual girls that were around at that time, Jeanette James, Karen & Lisa Warner, Andrea Banascoe, Susan Ambry and their little crew, who were as fit as you like and exceptionally smart dressers, head to toe in Aquascutum and Burberry get up. It was through these that when Pete was going out with Lisa in late 84, we struck up our friendship and started hanging out with each other, a friendship that remained solid up to this day.

For many of us through our early teens during the 1980s the weekends were mainly about the music and where the next party was, including how much gyal were going to be attending. At many of these shindigs, it seemed to be the usual faces everywhere you went and there were a lot of characters about for us back then. Players who you'd try to emulate, the way they dressed and how they talked, remember the exaggerated bowl everyone used to adopt during these casual days? The kids call it swagger nowadays but back then it was a bowl, we took pride in our garms. Looking REEM long before Joey Essex and the rest of them plastic cunts on TOWIE and none of this wearing your jeans around your knee cap bollocks either, showing off your under crackers? Smart and casual that was the look then, with the option of kickers or desert boots or them smart dual colour leather shoes when it was time to party.

Norwood halls at the time used to run every last Friday of the month. This concluded our weekly ritual of clubbing or partying in Carshalton, South Croydon, Penge, and on the odd occasion venturing up to the Lyceum in the Strand for Tony Blackburn's soul nights out. It was surprising how on £25 a week YTS money we could afford the extravagance of venturing up London. We began to learn many strokes back then to earn extra dough for beer money and clothes; like the Strimmer line and slot machine scam, scrap metal and general thieving from department stores. We also did an honest day's graft as well like cutting grass, painting fences and distributing leaflets door to door.

Inside the West End Venue, all the different factions went under one banner... Croydon boys would be quite strong in the club when you take into account the fact that going into West End firm handed with doormen using the old chestnut "Members only lads" was not quite the norm then as it was a soul thing and you can't refuse a brother into his own tribal gathering. But then again if memory serves me correct the doors were actually held by black guys and may have been the reason for the leniency. Going to Lyceum, Tony Blackburn and Steve Walsh rocked the gaff with in grooves like Lisa Lisa's *I wonder if I take you home,* which always had me daydreaming about her and her impressive rack. I'm sure we all applauded many an onstage performance from her at the time. We were big Dolly Parton fans as well.

The Soul Night out anthem Fatback band's *I found Loving* drops and Steve Walsh has everyone at it, "WOAH-OH, WOAH-OH, WOAH-OH, WOAH-OH, WOAH-OH", Having us all swaying our shirt tails and wet

6

looks. It was great going there and meeting fresh fanny from other areas who were game as a pebble and many of them. Interestingly, there never seemed to be a lot of aggro there for some reason, although we do recall a superb punch up, we are quite sure it was at the Lyceum, when a mass brawl between Arsenal and Chelsea broke out. I am sure it was not on a Soul Night out when this happened, we cannot quite remember but it was a blinding row like a scene out of *The OK Corral*.

The reason there weren't many skirmishes was maybe because we were all horny teenagers only interested in checking girls as it was a melting pot of North, East, South and West London posses in there but also possibly because we were all 'one nation under the groove and nothing would stop us...' as the song goes. At Norwood Halls on the other hand, we often had stand offs with different groups, possibly due to an alpha male thing and probably too much thunderbird. A terrace mentality of protecting our own would often lead to squabbles, which was noticeable over the years when often fights would break out between boys that had been pals not so long ago.

What it was that caused so much friction back then is unknown, but it could of course have been years of tension built up over the "Your mother..." jokes, which pathetically (and I'm laughing here), were remembering some of the outrageous cussing sessions you would hear around pool tables at youth clubs and on the night buses home from wherever. You might be unlucky enough to be on the wrong end of getting ruined by one of the kings of comedy back then, the likes of Wayne Lewin, Brass Tooth Neville, Carlton Bennett or Michael McLeary. People would disappear for weeks after falling victim to any of those people and it was never a pleasant scene to be bombarded with outrageous cusses that in turn would have a whole party or busload of associates and strangers belly laughing at your expense. Anyway, digressing a little bit, as I said Norwood Halls was a rowdy place on a Friday night.

At first we hadn't clocked on to who he was. There was this

notorious football lad from West Ham's Intercity firm called Cass Pennant that worked the door there, and after one occasion, we had bowled up there after a boozy journey on the bus from Croydon. As we were approaching the door after a few sips of Tennents and feeling a bit lively, one of the boys got a little bit lairy with the huge lumps controlling the door. He was generously offered by one of them a backhander if he carried on, which, wisely saw him melt a bit and back down. Days later after seeing the Hooligan doc on the telly about West Ham's Intercity Firm and seeing Cass on it we were so relieved at the fact that we'd escaped a hiding from ICF's main boy.

Before there was even a scene, musically, we were pretty much into a bit of everything. This would usually have us attending sound system clashes at Bally High in Streatham with King Stereograph or St Albans hall in Thornton heath, listening to Steppers and Jah Shaka dances on one week. Where it was strictly a skank out and a smoke as the baseline line fucked up our chests whenever you stood in front of these giant speaker boxes. I always enjoyed watching and hearing Shaka spinning some serious warrior style dub, like *Marshal* and *Kunta Kinte*, which had all of us going crazy with high kicks and shaking imaginary dreadlocks as we chanted down Babylon with all the real Rasta men at these events in tall tea cosy hats and trench coats shouting out their allegiance to The Most High Emperor Haile Selassie I, JAH RASTA FARI.

On the other hand, we would be all in Dr Jim's, Cinderella's or Cat's Whiskers on a Sunday night back on the soul boy tip. *Jingo* and *Southern Freeze* have the Thornton Heath Posse into their routine. The rest of us are sniffing out fanny and drinking Pernod and black, all very much part of the growing up process. At our age of innocence some of us are looking beyond our teenage years when we drop the best of our clobber when going out. Getting a snog and a fumble over the tight blouse of a Shrublands or an Elmers End doris was always considered a result that would have you boasting for weeks and showing off to pals to take a sniff of your index finger.

The other quality night out was the house party, where Watney's party packs, Double Diamond and Cinzano would be flowing and which were often, very, very messy occasions. This I believe was where I got my first bunk up on top of a pile of coats in a bedroom. These parties would always, 100% always, end up with Old Bill and vomit as we over indulge and cat fights break out between the girls or horrified parents return home with insurance assessors.

One thing that emerges constantly looking back at growing up in the eighties is that at certain points, in fact most points in time, when we went from rude boys and skinheads to football casuals, from B-boys to freaky Deakys to ragamuffin MCs, everything was based around you and the boys, the firm, the lads, the posse, the crew. We would scrap with different estates, different schools, and even different box boys of opposing sound systems, a way of life and mind-set that stood with me for most of my days.

CHAPTER 2

CHAMPION SOUND

Sometime between 1984 and 1985, I became one of the box boys with Sir Radics sound system and my mates and I had the opportunity to hang with older lads, smoke some weed and drink Tennents'. In today's climate such a thing would have been frowned upon, but we were not binge drinking, we drank to get a nice level while nodding our heads to some sweet reggae music.

Pete, Ade, Dinford, Andy P and Derrick Green had been their box boys since their early school days, Tony 'Noddy' Macdonald, Dave 'Frisky' Macdonald, Basil Grant, Harry the Snake and Curvis Butler ran the sound under the Thornton Heath banner and the sound was transported in an old brown Hovis truck.

It was our task to get the huge speaker boxes to and from the truck and venues. Each speaker box would require hands on each corner, a job that got a little bit tricky at 5 in the morning, when buzzing on weed and Tennents Super. The ride home in the back of the truck would also have had any health and safety executive developing major palpitations, not only regarding the risk of death by being flattened by a giant speaker box but also the carbon monoxide bellowing inside from the exhaust. We all wanted to prove we weren't pussies, so we never complained. Being a sound man was a badge of honour back then, some of us would even wear tracksuit tops with the sound system's name printed on the back to show everyone who you represented.

We also enjoyed the perks of free entry to many blues and sound clashes. Those were good times rocking at parties and dance halls, rubbing down rub-a-dub style with a bit of skirt to lovers' rock tunes which would often have us fending off the older Radics lads from pinching birds off us telling us we were too young.

At the time I joined them, Radics were not such the roots sound since they had re–invented themselves from their earlier Steppers Sound system days of the late 70s and Early 80s, playing at the Norwood Halls, The Mosque and St Albans Hall, where they played alongside some major players like Observer, Stereograph, Sufferer and Quaker City.

Dinford and Pete's stories of early Steppers dances detailed an era of heavy dub bass lines and clashes with other box boys and local youths in 'skank-offs', which was the same as a disco dance off instead to heavy dub, where they particularly remember Pete getting blazed by a back flip manoeuvre by one of Sir Lloyd's crew during a battle at the Mosque. The humiliation of losing was instilled for days, not helped by Dinford who had goaded Pete into taking on Sir Lloyd's reggae equivalent to Tony Manero (Saturday Night Fever) and the older Steppers boys light-hearted threats to throw him out the sound for losing.

Renaming the sound, Sir Radics were now catering more for the ladies and sweet boys who just wanted to sup a Canei or Special brew, have a spliff and tear off wallpapers while they danced intimately against the wall. A little niche was carved out when weekend after weekend we were on the road in the Hovis truck to New Addington, Norwood, Brixton and Streatham, including doing many wedding and christening parties. The air at many of the blues venues you could have mistaken for a smoke machine output as the aroma of Sensimilla would fill the room, alongside what at times seemed like hour upon hour of lovers' rock tunes by Winston Reedy, Alton Ellis, Sandra Cross and the likes, pumping and shaking the windows.

These were classic tunes but for us, all this rub a dub and lovers' rock was OK if there was a promise of some steamy sex at the end of it, which was never the case and for the most part you were usually left with just an embarrassing stiffy. So more often than not it would result in us as young boys struggling at times to stay energetic due to the boredom.

These parties were often an older crowd and the older lads, with eyes half closed, are putting in some back work and dipping into the scrub down with the women, which would also often have the crew in stitches as the daylight came if some of them had spent most of the night thinking they were in the arms of some fit goddess-like female, only to find an ugly-looking Lego beast.

When the sessions were in full swing and more up-tempo beats would interlude the slow jams, Radics would be slamming some good vinyl, that prompted MCs like Slackness, Paul Henry, Jiouxie Nice & Sgt Bilko to attack the microphone for us and even all the way back then, I was thinking this was something I could do.

Our involvement with sound systems and to some extent family parties had exposed us to the wonderful sounds coming out of Jamaica, the Studio One Label, King Tubby, Trojan and Greensleeve and UK originated labels like Lovers' Rock, Ariwa and Fashion typified a great era, but it wasn't until the huge dancehall influence of sounds like Saxon, Sir Coxson & Jam Down Rockers and the massive respect of Levi, Tippa Irie, Tenor Fly, IP and the likes, the turning point in our lives, influenced us to build our own Sound and put pen to paper to write lyrics.

Floating about in those days were cassette tape recordings of dance hall sessions that stoked our taste for MC'ing. From early Stereograph tapes with Chubba Youth, Marshall Lee and Diego Ranking to listening to battles between Saxon and Young Lion, where I remember listening repeatedly as the undisputed king Phillip Levi and his crew sounded out the upstart sound system which included Daddy Willy, Tony Ranks and Nigga Jimmy who dared cross swords with them, this along with Saxon v Coxson tapes, recordings of absolute lyrical genius.

A lot of the time we had written lyrics on the fly to a *Sleng -Teng* or a *Shank I Sheck* riddim, which in my opinion, we had developed into a real art where we could chat, and fill up a rhythm track with words to spare and flavoured most of our styles in line with the main top MCs we were listening to, many of these influences still used today with request like "who wants the reload?" and "rewind my selecta" where yesterday's equivalent was getting an audience to 'lik wood' and requesting, "If you love dem deh style shout FORWARD."

We formed Young Senator in early 1985, When the old box boys from Sir Radics and my sound crew Itrous Hi-Fi(a sound system formed by me and some Selhurst boys to play at friends parties) merged and became one of the best sounds in Croydon alongside Sir Radics, Observer & Justice. We were a young, up and coming sound, so we were more in competition with other young sounds like Shakedown Massive, Sierra and the likes of TK Massive, Quadraphonic and another sound run by Selhurst boys - Stephen Binnom, Paul Wright and White Rasta Dave, called Scorpion.

So from Sir Radics there was Pete, Ade, Dinford and later joined Terry, also known as The Face. In addition with the Itrous Sound boys which consisted of my elder brother Howard, also known as Colonel H, and Jason Gibbs, also known as Little Blue, who is the father of Arsenal's Kieran Gibbs, Roger Mapp, also known as TJB (acronym The Jazz Boy), Garfield Samuels also known as Beaver Banton, along with Steven & Roger Selman, also known as Hedgehog Lick-shot Neck & Madman respectively. Crucial Danny Palmer, Sugar Alex, Godfrey 'Jack it' Cochrane and myself completed the Young Senator line up.

I had known Pete (who wasn't Pete Nice at that time, he was nicknamed Spongy back then because of the big afro he had as a kid), Dinford, also known as Daddy Fatman and Ade, also known as Killa, since I was a schoolboy during the early 80s. They were all a year above me; I was at Selhurst School for boys, while they attended Lanfranc. An egotistical bunch, especially Dinford and Ade, they would often flex their muscles on us and were a regular source of mild animosity for me and some pals back then.

Ade used to nick our dinner money off of us on his way to school and with a name like Killa, we would obligingly hand over our readies. You would often see him harassing other lads en route, jacking them as they exited shops, tipping them upside down and shaking them until their money fell out of their pockets. Over the years he would remind us of those times when he would chase us just for a laugh, because that's how he was back then. He's still the same piss taker now with his verbal but back then this was something most boys had to endure growing up where older boys would give you digs to test your mettle, but nothing too heavy, just little slaps and the odd taxing.

Before I was mates with Pete, I knew him mostly through Killa but as was common back then, everybody knew everybody and acquaintances were made at most of the Thornton Heath parties, like the ones held at Paul Fuller's house and whenever I bumped into him in Croydon Whitgift shopping Centre where everybody used to hang out back then. Out of the three of them, he was the one that caused you less grief; his mum and my mum were also friends from work when they were both geriatric nurses at Queens Hospital.

As Young Senator, with an MC line up consisting of Beaver Banton, Colonel H, TJB, Spongy Irie, Little Boy Blue and myself, I had taken up the moniker Daddy Flux, telling everyone "Flux, meaning slick." We set on our quest to become the best reggae sound.

I never started heavy on the mic, I enjoyed selecting the tunes and saw this as my speciality, Crucial Danny & Daddy Fatman where the operators of the control tower and Sugar Alex was the soul selector. From very humble beginnings, we began by packing out house parties in the Selman's house and homes of friends who held birthday parties and along with regular parties came the regular mic checks, where we all gathered to review new music and for the MCs to fine tune lyrics ready for the next dance.

Daddy Fatman, Daddy Fatman you have to mix me proper
You, you are de King you are de ruler
Jah man me mek a living by being a hustler
Hustle Sensimilla in the Brixton area
(Beaver Banton Circa 1985)

There is no doubt in my opinion, that Beaver Banton, god rest his soul, would have been up there with the current rave scene MCs. We've always said this and we stand by it, because we reckon he would have flourished. His premature death when an underground train in South Kensington hit him left us all devastated. I remember bumping into him before he died in 1987, he was on his way to court when I was chatting to him at Thornton Heath bus garage. He said he was bringing his toothbrush because he was of the opinion that he was definitely going to do bird. It was the last time I saw him and it turned out eventually he was acquitted from the charge against him. I really wished he had done the bird for whatever the crime he had done, he was often in trouble with the law when we were kids, because I am sure he would have been alive today. I always think about him, it was a sad loss and we often reflect on the jokes and the laughs he gave us.

Especially about the time when a long-running feud he had with Mad Denzel, a member of our rival sound system Shakedown Massive. It was over some girl I think and it led into to a war of words bouncing around between them, resulting in Denzel sounding him out over the mic at a party one night. I remember we were cracking up about it to Beaver's displeasure but revenge was sweet for Beaver, at a packed-out party in Addiscombe, after hearing the news that Denzel got a custodial sentence for cutting a kid called Horse Mouth Winston with 2 ratchet knives. Beaver, grabbing the microphone, jumped on a version of Tenor Saw's *Golden Hen*, let off and took the roof off the house and had every last woman and man in stitches when he rang out a very funny lyrical verse about him getting locked up. He absolutely ruined him with lyrics about his girl, his out-of-date clothes and everything under the sun that fit into his rhymes.

As if it was not bad enough having the prospect of doing two and a half years for GBH and wounding with intent, having his reputation ripped to shreds in front of the whole of Croydon made it even worse. All Denzel's people were at the party and word would have got back to him that he was buried at that party. That was Beaver Banton. He was deadly on the mic and we all really miss him.

Going back to the years before his premature death, we were developing the sound system and having tested ourselves at more low-key parties and dance hall events, we were ready for a big event to challenge ourselves and take our abilities to the next level. After a dance that was supposed to feature Shakedown massive but for whatever reason they failed to show up, a lad called Trixter from Quadraphonic Sound System approached us to join in on a Sound Clash. Hedgehog and Colonel H thrashed out some basic negotiations and organised a slot for us with them at an upcoming dance at Winterbourne School's hall.

We now had a race against time to organise dub plates to make sure everyone knew Young Senator. The cream of these Dub plates was when we went to Jah Tubby's in North London and pressed a couple featuring a reggae star of that era called Dixie Peach. On the sound track to his original *Pure Worries* hit, he bellowed out a new version...

Dem have fe run dem have fe run
Senatah dem ah come...
Senatah ah come dem ah come
fe lick dem d-o-w-n

As he sang it out we said "Yesssss", this was going to let them know. Jah Tubby sent us packing with this and another track called *Slaughter,* which was a version of Nitty Gritty's *Hog in a minty* rhythm track, adapted to mention Young Senator Crew members. After we got the tracks home, we summoned Spongy and the other Senator MCs to Headquarters at the Selman's house to review the dub plates.

We were jumping up and down with joy and squabbling with sound members who were not mentioned on the acetate, but hey, you cannot please everybody. No one in the crew was immune to a backlash of cusses, when it was realised that I mispronounced the intro to the main dub plate, where I should have said "world's greatest singer." Ended up sounding more like "We – Earl greatest singer." So I had to endure my brother and the rest of the crew heckling me all night. We checked the microphone until the early hours until the influence of the weed and Canei kicked in, sending everyone home to get some much needed shuteye.

The night of the dance came. We rigorously went through the setup of the tower and the speakers to ensure that we dropped to our maximum capability. We were the first sound up, we dropped our intro to get the dance rolling, so the challenge was on but it would literally turn into a clash of sounds rather than a sound clash, the intention was to battle each other to see who was Croydon's finest sound. We knew it was us, but Quadraphonic Sound and TK Massive wanted to prove us wrong.

The dance was busy and we had pulled in a good crowd. We had a full crew out and had the main Radics boys in our corner to show us support. Although if truth be told, Quadro's Trixter and Sgt Bilko had for years MC'd for Sir Radics, so they was showing love for them too and probably one eye on us to see if we were going to be contenders for their crown. Along with most of Croydon and Thornton Heath faces, the Streatham lot had turned up looking menacing as they entered with crash helmets. This lot have the casual look, draped in Best company jumpers or sweatshirts and Ball jeans over spanking new Adidas and Diadora trainers, and they hold their corner right next to the Young Senator control tower. Yellow Baby and a few of his Brixton mob from the notorious Hang Man Posse were in there too, the control tower was rocking and looking at the crew around me, and I was beaming with pride...

"Ah my sound dis," I whispered to myself.

This was our chance now to let go our flow and show them we were the guvnors, but straight away Quadraphonic were giving it. At the very first rewind for Spongy to take up the microphone, Quadro began playing as they wanted their turn and didn't want to wait through our line-up of MCs.

"Dance mash up!" I announced over the mic, looking over at the offending Quadraphonic control tower. It is on now, this is my sound and we have not finished yet, so Fatman has beefed up the volume and a noisy clash of conflicting music ensues until they see sense and back off. Spongy grabs the mic again followed by Beaver and the whole dance is rocking when Beaver rocks a chant of "Ride, ride, ride, ride, ride de ridim." Fog horns whistles and general noise erupts to keep rewinding. The pattern is set and the dance turns into fierce battle of words when Quadro at every opportunity try to disrupt us.

"Fock arf bwoy, Fock arf!" Fatman releases a tirade of obscenities towards our opposing sound members. This echoes out over our speakers, when he lets the echo chamber continue its feedback, repeating 'Fock arf!' a million times during their set. By the time the last tune is played, all hospitality and niceties have completely gone out of the window. Our MCs goad them, leaving TK max feeling like gooseberries as Young Senator and Quadro continue to bait and bad mouth each other. At this point, I thought fuck the lyrics, we were going to weigh out their blood-clart. Daddy Fatman delays with bare treble until the signature bass line drops to the tune *Prophecy* by Fabian, **'PROPHECY...PROPHECEEEEEEEEEEEEEEEEEE'**

The dance goes ballistic when the mean bassline smashes out of the speakers. I use this opportunity along with Beaver, laughing at them and me digging them out saying they were nothing to us. I take it another step further, turning my attention on Trixter, saying, "It's your turn and we are playing what you gonna do?" I go even further by baiting him saying, "Come over here and fight...Come on!"

"CAN'T DO NOTHING!" I continued looking over towards their tower hoping for a response.

It had everyone in stitches, the crew looking at me all puzzled saying it seemed as though I was thinking I was at a football match. In all honesty, a little tear-up with them would have made my night but fuck it, I fronted it and they did not want to know and my sound ruled the dance that night.

Everyone was buzzing the next day. We congregated at my mum's house to listen back to the tape of the previous night. Beaver and Colonel H had set the dancehall rocking with their energy, Spongy had dropped some bad boy lyrics and that in truth, kept a professional edge on the proceedings, without being drawn into the cussing, he had kept out of the slanging. He was like that, always wanted to stay under the radar, whereas me, I wanted people to know this was Daddy Flux – young, brash and full of it and I probably would have smashed you in the face with a hammer to prove my point.

Growing up in South Norwood, Norbury and Thornton Heath as young lads, we always wanted to emulate the older lads or the so-called top faces. People like Nicky Allen, Lloyd Harper, Kevin Macdonald, Teddy Barnett & Noel Palmer and lads from football, like the Stewarts, Luis, Theo, Si, Yous and other top boys like that from The Whitehorse estate, South Croydon and Norbury. They always had the best clothes during the casual days and were always at the front of the action when things booted off at games.

People like Tank, Meat Axe and Freddy impressed us with big gold chains and chapparitas (Wrist bracelet). They carried off a kind of panache that reminded us of Freddie McGregor, who was the very definition of a cool operator in his Gabiccis and beaverskin hats. Seeing players like I mentioned rolling up to parties in impressive P6 Rover 3500 V8 and 635i BMW's, we all looked on envious at them stepping out and looking dead smart. Freddy also sold a wicked draw of weed and we remember many blues parties when Freddy would be holding court with all us youths, preaching to us and giving us guidance and jokes, he was a top bloke.

You also had your serial bullies and I will not mention any names out of respect for the dead and the fact that they do not deserve the extra taps on the Keyboard that spell out their names. Now do not get me wrong, as I mentioned before, it was a way of life that occasionally you would get your balls broken like how Killa used to during school days. An annoyance yes, but he was never sinister with it, just a giggle at our expense but certain gentlemen (and I use that term loosely) were like Beelzebub and we would not have been surprised if the 666 mark of the devil wasn't embossed on their heads neither.

The chaps (or one chap in particular) in question gave Pete and a few of the other youths about that time untold grief, him and the rest of his mob. All Pete had done was have a sister that blanked this fella when he asked her out and knowing Pete was the brother, felt the need to take it out on him instead. For the most part it were just verbals, often just sneering and the odd cuff to the head but it was obvious that whenever this lot turned up at parties or anywhere, everything just got tense.

One incident fresh in the memory bank, which afterwards almost turned into a conspiracy to inflict GBH, was in the summer of 1984. A load of us had more or less camped out at Luke Thomas's house for a fortnight when his parents were away. Killa and Andy P along with a few others were at the time two of the wickedest shoplifters about and were responsible for filling theirs and most of our wardrobes with the required Pringles, Fila, Aquascutum and Burberry.

One particular afternoon it came on top for them in Alders in Croydon. They had pilfered some Aquascutum and were literally legged by security out of the Whitgift Centre and all the way down Wellesley Road, where they only managed to lose them after Killa turned and drop kicked one of them. The bullies, from an unknown vantage point, had witnessed this and followed the two of them to Luke's house. Reaching the house breathless and hearing the bullies calling out to them to stop, they ran straight in and stashed the goods away in refrigerators in the basement.

This lot burst into the house, threatening everyone with chivs (knives). One of the lads and one of the girls with us received a couple of digs until we parted with the coats. I mean absolute toilet these cunts were, no honour amongst thieves as far as these nauseas were concerned. So now this would carry on over a few months taxing and bullying and just being out and out fanny parts, like one time Luke was relieved of a Benetton scarf by them and another lad called Roger T was deprived of a Burberry golf jacket that he got for his birthday.

They were also hijacking lads who had cars, people like Neville G who springs to mind who they used as their personal chauffeur as they made their rounds and attended weekly blues parties. On one occasion, they forced Killa into one of these hijacked vehicles as he made his way home from Croydon one evening. One of their main boys was making threats to him with a rather large knife, informing Killa of his dislike for his face and how he was tempted to make a mark on him.

Pete also details that soon after passing his driving test, he had this beat-up old mini he used to drive around in and after refusing two of them a lift from Croydon, they surrounded his car and forced their way in. Subsequently holding him for a few hours, they demanded he drive them around. After a while, following threats and abuse by them, Pete eventually, fed up, escaped from them leaving the car with the keys in it while at a set of traffic lights in Selhurst. "Fuck the 60 quid I paid for that pile of shit, they can keep it" was his response when he caught up with us later.

His actions resulted in Pete having to keep a low one from them for a while, even more so after getting a call from a school pal who told him where his car was. We later on retrieved the vehicle, which you were able to start up by using your front door key. This extended their fury as they let people know that they would catch up with Pete when they saw him again. Mad as fuck and fed up with the constant fear of losing their threads and at relentless intimidation, on one gathering, conversations were in place for revenge, to single them all out and pick them off systematically.

I am telling you, plans were at an advanced stage, even down to rope, gaffer tape and an A to Z of torture methods. However, the realisation of the aftermath must have seemed too daunting for the group, to say the least. The fact of the matter is, there was a reason these cunts were bullies and one reason only... safety in numbers and they were very strong in that department. In the end, the plan to attack this particular crew in a ninja style military operation never was implemented.

Pete would eventually get a pass from them, after reaching out to his older sister's boyfriend at the time, Jeffrey Portious, who was a face in Thornton Heath back then. They were told in no uncertain terms to back off and back off they did, but this didn't stop them from taking it out on other unfortunate individuals, such was their ability to be a right bunch of cunts.

Many people believe that life has its own way of meting out justice. Killa has a saying 'Reaction will hold you' and Karma has its ways to even things out and mention the point that someone else must have had a similar idea for retribution.

An incident at a Reggae Sun Splash concert in 1985 at Crystal Palace football stadium, following the actions acted out by this group the previous evening, the victim of that continued effort of bullying, sought after them at the packed event, which culminated in one of them being fatally stabbed. I never wish ill of the dead and luckily never had any real confrontations personally with them or him, but it was no surprise to see many youths on the street, including pals of mine, not feeling very sympathetic on the news of his passing; In fact, some were hoping that the culprit would get away on the grounds of doing a service to the community. Even an idea to call in a bomb scare at the wake was luckily talked down, as it was bad taste even for a jar like him. In all fairness to them, there were a couple of them that were game lads and I would see them often with the main firm at Palace a few times, but it still doesn't take away the fact that most of our lot hated them and wouldn't have pissed on them if they were on fire.

With the news of this passing things became a little more relaxed with the fact that the rest of that crew must have come to the realisation that you can only push people so far before they bite back. However, I do recall another incident, a few years after this. One of them stabbed a boy we knew called Vinyl, over nonsense. Vinyl stood his ground to one of them and got ambushed and then having to retreat screaming and running through Derby road estate in West Croydon with stab wounds. His brother Neville, the same Neville whose car used to be hijacked by them, another of our mates who had plotted up with everyone at Luke Thomas's house that summer, came down the Wilton Arms pub raging and attacked the geezer responsible.

As we all looked on, it seemed as though this fella was not such a tough guy now, when fronted on his own by Neville. He was squealing for help as Neville dragged him by his dreadlocks, attempting to force him out the pub door to avenge his hospitalised brother but also possibly for retribution on that period of intimidation, resulting in the geezer gripping the door frame, hanging on for dear life as he was half dragged out. His plight was over, fortunately for him, when Kevin Macdonald broke it up but it was hilarious hearing him squealing, "KEVIIIIN! KEVIIIIN!" as he desperately negotiated for his life, which was another proof that some people feel invincible because of who they hang with but proves in the end that most bullies are cowards.

Going back to Young Senator, as a crew now, we had enough to rebuff any nonsense from bullies. Strengthened by the Streatham gang, or Moped posse we called them, who were now in our corner, led by Jason L aka Psycho & Garry Allen along with Little T, Otis, Cecil, Peter Johns, Barry M and Nursey, we feared no foe. I remember one particular Young Senator dance in a social club in Mayfield road in Thornton Heath. Young Senator once again had drawn a good crowd and our MCs were on fire with Spongy, Colonel and Beaver smashing it as usual. The crowd was rocking to *Under me sleng teng* as we rewind and lik wood.

As the tune rewinds under the eruption of noise from the crowd's approval and as the next MC is ready to step up, all of a sudden there was a standoff in the middle of the dance floor. The usual pushing and shoving ensued, the moped posse and a rival group from Tulse Hill caused an opening in the crowd as people aware of the imminent altercation got out the way. They soon had the enemy on their toes when Cecil withdrew a concealed hammer from his jacket and struck the opposing crew's top boy, sending him screaming to the floor clutching a rapidly growing coco that was starting to appear on his forehead. This saw an early conclusion to the party, when the manager told everyone to fuck off home.

The Streatham boys were fearless and our growing reputation and regular dances began to develop a bit of a hostile atmosphere, as local and neighbouring posses would attend with many potential bad boys being put in their place by them. We would often compare them to a black Hell's Angels gang. The fact that they were on scooters rather than Harley Davidsons would have greasers laughing at the fact that a gang on mopeds would put fear in anyone, but you would laugh at them at your own peril.

Spongy even wrote an ode to the Streatham moped riders with his lyrics 'Youth dem nowadays moped crazy' and another that summed them up to a tee when he dropped his bad boy anthem called 'Flash dem Ratchets'. They all appreciated the respect and showed Spongy 'nuff love' and offered that they would always have his back. These were times when I bet he would have loved them bullies I mentioned before to try liberties at one of our dances, as I reckon it would have come well on top for them. There were a couple of incidents when there could have been a flash point with a few of that crew but the situation never escalated. I even recall Pete getting trappy with one of them knowing Streatham was behind him and was surprised to see them laugh it off, but they would have been wary at the time of the Streatham lot waiting for a reaction.

By now, Young Senator was getting a big reputation, which culminated in two more challenges to our crown. We played the first of these in Peckham on a Friday night. A notorious area for rude boys and ragamuffins, so I made sure we were tooled up because I was not ready to bend over to these just because they were North Peckham estate. That night we landed on the social club to play another young sound system, I can't quite recall the name but it was run by some fella I knew from work.

We had setup with the acoustics and bass all sounding crystal and with an array of fresh tunes, we had the almost packed out venue rocking. But as per usual, impatience from the other sound not willing to wait through our ever-impressive MC line up started baiting us, saying that we were not Saxon Sound and should stop trying to imitate them. This sent Spongy, who was fast becoming above and beyond, one of the best in our crew, uncharacteristically into a lyrical tirade towards them, lyrics with obscenities that had me instructing Fatman to dip the volume on the Taxi rhythm track to emphasise it over the speakers...

Dirty Little FUCKING CUNT
yes you me a tark,
Don't run up fe you mouth against Young Senetah
when your face favour horse,
breath stink like Skunk batty,
neck it long like Giraffe
Dirty little FUCKING CUNT
yes you me a tark.

This combined with Colonel H and me. We sent them packing with an incredible volley of burial lyrics that had most of the Peckham hardcore nodding their approval and my mate from work with the right hump. A great night for us in the end that should have finally put us on the map. Next on the list was Sir Radics, but instead of progress some unforeseen circumstances would halt the Sounds progression.

CHAPTER 3

DIRTY BABYLON

We must not forget during the 80s as black lads growing up, police in their SPG vans always targeted us, which makes me laugh when these youths of today complain about how times are hard for them and that the government oppresses them and blah blah blah, FUCK OFF, try getting pulled up on suss law and thrown into an SPG van and getting a shoeing as they taunt you with "Have some of this, you stinking black bastard!"

Nah mate, you kids have it easy today, because the SPG (Special Patrol Group) were horrible cunts who would head fuck you by driving slowly alongside you, staring you out, following you up the road and you could always hear the wankers giggling in their vans. Some lads would cave in and scream at them, "WHY THE FUCK ARE YOU FOLLOWING ME FOR? I HAVEN'T DONE ANYTHING!" This would usually be all they needed to come jumping out and asking "Where you been? where you going?" before sussing you out.

"Don't tell lies black boy, you're out thieving, what's in your pockets?" they shouted and seriously fucked with your head, but they wasn't exclusive to fucking with black people back then. They raised their profile with controversy, when during an Anti-Nazi league demonstration in Southall they battered a young demonstrator named Blair Peach to death, so they were actually, horrible murdering cunts.

God forbid if you were driving back in those days. I can recall many a time being passenger with Dinford, Sugar or my brother Howard, driving down the road and minding our business only to have fucking blue lights flash you up every time.

After half an hour giving you the bollock ache with their moody checks, they would serve you with 'producers'. The producer was a piece of paper ordering you to produce insurance and MOT documents within 14 days at a designated police station, where you would often find yourself in a queue at Croydon pig headquarters that you could easily mistake for a line for some jerk chicken. This was the norm in those days and on many occasions boys like my mates, who were legal, always carried driver documents wherever they went. This was a good way of getting up their noses. There was no point giving them any verbal back then or "Is it cos I is black?" Because that would just be confirming the obvious, so diplomacy was always our tactic.

"Is everything in order, officer?" we would enquire politely. Meanwhile, one of us would be whistling Smiley Culture's *Police Officer* theme tune, which would have them irked and telling you to fuck off home before they plant some shit and fit you up. Some would say this is tongue in cheek but it is a known fact that them no good cunts, especially Croydon borough's finest, would often stitch people up just to get a cuppa and a bacon sarnie back at the nick.

One of these incidents of police absolute cuntishness that was fresh in the memory was when we had a meet to attend a party where one of our rival sounds were playing at and Young Senator was going to attend mob handed. We all were waiting for Sugar Alex to pick us up from outside Thornton Heath bus garage, we had a few cars on the firm but were going to leave a couple and all jump into Fatman's car and also jump into Sugar's mini bus. Little T turns up on his scooter and tells us, "Sugar's at the Pond."

"For fuck sake. We said the bus garage not the Pond" was our collective response.

We jump in the motors to drive to the Pond to meet him, while others walked the short distance because he has got the meet location wrong. Fatman, Face, Spongy and I, we get out of the car to see Howard and my sister Sonia and her friends. Andrew Robinson, Charley Dacosta and Carl Taylor and a few more Thornton Heath faces were all there as well ready to go to the party. All of a sudden, SPG vans and a dozen police cars screech up and a plain clothes copper jumps out of the motor and steams into Spongy.

"This is him, come here you nigger." He grabs Spongy and slams him into the bonnet of Fatman's Ford Escort.

"I'VE GOT HIM!" he shouts. "Name please darkie?" He quizzed with clenched teeth, as I notice claret above his left eye.

Spongy was like, "Peter Spe..." but before he could even finish, plain-clothed copper interrupts abruptly,

"I'm arresting you for robbery, wounding with intent and assaulting a police officer."

"What the fuck? I have been with him all night, must be a mistake" I thought to myself.

After the initial shock as Spongy is manhandled into the van, we have all suddenly sprang into action. We are pleading with the police but with all the voices and the usual didgy (nervous) nature of white police officers when confronted by a load of blacks, out came the truncheons and all hell breaks loose. Fatman and Howard are grabbing the two officers that are trying to frogmarch Spongy into the van. Everyone is now getting involved; more Old Bill turn up and immediately start steaming in. My sister Sonia is sent flying over a wall with two coppers landing on top of her, just as a bus load of black youths on the 109 came passed, saw the commotion and were off the bus and the next thing we know, it's like a bad day in Beirut. Fists and truncheons are flying as police helmets and baseball caps are trampled on the pavement in the melee.

The police finally restore order with reinforcements and police dogs, but none of us are making sense of any of this, and Howard, Charlie, Andy, Sonia and others are all now under arrest. Spongy is sat on the bonnet of Fatman's car, having nicked him during all the commotion when the 10 minutes of mayhem had ensued. He realised he was sat in the SPG van and not even handcuffed, and the door left wide open. He gets out of the patrol wagon and continues to watch the chaos as Young Senator and a bus load of Thornton Heath bods have it with the boys in blue.

I was stood next to him and we are both thinking, "What the fuck is all this about? Robbery? Assaulting an officer? Something isn't right."

Meanwhile, the police looking like they are in a hurry to just get the fuck out of there. They have all the suspects they need and are about to slam the meat wagon door shut. Spongy taps him on the shoulder and said... "You've forgot one mate." leaving the officer looking all confused. "Get back on the pavement" he replies in a huff, so Spongy turns to another officer with stripes and says

"Listen, you lot have just had me in a headlock, smashed my head on a car bonnet and have accused me of all sorts. So please, can you tell this gentleman to put me in the back of the van so I can clear my name?"

The confused officer is reprimanded in front of everyone. He sheepishly opens the back door to the van to allow Spongy in to join Howard and the others inside. The original plain-clothes officer is again in Spongy's face, properly narked about something, but it was obvious to us that either he is off his head or is severely confused. So this is how it pans out.

Let us rewind back 40-odd minutes. So we have all originally met opposite Thornton Heath bus garage in Alma Place. Mr Plain Clothes copper has a doris he's knocking off in one of the flats in Alma place and hearing the usual noise from a congregating group of black youths, peers out of the window and sees us all just waiting about. So he sees 'niggers', he sees 3 cars, he sees Spongy with an Aquascutum scarf around his head protecting his recently shaven head from the cold night air, then, Mr Plain Clothes (Let's just call him PC Fuck-Face) goes back to knobbing his slag. 30 seconds later he has made himself a cuppa and has washed his cock, which takes us past another 9 and a half minutes. He peers out the window again but this time, there is only one car and at the same time, by sheer coincidence, he sees two niggers chasing a white youth and the driver of the car (another nigger) gets out and watches the youths run into the distance.

Fuck Face gets busy. He's out the door and sprints down the stairs, thinking the car and the niggers chasing the soon-to-be-robbed and stabbed white youth are connected. He now hears on his radio a call about a robbery and a stabbing. He runs up and makes a bee-line for the driver of a navy Ford Escort Mark 1, who is our very own Roger 'Madman' Selman, still sat in Alma place wondering why none of us has turned up, because we have all gone to the Pond to meet Sugar, who was at the wrong location (are you still with me?)

Madman only sees a white man looking like he was game for a bit of nigger bashing lunging towards him. His natural instinct, which is on par with any raving lunatic, is to grab a screwdriver and throw it at the oncoming white dude, striking him in the face before using a right hook, putting Fuck Face on his arse and driving off.

So the shout on radio plod was: "Robbery. Suspect IC3 (African/Caribbean)Male. Heading off towards Thornton heath pond... OFFICER DOWN,REPEAT,OFFICER DOWN... IC3 Male, BLACK, big lips, Aquascutum scarf, BLACK, armed with an Uzi, BLACK, made off in a tank with low profile tyres, BLACK, hung like a horse, BLACK." You get the drift?

PC Fuck Face is fuming now because he now thinks he's been done by a spade with a shaved head and an Aquascutum scarf used as a makeshift hat and totally confused with the descriptions. He has now basically caused a mini riot on Thornton Heath pond just because the cunt didn't have a fucking clue about nothing. Spongy, Howard, Sonia, Andrew, Charlie and others are all in Norbury police station charged with robbery, assault on an officer, wounding with intent and public order offences. Meanwhile, Beaver and Moped Posse gang member Barry M are also arrested, this time by police, who I guess, know how to do police work properly. Having interviewed the victim, he describes and names the two black youths who have chased him and confirms the youth that stabbed him.

Due to the police and the incompetence of many officers that night and the fact that they were out and out racist wankers back then, after synchronizing up their notes and police reports, they continue with the bullshit and had everyone going to court and wasting the taxpayer's money. With Spongy on £60,000 bail plus a 7pm nightly curfew and my sister nursing a fractured skull, the people versus 'any niggers we want' was presented to Croydon Crown Court on September the 22nd 1986.

With the help of the infamous Darcus Howe, who loves sticking the boot into the Old Bill at every opportunity and lawyers assigned by Sugar Alex's dad - a respected businessman - the whole case against the defence was laughed out of court, with the Judge, the Right Honourable Justice Mac-Kiddy Fiddler tearing all the arresting officers a new arsehole. Summing up, he said "blah, blah, blah you bunch of cunts," or something along those lines as Spongy and the others high-fived each other and our mothers directed some unrepeatable Jamaican curse words and cunted off the police as they sheepishly left the courthouse.

Beaver and Barry M, having been identified, arrested and charged 6 months prior to the case, were already both serving sentences for the robbery and attack on the youth. Meanwhile PC Fuck Face, having returned to his duties, was later sacked after being caught sucking a tramp's cock on Streatham Common.

CHAPTER 4

CROSS THE TRACKS

Young senator had become more and more less attractive during the autumn of 1986 when we became less focused. After seeing the sound break down on a couple of occasions, the worst of these being at a dance in St Jude's hall in Thornton Heath with our mentors and number 1 Croydon sound Sir Radics. This was after weeks of promise building up to it only to falter, going out with a whimper after being hampered by technical problems with our equipment.

There were also parties prematurely ending due to an outbreak of violence, usually started by the Streatham lot, Sugar Alex or myself and especially after the long drawn out bollocks with Norbury's finest cunstables; we wanted something else to do now so one weekend, Terry 'The Face' suggested we go to an LWR do in Tottenham.

"Valentino's, Valentino's." that is how the advert sang out on the pirate broadcast detailing the line-up of bad boy DJs from the Soul Syndicate and the vibes they would be spinning. We all met up after work, TJB, Face, Killa, myself and Spongy or Pete, as he often would point out that he was not a ragamuffin MC any more, having been disillusioned over the previous months, most noticeably by the lack of progress that had befallen Young Senator.

We put on our smartest jeans, a pair of shoes and headed out of the manor to pastures new. It had been a while since we had ventured out of Thornton Heath, let alone South London. We sped through the

West End, up through Camden before arriving. The Venue was an old pub/wine bar smack bang in the middle of Tottenham High Road. We were a bit didgy at first not knowing the territory and all that but the relaxed atmosphere and the sweet soul music pumping out eased our tensions as we propped up the bar drinking rum and black and brandy and Babycham. A huge fella standing near us offered me a spliff. We exchanged pleasantries and I vaguely remembered the dude saying he was a Gooner, when he and 'the artist formerly known as Spongy' eventually becoming enthralled in a conversation about the new Arsenal manager George Graham. We hadn't really had much interest in football for a while during the Young Senator period for whatever reason but this fella had us anxiously interested again as he openly slagged off the "Yid Cunts" on their manor. Going by the odd glance of disapproval (Yids, maybe?) and by looking at the persona and size of this gentleman I don't think they would have said or done anything anyway.

A couple of girls had approached me and we got talking. They knew this kid, saying he was a bit of a lunatic but really harmless, and happily danced and drank with us as Pete and this fella almost broke into full choruses of Arsenal football chants, until Face advised them to pipe down. Overall, it was a good do, the LWR DJs dropping the likes of Luther Vandross, Mary Jane girls, Loose Ends and Carl Anderson with an absolute floor classic, *Buttercup*, a tune we were especially fond of that Sugar Alex used to interlude our Ragga beats during Young Senator days. The journey home was funny, we talked about Spongy's new best friend, the cranky giant gooner, and discussed the girls we had met, especially the girl Sue whose digits I had clocked.

"Yeah maan, that was a wicked dance" I said, me and Face thumping fist in agreement.

We were all on a nice little buzz. We stopped at Emek's kebab shop on Whitehorse Road in South Norwood, which became a weekend ritual for years to come after that night, well, before the all night raves at least. The night ended with some banter between Killa and me, which had us all in pieces laughing. Eventually Emek kicked us out the shop to close up.

A few months after, we were following LWR DJs like Zak, Daddy Ernie and Jasper the vinyl junkie all over the place. DJ Elaine especially, she was my favourite because she was fit as fuck. She was like our own 80s version of Beyoncé, such a sexy voice we would hear on the radio, seeing her in the flesh we were all like "WOW". So now, we are following them around West End and other London venues but mainly North and East London, Tottenham, Stoke Newington and Dalston. Places like Gossips and Trends were popular for us at the time because it was proving difficult to go five handed into most West End nightclubs.

We were becoming a bit cocky now as we had become a tight group having spent every weekend in early 1987 clubbing it together, so with an air of invincibility I used to get the hump with lumps on these doors refusing us entry and would often front them. "Why don't you just say NO FUCKING WOGS ALLOWED? Fuckin' members only?" This would often require Killa or Face to drag me away as I continue with my tirade, "What the fuck are they gonna do? Steroid pricks! I don't business."

Thankfully it was usually a front out of frustration. I would usually come to my senses because the size of some of those meatheads was impressive. I should thank my lucky stars really because the likes of Lenny Maclean and Dave Courtney I believe were main holders of these West End doors back then, so someone must have been looking down on me and prevented me and the boys from a possible annihilation.

Wag Club on Wardour Street in the beginning became as difficult as you could get to get in, you'd have thought it was Fort Knox. Although this seemed to be a more clique thing, 'if your face fits' turnout but it still seemed a difficult task for 5 moody-looking black boys to enter this establishment, although we did get in once or twice it wasn't all that we thought.

One club that we did attend regularly was Ambassadors in the Ambassador hotel in Euston. This club was a doddle to get into because RAT, a notorious security outfit, controlled the doors and consisted of predominantly black personnel. Ambassadors was where

LWR DJ Jazzy M, 'The Jack Master', had the Jacking Zone introducing us to the sounds coming out of Chicago. Tunes like Steve Silk Hurley's *Jack your body* was blended in nicely along with the usual rare groove slammers.

As we entered this club, the ragamuffin football casual hybrid look from the past few years was no longer our style, our attire now consisted of Doc Marten shoes, Levi 501 jeans, White T or Polo shirt with a nice cool casual jacket either denim or cloth. Me, Pete and Face had also grown little dreads on the top combined with number 1 haircut on the sides; this was the start of the Soul II Soul inspired funky dread era. Killa opted for a more US KRS1 style and TJB sported a quiff and went for a James Dean look complete with the red bomber jacket. He was also scoring with the women on a regular basis; he was the prince of chat and had the gift of the gab when it came to picking up birds.

Staying in Stoke Newington and Hackney until well into 1987 we began meeting different groups of girls every week, TJB and myself grabbing the most as we carried off this confident 'Ragga-swagger' whilst we were out that the girls seemed to like. One of many we had met at the time was a firm of girls from Southgate, Louise, Mary, Kim and Penelope - which was not her real name but she reminded us of Penelope Pitstop from the cartoon Whacky Races. She also drove a souped-up Ford Escort RS Turbo similar to TJB's. His was an orange beast, which we nicknamed the Thunderdome due to the extremely loud exhaust. These girls would school us about the hip do's going on and would eventually end up meeting up with us to go clubbing in the West End, and where we had girls on our arms this time around, the doormen reluctantly let us all in.

They were a good set of girls, a great laugh to hang out with and great dressers. We met them often at places like Mad Hatter parties and Soul II Soul at the Africa Centre. Pete started dating Louise, who I thought was really gobby, funny but gobby, and had a huge pair of tits. Mary was a mixed race girl, tall and sexy as hell (and also had a nice pair of tits) but none of us stood a chance with her, she made that very clear as we all tried it on when we first bumped into them. Kim was a short, cute, funky dressed little sort, which I met on a weekly basis for a bunk up when TJB and me met her and Penelope, one of our many regular rendezvous with sorts we were pulling back then.

Another pair of fit and funky dressed birds were from over Thamesmead/Abbey Wood way in South East London. Another me and TJB combo, where even to this day I had been racking my brains trying to remember their names. This is a common issue, because most of the time and over many years we'd usually have nicknames for a lot of them like Suck-a-deuce (she gave good head), Herman (Munster), You-bad-so, Old hat, Willie Young (good header), Disrespect and Yard Batty, to name a few of the outrageous nicknames dished out. Anyway, these two birds we had met during a little Saturday afternoon club in the West End that we ended up in during a shopping trip to Oxford Street for some garms.

The one I was seeing was of Middle Eastern origin, Palestinian if I remember right and one of the best fucks I ever had, a real toe curler (and I can't even remember her name). She was a great dancer as well. TJB was on it to begin with but ended up slipping into her mate, we nicknamed her Walid Jumblatt at the time after the leader of the Druze militia who was always in the news back then.

Going to Thamesmead to meet them on the few occasions is the reason why we always refer to that part of South London as Terry Waite country, an area we were not familiar with but always used to childishly joke about getting kidnapped by PLO and other inappropriate jokes like that in front of them, all politically and factually incorrect as Palestine and Lebanon, we now know, have fuck all to do with each other. She never used to mind, it was all light-hearted banter, because she was a kinky little filthy slut as well and used to call me her big black slave, Mandingo cock and shit like that during sex.

Time seemed to fly by during those days. We cracked out the working week, burning the candle at both ends as we tried to accommodate as many weekly exploits as possible. I was still also with

Sue, the girl I had met at Valentino'. She was more your typical nice girl next door, and had made me wait an eternity before I got my end away. At the time she was friendly with my mum and got on really well with her, which made things a bit difficult. Mum would always reluctantly have to cover for me and lie to her and say I was out whilst I was fumbling away between the sheets with other sorts (nice one mum).

The revival of the funk and the soul of 70s, ignited the rare groove scene, do's we'd go to we were shuffling to James Brown, Maceo and the Macs, The Jackson sisters and other top tunes from artists of that period, but also some legendary hip hop sounds were getting dropped when Public Enemy was unleashed... "Yesssss... The rhythm the rebel", together with the unforgettable break-beat of *Rebel without a pause* and *Bring the noise* that cut through the club speakers. This would always send us and other Rare Groove dance floor connoisseurs into an almost robotic head ritual, a dance style copied by John Barnes during his '*World in motion*' rap. Eric B and Rakeem and Big Daddy Kane also provided a complementary alternative to the regular funk beats, due to the fact that it was the sample of many of the classic rare groove tunes and James Brown riffs that were making these tunes and launching many rap careers.

It was around about 1987 when we also began going back to football. Although Face was a Chelsea fan, TJB Liverpool, I was Crystal Palace and Killa wasn't really affiliated to any club, for whatever the reason, so we all went to watch Arsenal. Pete was a big Arsenal fan and was excited with the likes of Paul Davis, David Rocastle, Tony Adams and Paul Merson breaking through the ranks, not to mention Gus Caesar (laughs out loud). This saw us taking in most games, home and away, especially during the 1988/89 season.

On a few Saturdays, seeing that we'd be partying somewhere in North London, we'd take in a game and plot up in a restaurant or wine bar before venturing out to where ever Rap-attack or LWR DJs were. I was also meeting up with some old school friends and going to Crystal

Palace and on the odd occasion, getting involved in a bit of mischief. I had been going down there on and off since about 1985 usually going on my tod. I'd become a keen observer of lads I knew from around the area having it with rival mobs.

Every so often, when any of our bitter rivals were attending Selhurst Park, you would get some major disorder going off in and around the area. I will get into more details about some of these incidents in later chapters. More recently around this period, after attending any Palace games, I started frequenting the Wilton Arms on Thornton Heath High Street with some of the Palace boys I knew for a few jars or many. We would eventually use it as a meeting point for the boys to pick me up before we went out clubbing, and as the years progressed we began attending some legendary raves.

This was a great time for clubbing because having been so long indulged in the reggae and dancehall vibe, we were now bang into Reuben Wilson, Johnny Hammond, James Mason, Dexter Wansel, Norman Connors, Roy Ayres, Donald Byrd and Cymande, and his classic *Brothers on the slide* and *The Message* triggered many slick moves on many dance floors. The list of grooves were endless. We attended HQ's in Camden, Car Wash in Blackfriars and spent regular Sunday nights in Africa Centre with Soul II Soul who play Fun boy 3's *Faith and Hope and Charity,* which became our Funky Dread anthem along with *Nightlife* by Blair.

It was an infectious atmosphere inside the centre of the world, with a kind of blues-ish vibe by design (and the red stripe on sale at the bar) you would have thought Jazzy B, Haitch and the boys could have easily got away with dropping a few dance hall tracks on some nights as they drop bass lines in there that often shook the place to the rafters. Brothers dance off in the middle of dance floors, girls freak out to Prince's *Sign of the Times.* Combined with some seriously heavy funk, the vibes at many of these events were electric and the clobber at times eccentric. Girls were dropping puff ball skirts and mad stripy tights, Madonna type tops, tweed or baggy suit jackets with bright red lipstick, which surprisingly looked dead sexy on many chicks we saw in clubland in them days.

I have to dig Killa and Face out here when it comes to clubwear. One night they walked into the Wilton to pick me up, and some pals of mine could be seen trying to hold back tears of laughter after spitting out gulps of beer at the sight of them. Face bowls in with a whistle on with the strides altered into knee length shorts, while Killa has bondage trousers on and some crazy mad max style boots. I mean we were funky in them days but they took it a bit too far at times. After the ridicule, which we often used to banter with each other about, Face refused to don that get-up ever again. However, Killa being Killa couldn't give a fuck and was the more eccentric out of the 5 of us when it came to garments. Although in West End clubland at that time, his dress was a little understated compared to some.

People experimented with rare pieces of attire from Portobello Road market and second-hand shops and it seemed the more ruined the 501 jeans the better they looked. There was also this crew of black boys on the circuit that I remember back then that all had short-cropped blonde hair, wore green MA1 jackets and ripped 501s. They looked really cool, were wicked dancers and they always had fit birds around them.

It must have been a thing with the girls back then, they seemed to influence the way the boys dressed. I remember Louise was always buying Pete bits and pieces she would find in Camden Market and I'm quite sure it was her that first got Pete to start locksing up funky dread style, which would then influence us. We were often out shopping with girls back then as well and then would be meeting them again in the clubs.

These were great nights out. A friend of ours called Heidi who we met in Babylon still has many of the flyers from back then and we all remember the enjoyable nights we spent at Borderline off Charing Cross road, Go Global and Delirium at the Astoria and Pig Club in Holborn.

The main pick was Thursday nights in Babylon at Heaven Night club in Villiers Street. Traditionally it was a poofters' gaff but on a heterosexual night like Babylon nights it was excellent for everything related to music and birds. The boys, including myself, were often falling in love after meeting some good sorts and getting off with them in the many dark archways that separated the dance floor and the corridor. Over the years we have had many a great night but we absolutely loved these Thursday night adventures to start off our weekends. Babylon was our regular stop on a Thursday night from late 87 and well into 1988. Here we would also meet another great group of girls from Wood Green, Mehtap & Sherene, two beautiful Turkish sisters and their friend Donna and a couple of others whose names escape me right now. They introduced us to shopping on the Kings road and restaurants in Covent Garden as TJB and Pete upped the game with the quality of sorts we were pulling.

Pete and I often reminisce when shooting the shit about the old days and he feels a tad guilty about his time with Mehtap, admitting he was totally wrong for her. I reckon it was only due to the fact that he took her cherry, even though she was 25 at the time he was seeing her and after she took big risks with her family by dating him, only for him to fuck her off. In our selfish chauvinistic world at that moment in time we were not up for most of the girls we had met to be taking us home to meet their parents, or husbands in some cases.

At the time I was getting hold of a local girl who was just getting started on a modelling career. Now with her, I would have been more than happy to meet the parents and drop down on one knee and hold up an expensive sparkler too. She was so fit and a girl who would turn me into a blubbering melt whenever she curled my toes with the sweetness of that velvet cavity between her thighs, damn she was good. Now her name I do remember, but she was also dating a dangerous individual on the manor, so she'll remain anonymous.

We were slipping into a few girls during these nights out and after clocking their digits we would all go on regular weekday missions meeting them and then telling each other stories of our exploits. We were hearing some incredible shit because some of these birds were not the regular type we used to meet in our younger days, we were meeting some game sorts young and old and had plenty of stories that made the car journeys a fucking good crack, as other than bestiality we got up to some nasty shit.

Around that time we started referring to ourselves as The Family and were often thinking up schemes to make a bit of money. We were all working in fairly decent jobs, earning enough money to splash out on clobber and nights out. We were often carried away with our imagination, but we still wanted it to be something legit. TJB however, suggested we should take on a protection racket, but we had to remind him that there were nastier cunts than us already covering that game. Killa being the piss taker he is, ripped him to shreds with that infectious belly laugh of his. We often look back on this time and take note because later on TJB had some mental health issues due to stress of work and also the cause of most men's mental issues... women. Looking back, we often see this period as the start of him going doolally, and I will tell you why.

At the time, there was a mini-series on ITV about a little firm out of North London. The series was called The Fear and the basis of the story was a wannabe gang leader called Carl Galton who was running protection on local businesses and wanted to move up in the game by taking on some big boys. It was a good programme and we was all in to it, but TJB, for some reason was obsessed with the main character and even started introducing himself to birds using Galton as his surname and getting wrapped up in the character. This had brought him to suggest that we too could run a protection racket operation.

At the end of the day, we were a confident group of lads and could stand up when tested, but trying to dabble in the age old art of protection was in another league. The only criminal activity of sorts I was up to back then was with my new found group of pals in the Wilton Arms getting into tear-ups at Palace games or serving up the few mouthy cunts that got lairy with us when we was out clubbing.

One such incident was at the end of a do in Busby's. There was a bit of a crush to get out of the building. Galton, as we would now bait TJB with, got the hump with Killa, who would not let it lie about him mimicking the TV character. Some fella piped up about Killa's loud laugh, something about it sounding like what you'd hear in a zoo or something on them lines, from which the old red mist descended and I launched myself at the geezer. Before we knew it, a little opening had appeared as men and women moved out the way. Anyway, this fella had a small team with him but the battle was all over after I unleashed a ferocious verbal attack on the lairy cunt.

This led to several door attendants sprinting down and causing a little stand off as they tried to understand what had caused the exit tailback to disperse so quickly.

"No problem gentlemen" Face said quickly, defusing the situation, "Just a little misunderstanding. We'll take it outside and away from this fine establishment."

At the same time, we could see these lads were starting to severely melt and were trying to, at all cost, let the bouncers do them a favour and keep them in there. Making our way up the stairs and out of the building, a group of girls we had met earlier approached us and asked, "what the fuck was all that about?" TJB started to explain. He must have got as far as... "These geezers..." when mid-sentence, these fellas, with newly found bollocks, came bouncing across. "Come on 'en!" One of them offers, with the customary hands out wide gesture.

Little did these soon to be ironed out pricks know, en route out of the club, I had sneaked an empty Grolsch bottle under my coat. Face went flying into them and half chased them up this little alley beside the club. He drop kicked one, whilst Killa had another turfed out with a couple of sweet jabs and their main mouthpiece left in a heap and sobbing like a little bitch after I'd introduced him to the bottle, and then we all, as cool as you like, walked and half jogged back onto the street. One of the guys by now had tried to melt into the background of ravers and revellers. He was approached by TJB, in full Carl Galton mode, who calmly said to him, "Tell your boys you've just met The Family." He gave him one of them double tap slaps on the cheek and winked at the two birds that were standing close by beside the crossing.

That was the icing on the cake. After getting back to the comfort of the motor parked off of Tottenham Court road we was all absolutely in tears. "Where the fuck did that come from mate?" I said, holding my sides with laughter. Although he was acting out his idol on TV it was a peach of a line and I bet it had made them two birds knickers wet, but we never did get to find that out.

Another incident occurred when we had left the manor and headed to Babylon and driven up to Charing Cross. We parked the Thunderdome up in our usual parking spot just off the Strand and took the small walk down to the club. I could see these chaps eyeballing us and through experience, I just knew they were looking for bother. Out of nothing, this group of very well spoken gentlemen were giving me and TJB some verbal, all jokingly to begin with but at a guess they were thinking we were a couple of muggy homos. Face, Pete and Killa were a short distance behind us and only witnessed an exchange of words. It went quickly the other way when they started digging TJB out for what he was wearing and if I remember, he was starting to resemble a black Luke Goss from Bros. They were soon on their toes when we unleashed a vicious onslaught on them and even unluckier for them, they ran straight into Face, Killa and Pete and took double the beating.

After the incident, we half-legged it down the slope to Heaven as we could hear the gavvers coming. We left the four men laid out on the West End sidewalk picking teeth up and nursing bruises. In the end after a few bevvies, chatting up a few honeys and some two-footed wizardry on the upstairs dance floor, we ended up having a fantastic night. Now I don't want it to sound as though we were trouble makers or anything like that, I suppose we were still adapting to West End life, because we always seemed to run into obnoxious people or people who would think they could talk to us like shit and take the piss, especially the kind of public schoolboy Eton type who think the world should eat shit from them, well maybe some people do, but not my crew.

43

So we had a few little skirmishes like this up town on a few occasions at that time. I do not know what it was, maybe it was the Young Senator thing still in us, or just me at least, as it always seemed to revolve around me, so everyone used to tell me. On one occasion in 1987 it even helped us with an alibi when Croydon Borough's finest law enforcement was once again looking for people to fit up. We were all surprised to get an early morning knock. As I lay in bed my mother was shouting up to me saying the police were at my front door, but it wasn't until some lanky prick from CID ruffled my covers and told me to get dressed that I realised this wasn't a wind up. At four more addresses there was the same thing happening, Face, Killa, TJB and Pete were all bundled into police cars arrested on suspicion of the murder of a prison officer. Well you could imagine the fucking relief when the copper in the interview room asks what I was doing on Saturday 14th March at 2200 hours. At that exact time, we were having a tear-up in an amusement arcade off Shaftsbury Avenue that night as we waited for the girls from Southgate to meet us to go to a do. A night that stuck clearly in our heads as we giggled about the altercation which in the end had police turning up to give us all a slap on the wrist. What a touch, they're not going to pin no murder on us, I thought. Because meanwhile on the same evening, outside the Prince of Wales pub in Thornton Heath, an off-duty prison officer was stabbed to death by a black male matching any nigger's description, going by how hard they were trying to pin it on us after the event. All of our alibis were the same because it was stuck in our memories at the time, so fuck you officer.

I know there are people thinking that the police are not in the business of serving up that kind of injustice, but believe me, it wasn't until they captured the real suspect, some black geezer from Tooting, that my arse went back to normal. It was funny because when they lifted Pete, Pete was thinking that these officers must have come from the shittiest academy of shit bad cop/good cop actors as they entered his house and tried to confiscate a kitchen knife out of his mother's kitchen,

"AH–HA!" one of the officers said all smugly, reminding Pete of Paul Daniels completing one of his not so fabulous magic tricks. "Is this the murder weapon?" Pete is now thinking Lieutenant Columbo here is on a roll.

"PUT BACK ME BOMBO CLAART KNIFE" came the hostile response from Pete's mother, who had just come down in time wondering what the fuck the police wanted with her son again. This had the PC dropping the knife quick time all red faced. I mean seriously, don't all kitchens have knives? And even more hilarious, after 2 hours of questioning at Croydon Police Station and trying to put the frighteners on Pete, the same officer returns to the interview room with his face full of glee.

"It's OK your friend Killer has confessed to the murder," he resounds in a matter of fact kind of way. This sends Pete into hysterics at the officer's poor attempt. His two interviewing colleagues roll their eyes and give the officer that 'you silly cunt' look. It turned out that we had all had the same interrogation.

"Why is he called Killer then?"

Which is unbelievable, the level of police work it must have taken to come up with that as a motive for the crime. We had offered various explanations but Pete knew him the longest and educated the officers that it was not because he was a homicidal maniac, but it was because, when Adesola started the 3rd year of school at Lanfranc, he was a scruffy cunt that everyone tried to pick on. "He looked like he had just arrived on a banana boat" he explained.

However, in a period of two weeks, Ade sought retribution and bashed up everyone that picked on him. So now that everyone witnessed that he could have a row, our mate Dinford gave him the tag 'Killa' and when Killa started boxing, he deserved that moniker even more so, and even though he lost every fight in the ring, the name stuck. Although he has tried to change it over time to 'The Adesola Experience' amongst other things, everyone calls him Killa.

Thankfully there was no hard feelings as we were all called or visited a few weeks later saying the investigations into the murder were concluded and the suspect was on remand in Brixton or wherever the fuck. It turned out that during the 6-month long investigation, it was rumoured to be just targeting ex-members from Young Senator. Maybe it was Norbury police trying to get their own back on that fuck up detailed in the last chapter, but we eventually learned they had targeted most of Thornton Heath's black youth aged between 16 and 20 at the time, which goes to show, all us darkies must really look the same.

CHAPTER 5

WILTON ARMS GOONERS

As 1988 rolled into 1989, we began to use the Wilton Arms more and more on nights we went out partying and also for football. I was now going up the Palace more regularly and was enjoying being involved in public disorder events, involving different mobs that would come down and expect to take liberties. We were also causing a few liberties ourselves when we travelled away; my pick of events, was the away game at Bournemouth at the back end of 1987. We had it all day long with locals, stewards and their local constabulary with 36 Palace being arrested for a selection of public order offences, including letting off a flare gun in the stadium. It was funny on the train journey back to London, cracking up about stewards running for cover shouting, "They're worse than Millwall."

On our regular trips to Arsenal, Me, Pete, TJB, Face and Killa, had gone to see them several times, including Spurs away. Taking the journey down there and parking up near Seven Sisters road, we walked down Tottenham high street without a care in the world. As we passed some main Tottenham boozers, I noticed a couple of shifty looks, it was as though they were not sure what to make of these five boys bowling about as if it was their own manor. If there was any slight suspicions in their mind, we were already past them and continued to the White Hart Lane stadium, where we witnessed a well fought out 3-

2 win to the Arsenal, and a pitch littered with Mars bars after the away end targeted at Paul Gascoigne on his home league debut.

We weren't part of any firm at Arsenal, we pretty much kept ourselves to ourselves, but we would often get a few stares from bods that were main boys, and Pete recognised the odd face from the North Bank he was acquainted with during the early years when football was fashionable. We also recognised a few familiar faces who nodded in acknowledgement but looking at us - 3 of us with funky dread haircuts, 1 black James Dean lookalike and a mad African, all of us dressed in either leather bomber jackets, Denim or MA1 Jackets, ripped 501 jeans and desert boots or DM shoes - We did not look like your typical firm and obviously the reason that nothing came about from the inquisitive looks outside the Yid boozers we passed on the way.

That did not stop us from giving the odd outburst to opposing fans, as you well know, football fans do 'give it', which in hindsight was a bit foolish, if you're not sure what the opposition has and also whether anyone outside of the family has your back. Like I said, we weren't part of any Arsenal mob, who at the time had a good reputation, but we also weren't looking at the fact that we could get severely done by the likes of the Yids or Man United, so we weren't standing about hoping we wouldn't get noticed, we always went and enjoyed the games.

As I talk about not being noticed, this is a little hypocritical considering. I'm reminded of the trip we all took to Millwall in February 1989. Pete was working for BT at the time and acquired the tickets midweek for Arsenal's game against them that weekend. On the way down, Pete was saying, "We need to be careful".

Most of the lads at his work went, including a Bermondsey lad from 'The Blue' called Kevin, who was a staunch Millwall fan. He had warned him to be careful, of not only the Bushwhackers, but also the local loony tunes off the estates. With this and the usual horror stories you often used to hear about opposing fans attending Cold Blow lane, we were a bit dubious and thinking it might be a bad idea.

Driving down, after meeting Pete at Borough tube, we drove off the

Old Kent Road and through the back routes he had learned on his daily rounds at work and found a spot that was close to Ilderton Road but was still a fair old walk, with enough opportunity to run into unwanted aggravation. After a few minutes of hesitation, we all looked at each other with a kind of reassurance that we stay tightly together and took the brief walk down Ilderton and across toward the moody Old Den.

Halfway to the ground, this fella approached us, on his Jack Jones looking all excited. He said, "It's all going fucking mental down the Old Kent road, Arsenal are getting cut to pieces."

He wasn't a big fella, but had that typical Millwall-Bermondsey swagger about him, you could tell he'd be a handful, as you could imagine, this was the last thing we needed, as we cast eyes at the excited lunatic and at the little gangways and openings, which looked prime location to be caught up in an ambush. We half ignored him and carried on walking, when Killa said, "Yeah... Well what you doing around here then eh?"

The geezer stopped, as if surprised at Killa's inquest, looked us up and down, it was as if he had a Gooner radar on, then he got all excited again. "It's youz lot isn't it? YOU'RE ARSENAL, YOU'RE ARSENAL!"

I took a step towards him, thinking I had better silence this cunt, but TJB and Pete held me back. Even though the fella was on his tod, he was bouncing, light-footedly doing the Ali shuffle and smiling all the time at us. He was a game cunt I give him that.

"Just leave the breddah" Face was warning me, as Pete tugged on my jacket, becoming anxiously wary that this could be a set up. "Let's just get the fuck to the ground."

Walking backwards, I continued looking back in the direction that we came, and watched as Bermondsey Billy continued about his business. We trotted by the rest of the way, luckily without anyone picking us out any further, as we teased each other about who was shitting themselves the most. It was quite a relief in a way because we were sure your typical Millwall would have enjoyed jumping up and down on the heads of 5 Gooner spades, if we were unlucky enough to run into a mob of Bushwhackers.

Maybe that is a bit unfair about Millwall, who were at the time one of the most feared mobs in the land. They had a few game black lads that rolled with them in the 80s, even a notorious and legendary black top lad named Tiny, who was in amongst it all with Harry the dog and the original F troop, so they were never really in my eyes, as right wing as many people would have you believe, well, no more than any other London outfit anyway.

After getting into the relative safety of the away end, entering with the rest of the away support via that intimidating tunnel/archway bit which led to the ground, we watched an eventful 2-1 win to the Gunners. The away end was bouncing after Alan 'Smudger' Smith scrambled home the winner and unified in chorus as we taunted the home fans with, "You're not singing any more, You're not singing any more!" after seeing them take and concede an early lead. This sent most of the Lions fans into psycho mode, which was not difficult by all accounts as their support are notorious for absolute horrible cunts, which is Millwall by definition.

After the game, we were held in for 30 minutes. This was to allow the Wall animals to fuck off back into their caves. When we were finally let out of the ground, we suddenly realised we would have to leave the safety of the police escort. This would take the majority of the away section, which in fairness had a good selection of game looking boys wrapped up, towards New Cross, where we would have to venture back in the opposite direction to where Pete had parked the car. As we crossed the road, a busy copper said we had better do ourselves a favour and get back in the escort. Kissing his teeth, Pete replied in a strong Jamaican accent and said, "Listen y 'hear Babylon, we no 'fraid fe no bloodclaaart white man y'know."

Actually, what we really said was "Our car is parked in Ilderton road officer, we have to go this way."

We also drew some inquisitive looks, as if to suggest we were

Millwall infiltrators or something, or maybe, considering our plight, they could have been possibly thinking, "Fuck your luck walking back into bandit country on your jack."

We nervously continued off walking in the direction of the car, which luckily for us was uneventful. There were pockets of Lions fans with scarves on and young lads clinging onto their dads' hands as they skipped in between cars on the busy main road. We realised no Millwall of the notorious hooligan variety would really be hanging about after 30 minutes looking for Gooners along the Old Kent road and would instead be trying their luck further up the road around New Cross station.

We relaxed again, TJB and Killa were joking about and largeing it saying that we had enough about us to do Millwall anyway. So other than a few inquisitive eyes by tough looking, big beer-bellied men standing outside the Canterbury Arms and betting shops, we walked back down the Old Kent road probably just looking like a bunch of black guys and nothing to do with football, relieved in the end to see Pete's light blue Ford Granada.

We got in the car and away unscathed and I'm still going to go with the fact on record, that we came to Millwall's patch 5 handed and took the piss all day long, so I don't really know what all the fuss was about. Anyway, all joking aside, we were pulling away when we decided to stop at an offy to get some drinks. As I walked into the shop I could hear these two lads giving the Pakistani owner a hard time and being a general pair of pricks. I sort of barged one out of the way to get to the till when one of the lads kissed his teeth, in a kind of Jim Davidson way, giving it the old "Chalky" chestnut and as I spun around to confront him, he was giving it proper. "You're a bit brave yoo caant, we're Miillwool," he said with a constipated grimace on his face.

Bless him, you could tell he must have used that statement every day of his life to strike complete and utter fear into people. I tried to think of something witty and sarcastic as a response, like "Does your mum fuck black geezers by any chance?", but instead, at the request (more like desperate pleas) of the shop owner, I paid for the drinks and began to walk towards the door. The geezer started eyeballing me some more, and I could feel it wasn't going to end peacefully with this scruffy young runt. I just knew it was going to come, so I prepped the plastic bag of cans...

"NIGG..."

WHAM! Straight in the mooey with the bag, sending him sprawling sideways into the shelves. Before his pal could react, I jogged back out to the car. "Quick, drive you cunt, Millwall, Drive!" I said, laughing out loud as we sped away, with me shouting "WAAAANKERRS!" out of the window to Pete's disbelief.

I explained what had happened, detailing the sound and reaction of the lairy geezer toppling into the row of tinned corned beef and soup cans, with the shop owner shouting "Get atta my shap." which had us all laughing, that typically, I would be the one crazy enough to start on some cunt when we had spent all day trying to keep incognito.

Going Palace was a different kettle of fish from when I went to Arsenal with the others. Whereas Arsenal was Pete's team and I did enjoy watching them, Palace was my team and it was also a bit more eventful getting involved in the odd skirmish with the boys and the beer monsters out of the Wilton Arms. It was around this time that I first met Reggie Anderson, a menacing looking lad from Catford who was living in Brighton at the time. A printer by trade and earning a fair few bob on fraud and other capers, it was rumoured that he had a nice lump of dough wrapped around him. He was always flashing the cash about, and he also had a reputation as a nut job down the Palace, who loved to flash a blade or two.

He had recently been released from prison for firearms, and I first noticed him eyeballing Pete and me at a game against Ipswich. Pete was with me that afternoon to clap his eyes on the main man Ian Wright who was forming a formidable partnership with Mark Bright as they combined to score a hatful of goals that season. Reggie approached another lad I knew asking him who the two "Schwartzes" were, and the fella replied, "Who, Black Rodney and his pal? They're sweet, Gooners I've heard, and they love a tear-up."

Learning this years later, it is funny how people would hear rumours and by the time it gets back to others how exaggerated it can get. It seemed that people hearing about a few skirmishes on nights out up town added to the fact we were regularly down the Arsenal added the 2 together. We weren't complaining as sometimes it's good to live off a good reputation like this one, as we would learn later on.

I would see Reggie at a few games and began to hit it off with him. He was a good laugh and we would always have a lot of banter with him. He was always bringing up the black man-big cock topic, amongst other things, claiming it was a myth and stuff like how us black boys don't like plating women, which we assured him was all bollocks. Almost the whole pub would get involved in our debates including us trying to get the barmaid Mary, who was a sexy middle-aged Irish MILF, to give her opinion but she would decline, all embarrassed.

Most weekends we would always end up in Wilton Arms for a few beers after the games and it is also where I began chatting with a young group of lads, headed up by a chap called Dee. He and his brother Liam and their little crew were good lads and I'd often end up drinking with them and having a few laughs and often we would give the landlord Terry some grief, usually ending in us getting barred because in a drunken state, we would always go too far with the personal digs at him. He was always OK the next weekend after we had apologised, blaming it on the beer.

I suppose I should also mention a little bit of history about The Wilton Arms, which was a notorious pub in Thornton Heath; it made the headlines during the race disturbance of 1982. Back then, black youths, which included some of the older guys around during the Sir Radics sound system days, used to congregate at the Parchmore Youth Club. Mainly playing pool and listening to reggae music, it was just a general hang out. One night, skinheads attacked a group of lads who had left the Parchmore club to go home, with a couple being seriously injured after the assault. It was believed at the time, that they were National Front skins from the NF headquarters that was based on Pawsons Road.

Pete used to tell me stories of skinheads chasing him on his bike when he was doing his paper round down there when he was younger in the late 70s and for years swerved going anywhere near the place. Cowardly cunts, considering Pete must have been no more than 8 or 9 years old at the time, yet brave NF cunts thought they were tough chasing a little black boy down the road and hurling bricks, along with a barrage of the usual racial abuse. That is how things were back in them days; you were often chased or spat at by racist pricks because that was seen as the norm. You would often see graffiti with KEEP BRITAIN WHITE, WOGS OUT, NF and all sorts on walls and bus shelters around Croydon and Thornton Heath and repeatedly told to "Fuck off back to your own country sambo!"

You would probably find it unbelievable today, when you look at the makeup of the area now, so I bet them cunts feel gutted today that they did not get their wish.

Following the skinheads attack, the next night at the youth club, it is rumoured that the elders of the community were trying to keep the youths off the street but how it panned out, a massive mob of black youths from Thornton Heath and the surrounding areas had descended to the Parchmore Club. The atmosphere was described as hostile and rumours of tools hidden in alleyways and under cars, something was surely going to kick off. The evening ended up with running battles with police and skinheads as a herd of youths descended towards Pawsons Road, intent on steaming the skinhead gangs and smashing up the NF headquarters. I was very young at the time and cannot remember all the details but one group had rushed the Wilton Arms, attacking the drinkers in there, and they reportedly stood and gave some back. The aftermath saw a lad called Robbie Kennet having his arm almost severed by a machete-wielding youth. Sadly, another or maybe the same group, having chased a man on a motorbike, dragged him off and as the partially crippled victim ran for his life, he was set upon by a marauding mob and killed.

Like I said, I do not know the full extent but I remember it on the news and seeing the landlord Terry Lawrence interviewed on Thames News on interethnic relations in the area - including the activities of the National Front, following an attack on the pub and the murder of Terry May outside it. We later learned that the incident was highly unfortunate for young Terry, who was just in the wrong place at the wrong time. Having grown up and been schooled locally, he had many black pals and was heavily into reggae music. He was an avid biker who was unlucky that day to have been riding pillion when having a nose about with a pal. He was flung off as the bike was fumbled when the mob sought after them.

The machete attack survivor Robbie Kennet died in 2008 just after our Sydenham trial. I got to know him over the years down the Palace, a proper lad and game as well. He was attacked for the sheer fact that he was a drinker in the Wilton, which was mistakenly labelled as an NF Pub but was plainly just a football pub, where many Palace lads have drunk through the years.

So this is now my local, our main boozer. Reggie and I would often meet for a pint and discuss business ideas and the odd plans on hurting people he had fallen out with. It would be a while yet before anything came about. I will explain later and I will also divulge a little bit more of my involvement with the main firm at CPFC.

CHAPTER 6

ACID MAN

It was the middle of 1988, and recently the boys and I had been hearing rumours of a new dance phenomenon. There was the weekly event at the Astoria called the trip, which saw the place always filled to the rafters. Some of the tunes were played in many of the places we attended. Inner City's *Big Fun* and *Good Life* were tunes we often heard out but it seemed the discovery of the TB303 was sending London club life to another extreme. We were so into our rare groove at the time we were not that bothered about it, but literally, we would stumble upon it by sheer accident.

Pete and I always had rows with our girlfriends at the time, because we were always out from Thursday nights to Sunday nights with the boys. Added in to that, the mid-week football matches and rendezvous with existing or new fanny we had pulled, they would give us the usual ear-bending whenever anything distracted us from giving them 100% attention. Around that time, we were seeing these two Jewish girls from North London called Suzanne and Amanda. Our 4b2s we would later nickname them, and if you saw them, you would imagine butter wouldn't melt, yeah? Well maybe in their parent's eyes, because as far as we were concerned, they were sex crazy nymphomaniacs who Pete and me had met after Pete had recently split up from a sort he was bang in love with from over Blackheath named Katrina.

This Katrina, was the first girl I'd known him to get so emotional about. He said it was love at first sight after pulling her at one of our regular jaunts in Babylon and I remember him talking about her constantly, like he had done with no other since I had known him to at that time. She was probably his toe curler and he was going on about stuff like 'she was the payback' sent by some godly protector of women or some bollocks, payback for how he treated Mehtap, who he had left her for, fuck knows. He was down, he was my best pal and it was my duty, so to cheer him up one night, we went up to a midweek do in The Astoria.

A Wednesday night was not a regular raving night for us at the time, so it was not a busy night when we first clocked them at the bar. We knew by looking at them that they might be hard work but as we were accustomed back then, we had to at least try our luck. Pete was sceptical, he did not think he was up to dropping any smooth lyrics on these and just wanted to drown his sorrows after his breakup. As I said, I do not know what it was about this girl, Pete could be a cold-hearted bastard towards birds at times, but this one, he was besotted with and I was struggling to liven him up.

Anyways, back to the four-be-twos. They looked fucking lovely, average age 22-23, both with blonde curly hair, similar in size, great tits and banging arses. They stood there sipping drinks from straws, dressed smart in skirts and suit jackets, with low-cut tops that made the fluorescent lighting shimmer off their heaving cleavages. Looking like they had just stepped out from a posh office building, they were smart, sexy but somewhat slaggy at the same time. They had that sluttish look, where if this was a porn set, they would be the office secretaries with the hair tied up with the bins on.

Every so often, they took a sip of their drinks, while glancing over at whoever. They danced as I was undressing the pair of them slowly and even prepared to send Pete packing, fearing his sadness over another bird might scare them off. I'm picturing a gangbang on the cards if that was the case but by now, I could sense the other hungry wolves in the club clocking them too.

"Fuck it, I'm going in," I said.

Pete had the look of 'leave it out' on his boat race as they walked towards us but as they approached to walk out the door to the stairs, I was uncharacteristically lost for words.

"Wh... Wh... Whe... Where you going?" I stammered, sending Pete into a fit of laughter.

"You fuckin' sure?" he said trying his hardest not to piss himself.

It seemed that my lame-arsed, tongue-twisted, stuttering chat line and Pete's million-dollar smile had broken the ice with the girls because we had a good time after that, whispering sweet nothings into their ears for the rest of the night. We offered them the world, if they took up the proposals of being our babes, our main squeezes. Pete seemed to take a shine to his after a very short time chatting her up and his recent breakup was all but forgotten. We smooched with them to some Leroy Burges who was PA'ing that night.

The night ended with us desperately trying not to come over as desperate, as we clocked the digits, struggling at times to write the numbers onto a soggy beer mat.

"You gonna ring me right?" I said to Amanda, unsure of whether our paths would cross again.

To our relief they kept in touch, so now we were often wandering up to North London to meet them when they became our regulars. I had my suspicions about Amanda and up to this day, I still believe she was a married woman. She lived in Golders Green, which is a main rabbi jewellers' manor, a place I never had the privilege to visit and more often than not, she would drive down to meet me, which would consist of picking me up from work and back to my flat, which I was renting from my sister Sonia in Elmwood Road Croydon, a flat that turned into a fuckfest venue on my regular meetings with Amanda.

If she was married then she wasn't getting much indoors, because she was starving and would often have my cock out before I could get the keys to the drum out of my pocket. Pete would ring me the next day after we had been on double dates with them and we would both natter like two old ladies. He would explain that Suzanne would leave him fucked, as if he had done 12 rounds with Tyson; they both had skills, Premiership pussy in my eyes and boy-oh-boy if you needed to crash test Viagra tablets, they would have been perfect candidates, making me half gutted that Viagra was not about in them days for me to cope with Amanda's insatiable appetite.

So me and the boys, we had our routines and it was not long before it began to piss the girls off. Yes, granted in the beginning we would go down to Dingwall's in Camden Lock, HQ Club and fancy bars and shopping with them, but that was because we was babes-ing. This is a term we used that described the part of the mating ritual you would undertake before finally getting to fuck them, but now, if we are out with the boys, then we are out with the boys, what the fuck? It's funny because over the years we would have the same old tired old arguments with birds over and over.

One Friday night we met the girls over Kings Road or Knightsbridge, I don't know, in some poncey wine bar or another, when off they started on us with words which I can barely recall like attention, feelings, neglected, selfish, blah, blah, blah, yada, yada, yada. When the lecture was over, we broke our silence and together decided, "Fuck this for a Friday night, let's go."

We left them with their screwed-up faces and headed back to the hood. As we drove through Kennington, we see this fella from the manor called 'Pin' outside some gaff. We pulled up to see what the crack was, with flyers in hand, and he said there was a little warehouse do going mental around the corner, £10 to get in, so we headed down there paid our cockle (and hen)and went in. The place was going off ballistic, we'd not heard these sounds live like this before. We heard the odd one on the pirate stations LWR and Kiss FM. This was mid-88, we were still bang into our rare groove but the people in there and the atmosphere was fucking bang on. This was our first exposure to the house that is acid and Pete's first words as we watched the mad crowd dance in a trance was, "No chance of pulling any sorts in here then".

At that same time(funnily enough) we clocked these two lovely birds. They were fit as fuck, in little tight dresses and the way they danced had Pete and me hypnotised. Without muttering a word they was over with us, gyrating around us, as me and Pete looked at each other bewildered. This carried on for what seemed like ages before they spoke as the next track came up.

"Hello lovelies" said one of them. They introduced themselves as Tracey and Trudy. We were quite taken aback by how friendly they were because unknown to us at the time, they were heightened by little yellow Californias they had taken and we listened intrigued as they explained the beautiful sense of aurora they were feeling. "I have the same sensations in my cock" I thought to myself.

They offered us half each of a tablet that Tracey had pulled from her bum bag, which seemed to be perched on top of her perfect arse before spinning it around to offer us the E. Them days, the only drug we had taken was in a spliff, the good Sensimilla and the odd Moroccan black is all we'd been used to up to this point, not this type of chemistry experiment. We were dubious, so we declined the offer.

As the night went on, the two of us being in usual pulling mode, we continued our pursuit oblivious to the fact that they were smashed on the Es, but fuck it, Tracy was hot as you like, devilishly sexy with her short hair, the figure-hugging dress and ankle boots ensemble complemented her curves, constantly rubbing up against me, I so desperately wanted to smash her back doors in, E'd up or not.

We didn't do too bad by all accounts, clocked their digits and thought at least we would get to fight another day, hopefully when the hippy bollocks was out of their system. By the end of the night, after a few cans of Red Stripe, we seemed to be getting on the tunes that was lashing out.

"ACID MAN, ACID MAN, ACID MAAAAN... YEAH" I shout happily as we are now getting the vibe and the atmosphere.

The D-Mob *we call it aciiiiied* chorus rings out and the whole building is screaming it. I was laughing about with Pete, who by now was mixing up a little James Brown slide foot move to the acid house beat. We finally rolled out the gaff about 6 o'clock in the morning after saying our farewells to our newly-found conquest and were hoping to see them very soon.

On the Saturday, I was too fucked for the football and having avoided Amanda's phone calls all day, I was on the phone to all the boys, Face, Killa and TJB, who by now had found out from Pete that we'd had a blinding night at an acid house do. TJB decided that we venture that night to another one in Clink Street, which some bird he was seeing was banging on about.

Located near Borough High Street, we'd parked up near a convoy of BT vehicles where a few of Pete's pals were working a night shift. We stopped to have a laugh and a joke with them as they teased us about seeing space ships or some bollocks, but we weren't drug takers, apart from the spliff we shared with the two outspoken telephone technicians, we were clubbers, here to experience something a little bit different.

I remember going there and sweating our bollocks off all night, as the heat in that place was almost like a furnace and it slapped you in the face as soon as you entered, but we didn't mind, as we danced away to these new sounds. Hearing *Definition of a track* by The Backroom, was one of them clubbing defining moments for me when that tune dropped in there. With its almost dub wise make you want to skank type beat, this I have to admit was a different experience from the previous night. It was less TB303 and more Synthy based, smooth dark vocal type tunes with DJ Evil Eddie Richards spinning some amazing stuff. The crowd was as energetic as it was at our last event 24 hrs ago. It was an absolutely blinding night and we were drenched at the end of it.

What set the acid house sessions in Clink Street apart, when I think about it, was that you could tell that some of the clientele in there were naughty. It's almost like an instinctive thing with us, we'd acknowledge certain people in there and over the next couple of weeks,

61

seeing these faces and talking to people we'd got friendly with, it became evident that these were football faces, like a few Gooners and the odd Chelsea, Luton and Tottenham in there who we met, all being the salt of the earth. People just like us, as was the case with the Fitness centre on Southwark Street with its Millwall links.

Despite all this though, there was never a single out of place look or anything sinister experienced at any of these events and they were probably some of the most enjoyable clubbing experiences you could imagine, enhanced by the power of the E no doubt. The same could be said of the Centre Force run Dungeons in Lea Bridge Road, where we attended during 1989. This was a rave with heavy connections to West Ham's Inter City Firm.

By the winter of 1988, we were back on the rare groove tip, Dance Wicked were doing regular weekly events and dropping some cream beats, and we would often meet up with Heidi and her friends for a good old boogie. Heidi was a girl Pete had met at Babylon earlier that year, and we always found it funny recalling when and how we met them. Heidi and her mate Irini (who later on became a leading UK R&B artist with her release *24/7 Love*) were in there together one night. Pete and TJB looked like they were copping on to another set of conquests, that was the standard for us back then.

I remembered clocking them at the time. They were both stunningly pretty with the look of mischief and mystery about them, the kind of challenge me and the boys were always up for, so after the customary exchanging of numbers as was our thing back in them days, it was mission accomplished. After leaving it a few days, as you do, keep them keen and all that, Pete belled Heidi up. During their long telephone conversation about the scene, music, the usual chit chat and him working his way for a meet, she confessed to him that she was only 15 years old and still at school.

Pete was kind of in a panic as we headed out clubbing that night after TJB enquired to whether he had made contact yet because he'd not had any luck getting hold of Irini. "She told me she was 19 when I met her" he said all worried, as the car rocked with laughter. In fairness to Heidi or how Pete explained it, the conversation when he met her was probably like how most initial spiel goes when giving it all the chat in the club ...

"'Ello Darling' what's your name?"

"Heidi"

"Where you from?"

"Hackney."

"You look really nice, How old are yah?"

"How old do I look?"

"19."

If at all a conversation like that about age ever even came up, when hitting on chicks in the clubs. But for me, this was a great opportunity to rip the piss out of him, calling him 'handcuffs', which was a term we used during the Senator days when some of the boys were accommodating the attention of some of our young female followers, or jailbait, as they were referred to. Even though most of us were between 16–18 at the time, Pete was always one of those that would be cussing the boys and sounding them out over the mic for doing it. He would rap over the microphone and even to this day, I have a dig at him for unfairly naming me, when he dropped his anthem that went something like...

Shark Business, dem under shark business,
Cos my posse nowadays a check de' young school kid
That is something I don't want get involved wid
Warned Crucial Danny yes I did, yes I did
Warned Fluxie, Colonel and Sugar Alex,
Warned Daddy Fatman but him don't give a shit,
Shark Business, dem under shark business.

So now this situation of him, a big old 22-year-old man, chatting up an under-aged Heidi in Babylon gave me a good few weeks of piss take at

Pete's expense. Although they never got together in the usual sense, we still questioned his intentions as we found it childishly hilarious at the time. She would even play along with us when we were in the club, like trying to hold his hand and pretend to be all over him. Above all that, they became very good friends after and have remained good friends even to this day 26 years later.

This puts a little shine onto this story, that it wasn't all wham bam thank you mam with all the girls that we met over the years, hard as we tried. Because after this, we would see them out often and began meeting up with them plus Irini's sister Marina and Heidi's sister Hayley and all their pals, like Lisa, Brenda and Jennifer, on a regular basis. A good set of girls, who were proper ravers, a good crack and great company as we drank and partied with them on many occasions at Pig, Babylon, Dingwall's and many Dance wicked events.

Without sounding too big-headed or anything, at the time we were copping off with more girls than we could handle, because we were greedy like that. We were often in clubs when most or all of them were in the same building at the same time. At this point though, we wasn't that fussed, such was our arrogance. Pete was pulling up to clubs with us in his white BMW 320i, he was doing well at BT and we were thinking we were the bollocks as we simulated a drive by. We slowly drove past the queues to clubs, music thumping, making sure we were clocked before approaching the venue.

TJB/Galton was also in full swing with his pseudo personality, telling birds that he was a photographer now. In all fairness, they fell for it. We enjoyed reviewing his handy snaps and some of them wouldn't have fallen short as proper masturbation material as he talked them into semi-nude & erotic positions in front of his lens. He was also a sucker for Mickey Rourke and his nine and a half weeks character that the rest of us also confess to being inspired by when luring our intended targets under the sheets. Remember, we were young, in our early 20s, cool dressing funky dreads, with egos as big as a female jazz singer's arse, as Eddie Murphy quite eloquently puts it, these were our 'fuck years'.

We were in full flow by the end of 1988 and slowly, I was getting a taste for violence. We were booting off regularly at Palace with the Wilton arms mob. It seemed at the time that it drove up the sex appeal, especially with Amanda, who always wanted to hear the stories about me putting the boot in and running with a hooligan firm. It made her exceptionally wet. Now don't get me wrong, I'm not saying that I went around bashing people up for no reason when we were out clubbing, but we would often get silly cunts wherever we went and occasionally, people tried to test us and were more often than not left in a heap.

Leading up to Xmas, I had a few rendezvous with Tracey from the Kennington acid house party where I had some fun nights with her as she was bang on expectations, fit as fuck and impressive under the sheets, always a good thing. I could have easily begun to get the impression that this was the one. Don't get me wrong, she was a lovely girl as well and really good company, but back in them days, that was way down on the priorities, it was all about the bedroom skills.

We also had a couple of combo hookups with Pete and Trudy, where if I remember correctly, being quite taken aback as I'm sure she was teasing for a threesome with them both. I don't know, maybe it was just me but I vaguely remembered her putting it on him with a few little compliments here and there and the odd hint. Pete in all fairness didn't bite on it, we were pals, there was an unwritten code of honour and unless both of them were game for a gangbang then it wasn't going to happen. Pete would confess that he was tempted to breach that code for a split second (who wouldn't? she was fucking fit) and reluctantly having to play dumb to the advances. We also recall that it may even have caused a rift between the girls. I guess they had a code too but don't quote me on that, I'm just trying to get things clear in my head, the reasons why a bird as fit as she was wasn't on my contact sheet for much longer after this.

Trudy however, was bang into Pete and as we went our separate ways that Xmas night, I imagined she was going to give him a nice Xmas present to see the night out, whilst me on the other hand, I had to settle for a romp with Tracy, paranoid to the fact that she was probably imagining Pete there instead of me. Pete wasn't shy on detailing his intimate evening with Trudy when we all met up with TJB, Face and Killa on Boxing Day to watch Charlton V Arsenal at Selhurst Park. Back then, the gyppos were ground sharing with us (Crystal Palace).

I remember it being a very subdued atmosphere during Arsenal's 3-2 win down there. It seemed as though everyone was still worn out and over-indulged from the Christmas, and looking at Pete, It looked as though he'd over indulged after eating some good bird himself last Christmas night.

Pete was seeing this Trudy on a regular basis for a while, but he was also in and out of relationships with his sweetheart from over Blackheath. Whereas me, at the same time, along with Tracey for that short period, I was still seeing Amanda on and off but was also getting my end away with a girl called Carla and also a girl called Kay. So weekdays mostly we were patching up, making up or making out with our girls trying to keep as much of the peace, so we were free to continue our ritual of hitting the clubs at the weekend. Trudy had introduced Pete to a fella called Dave from Brixton. He and his mate Paul were main ticket agents for Sunrise Back to the Future, Westworld, Energy and Genesis dos.

The pair of them (Tracey and Trudy) had both told us about Sunrise events and promised us that if we went, that we would absolutely love it, pills or no pills. Just the excitement and the secrecy of it all was a buzz in itself. On this recommendation, we'd agreed we'd give it a go but it was tough parting with 25 Sovs for a party, I can tell you.

"This party best be the bollocks, and I expect to get my cock sucked by Lady Fuckface of Kensington for that money as well" I said jokingly when Pete rang me after he had shelled out £125 large for all our tickets. There was no address or fuck all for the do, just an 0836 phone number and the instructions from Trudy to meet at the Windmill pub on Clapham Common. So the night of the 20th May 1989, Sunrise Once in a blue moon, held in aircraft hangar at Santa Pod racetrack, we attended and we were blown away. "Whaaaat... Fucking blinding!" was our unified chorus.

We scoped the venue out, which was rocking to *Rock to the beat* and Doug Lazy *Let it roll*. Tunes we heard before in the back room of Dance wicked but when the 2 in a room tune dropped with the intro

10... 9... 8... 7,6,5,4321...
Someone in the house say yeah!

It had the place and us going mental. Double Trouble and the Rebel MCs *just keep rocking* track slams the arena as the Rebel rhymes 'All night business the intention' culminated in people standing on platforms and on speakers and going for it flat out. This party got us hooked all right and every other tune reincarnated our past rare groove 'I'm a wicked dancer' shuffle into an 'I don't give a fuck' bounce. These tunes were blinding yet so simple, a drum machine and a bass line. It just made you want to smile. Amidst the entire crowd we see Trudy and Tracey; they were spun off their nuts so we left them to it. We were bumping into bods we knew as well. Main Croydon faces like Lloyd Harper with a little team in there from the manor. Clive, who was a main face at Palace, Little Nick and a few others were there also, we greeted each other with bear hugs as they explained that a small contingent from the manor had travelled up after meeting at the Swan and Sugar loaf pub in South Croydon.

I knew these lads from Palace. The weekend before, they were fending off a marauding mob of Birmingham City Zulus in Tutus and gorilla suits in the Arthur Wait stand, throwing fists with a menacing growl. Now they had their hands in the air and were grinning and rolling their eyes around in the back of their heads. This plus the feelgood atmosphere, almost subconsciously, had all of us doing the same thing, throwing our hands up and having it; this was well worth the 25 quid and had me curious for the chemistry that was the E.

"I might yam one of these Es to see what it's like" I said to Face,

67

who then looked at me, just as my dad would look at me if I'd asked him to lend me a score.

"You're off your head already you cunt, you don't need drugs." he laughed.

By the morning, we were standing around watching people gurn on the fairground rides. We were totally in awe of it all, how birds were all friendly and coming up to us, some blatantly asking for a bunk up in the hay stack, which took us aback strangely enough as we were more used to having to graft for it, but hey ho, I make no bones of the fact. When curiosity got the better of me and after sneakily necking two halves of an E during the night that Palace Clive had given me earlier, I began to understand what it was all about, but oh mate, it wasn't just the music I was feeling. This had created an unbelievable party in my boxers and she must have seen that it was love season because she was all over me. We were on the same kind of level, I had no idea what that level was but every stroke, as she caressed my back and that sexy bass line thrashing out, seemed to be too much for us to control our urges. I was beckoned and obligingly followed this posh sounding, media arty-farty type bird behind the tents and in between the generators to bang her doggy style. She was gripping the rope and hanging on for dear life as I smashed my E excited dingaling in and out of her splashy quim as KLF's *What time is love* played in the background. I thought it had only lasted a few minutes, 10 at the most, but Pete later said (and swears this as gospel) that I had disappeared with Tracey and was gone for at least two hours. I reckoned he was either on one himself, or he was on a wind up, Tracey wasn't even posh. Up to this day I still wonder what her name was, it definitely wasn't Tracey and we even exchanged numbers at the end, she may have been Lady Fuck-Face of Kensington for all I could remember it was a moment we shared and was probably all it were meant to be, but imagined I'd recognise her again if I happened to see a posh tart walking like John Wayne.

The following Monday as my senses started to come back to me and my erection finally went away, we were all waxing lyrical to whoever would listen about the amazing time we had at Sunrise. Who'd have thought you could have such a fucking blast in a dusty old warehouse where people would embrace one another, man and woman, who would tell you to "get right on one matey". It signalled a new era for all of us, from the way that we dressed to our attitude towards mankind, that I'm sure many people look back on as our Woodstock.

CHAPTER 7

ZULUS IN TUTUS

It was now into a really hot summer. The 88-89 football season was finished now and was a really good season for Palace. We had clinched promotion via the playoffs against Blackburn Rovers where we overturned a 3-1 deficit on the away leg. The packed in 30,000 Selhurst Park attendance saw after 2-0 at full time and 3-3 on aggregate, Ian Wright pop up on 117 minutes to head the winning goal to spark a mass pitch invasion. I remember deliberately trying to trip up the Blackburn keeper but missed and stacked it onto the turf, styling it out with a roly-poly of joy. I also enjoyed the odd skirmish after the game, and running what was accounted as their mob, all around Selhurst that afternoon as well.

It was also a good season, with Arsenal winning the league title. However, it was also the year we had all witnessed the disaster at Hillsborough. This rather brought home how a waste of life could happen at football. We've all been there, squashed up against the fence or the barriers on the terraces during offs and with goal celebrations, so how more incidents like this never occurred must have been a miracle. As we witnessed the events unfold, 96 poor souls lost their lives.

Due to hard partying, our finances were taking a battering, so we decided on taking it easy for the last few games that season as we flittered between visits to Selhurst Park and Highbury. The last game we went to that season at Highbury was Arsenal v Norwich. Arsenal had thumped them five nil but if we had known, in hindsight, how the final game would finish, we would have loved to take the journey to Anfield. Instead we watched on TV the unbelievable event unfold. With the very last kick of the game, to see my best pal Pete so elated to the point where he could have cried, it was up for grabs as the ITV match commentator Brian Moore screamed... "THOMAAAAS!"

Pete was on his feet. "YEEEEEEEEESSSSSSSSSSSS"......FUCKING YEAAAAAAAAAAAAAAAAAAAAHHHHHHHHHH!" he screamed, in a manner I thought he could only reach with Suzanne, or Katrina for that matter. He ran out into his mother's back garden, passing TJB, whose tears of sadness flowed as he witnessed his Liverpool team concede the title on this unbelievable climax to a league season. Pete's mum came in after hearing the commotion and after clocking TJB's boat, said in her sweet Jamaican tongue and quizzed, "Is wha' you all do to Roger, why him a bawl fah?"

This had Killa, Face and Me rolling on the floor roaring with laughter at the thought that TJB had got so upset that Pete's mum thought it was us that had caused his despair and we were chuckling even louder as he skulked off home. The rest of us ended up that night outside Highbury, when Fatman, who we had not seen in a while, had come round to Pete's house to watch the game with us. We drove up through the streets of Islington with beeping car horns going off everywhere and celebrations outside the ground. Even as a non-Arsenal fan it was special, especially doing the scousers 2-nil at fortress Anfield in that manner. Many Gooners claimed this as their best night ever, even ahead of their weddings and birth of children. We sat on the pavement opposite the grand façade of the stadium and watched people jumping around, Pete just sat there quietly sipping a can of Hofmeister and singing, "We love you Arsenal we do". He said with regret, "Fucking wish we had gone up there man".

It had been a great year for all of us up to that point. We had had so much fun, although Pete was hurting for the most part as his relationship with Katrina was back and forth. Out of the blue she had told him a couple of weeks back that she was getting married to some fella and had also told him previously that she had slept with her ex while Pete was away on a training course in Edinburgh. This kind of choked the boy up if truth be told. OK granted, he was banging other birds like Trudy and Suzanne in between their on and off periods.

Neither of us were at the settling-down stage, but he was really into her in a mad way that over the years, we always had that kind of emotional tie with certain girls, so I knew where he was at with it all. I always had his ear and he always had mine. For years now he had been my best pal and tonight he could forget all that shit. Tonight he was happy with the love affair that is a man and his football team. A woman would never understand it.

That season also climaxed with an end-of-season battle at Palace v Birmingham. Everyone was out early doors for this one and I was surprised entering the Wilton and seeing it filled with Blue noses, with the few Palace that were in there looking awkward at this incursion. It only took a few minutes of being in there, when wound up by the silence of the Wilton boys, I slammed a pool cue on the bar and let everyone know, "THIS IS OUR FUCKING PUB!"

Surprisingly, the Birmingham supporters all just upped and left, followed by a couple of pint glasses courtesy of some fella called Spud. As I had mentioned earlier, Brummies had all come down in fancy dress, dressed as Charlie Chaplins, ballerinas and sailors, and some were in monkey suits and dressed as Fred Flintstone, when they came down for a pre-planned end of season relegation party. It all went berserk when Ian Wright scored in the 12th minute. The ensuing pitch invasion saw Zulus and Palace clashing, with Palace lads getting fronted as they walked into the gaff by Brummies' droning voices with the offers of, "C'mon Palace ... where's your firm?" In addition, "we'll see you at Victoria!"

One of our lot from the Wilton responded with, "I'll see you now you cunt!" and puts one on one of them, sending the Zulus into action.

I was in the seats in the Arthur Waite with Reggie, Gary Pitcher,

Dave, Richard a few other Wilton boys and a number of Nifty 50 lads including a lad I knew from our school days called Frankie who had missed most of the trouble but joined us later on. Zulus steamed across battering all in site, Hooligans and scarfers, as we stood and had it with them. What you see from the news footage of the game was Zulus on the pitch giving a slap to some Palace who fronted it, but further up in the stands it was going off proper. We were holding our own until we were finally over-whelmed as we battled and clamoured over our own scarfers, who were happy to have us as their saviours that day. Zulus were running amok as we got a few digs for our troubles and as bedlam continued in the stands and on the pitch I noticed a Zulu in a nun or vicar outfit, sprawled across the seats screaming, high pitched, "Some kont's knoifed me," clutching his cheek, which was pissing with claret as he was helped up by his fellow BCFC supporter.

"Have some of that you cunt" I said as the oncoming Zulus in tutus backed us off. I clocked Reggie slipping off now after doing damage to the Zulu's face. I had guessed he was the culprit. He confirmed later that he had rammed a small penknife into the fella's cheek. "Cunt took a swing and banged me in the moosh, so I stuck my pen knife in the cunt's face" he said with a mad Frankie Frazer look, a look and a phrase that would become a familiar theme and I would hear many times in years to come.

It was kicking off all over the place that day and we held our own in all honesty. The main Nifty 50 lot when they had all mobbed up back at the Whitehorse had it on and off with coaches and minibus loads of Zulus. This also sums up the main point about Palace, that we were often split between mobs at home, where if we were all together 150-200 lads having it with these main mobs we would have probably got more respect and recognition. On the other hand, it's OK hiding behind your 200, 300-strong firms but getting in the thick of things when you're 25-handed is a different kettle of fish where you have to get your hands dirty, and we did.

Another funny incident that day was later on, having convened back at the Wilton, pockets of Blues were intimidated on the high street as evening fell, when drunk and disgruntled lads got some payback on smaller mobs of Zulus. One lad called Don was terrorising whoever he didn't identify as local. A couple of dudes with rucksacks on were fronted by him from across the road as he asked them who the fuck they were …

"We're from New York, Maan," one hollered back. An enraged Donald, making his way across the road to them, screamed, "Cunt, then you ain't from Thornton Heath" and proceeded in steaming into them, which had everyone in pieces as he chased them up the road. We were all shouting for him to leave it out, that they were only tourists, but his head was gone by then as we stood by pissing ourselves.

I was now getting heavily involved with it all and people were starting to notice Reggie and me together standing firm when the time came. Although Reggie's bigger than life personality and tendencies to go OTT with blades was a little concerning to some, it was after the trouble with the Zulus later on the following season when Frankie, who I was with that day, invited me for a drink over the Cherry Trees in South Norwood. This would take my involvement with football violence to another level when he introduced me to the main boys, the Nifty 50.

I had been witness to and also been in a few scrapes and battles with most of them before at Palace and they knew of me, especially the main lads, who were a very tight unit and did not suffer any fools. They knew I was game for a tear-up after seeing me involved with the Wilton lot over the past few years, but a game against Charlton comes to mind. We'd had many running battles with them snide cunts for many years and evenly matched to be brutally honest, but for some reason when it comes to rows with us, our friendly neighbours over there have had selective memories, as a lot of them regularly seem to forget the incident at the Goat House.

From memory of that day, I was not going to football regularly, but being a youth of the street would occasionally, if you were in the right place at the right time, end up in fisticuffs in honour of defending the manor. Before the game there had been a few bits and bobs going off in Thornton Heath and Norwood, as you can gather those days without mobile phones and internet you would get the main news on the terraces of what went on before and what would be planned for after the games.

I left a little bit before full time, this would have been around 1985 season. I left the game to meet with some of the Streatham moped crew. Trying to tie it all up this would have been during my Sound System days as well, so I was meeting them for whatever reason I can't recall. Anyway I was walking back up the hill towards the Penge Road. The main Whitehorse and South Croydon boys were bowling up towards the Goathouse looking like they were on a mission. I knew most of them from school so this lot would have been 17 upwards, with the South Croydon lot being a little bit older, but I guess they would have been classed as youth in today's hooligan climate.

Soon after, about 40 or so of the Nifty had a pop at an even number of Charlton. These were their main boys, their older lot as well, and when it all kicked off I went steaming into the Charlton mob. A few of them, each time there was a standoff, were giving it the usual bollocks, black this, nigger that, towards me and the other lads of colour that were battling, including a few of that lot that were terrorising pals of mine I mentioned earlier in the book.

We eventually had them backed off as we chased them back down the Penge Road. As the row stopped and started, they tried to regroup but continued to get smashed and on the back foot. I enjoyed catching the odd one and giving them a volley of abuse in Jamaican, something that I must have picked up from my old man when he would beat us when we were kids for being naughty. "Hold dis you lickle bloodclaaart", as I smash one sweetly on the jaw.

I also remember one of their main fellas, some big old lump with a beard. Strangely when we were all over them at certain points, he kept wanting to shake hands with our lot but every time he did he would get smashed in the head with a lump of wood. It was really bizarre but this was a top row with tools, bricks, bottles, the works as we have them backed off all the way down to the railway bridge. At the end of the day, they can say what they like about Palace but I witnessed a game mob representing Palace that day, we were tight, organised and smashed Charlton's main boys up until that point.

When their numbers increased, this gave the first lot of Charlton second wind. We continued going toe to toe with them for a few more minutes, and they began to get the upper hand on us slightly. They returned many of the missiles we had already rained on them, so we had to back up a little. With numbers on their side they were reluctant I am quite sure, maybe it was seeing the whites of a few angry darkies eyes, looking like they wanted a piece of some right-wing meat. This had them a little hesitant. They could smell a bit of a result having been battered and run several times during the skirmish, but their initiative was short lived as the Old Bill arrived, jumping out of SPG vans and swinging batons to contain the two rival groups.

Nifty 50 were holding their own and were prominent as our main casual mob. Despite what people from other firms think of us, back then we were having it proper, between 1984 and 1987 especially, and were at the top of our game as far as the organised violence went. The only time I understood some to start losing it was after the dawn raids from Operation Whitehorse in 1987, where several members were looking at big sentences. 32 Palace lads were arrested as the authorities tried to clamp down on the English decease, if I remember rightly, occurring at the same time as the ICF raids, part of Operation Backyard.

After a few weeks in court, all the cases brought to courts at that time were thrown out due to unreliable evidence produced by the police (hmm... now where have I heard that one before?) and actions of police infiltrators assigned to these mobs. This had left many lads paranoid after the events because many were also up to a few bits of villainy as well, so every new face from now on was potential Old Bill.

I knew most of them from school, mostly boys who went to Ingram or Norbury Manor went to Selhurst School after the third year and that's where I knew most of the Whitehorse lot. Lads like Frankie were good pals with the Fuller brothers that I knew and I remember being at some blues parties where he would be the only white boy in the building, but this never fazed him and he was as game as they come.

Clive, Matt, Mickey and Little Nick were also fellas that I knew, that were among the main boys in the firm. In fact, all the main boys I had looked up to for a few years because they had that way about them, don't get me wrong, we were all around the same age more or less but this was a football thing and in my opinion, when they were all together, they looked as good as the ICF, Chelsea and Yid firms I used to see and cream about when I was back in school, especially the South Croydon-St Joseph's lot, which was a school Billy, Si, Yous and the other top boys attended when they were younger. They looked the part, dressed smart and were game, all could have a row and because they had been solid for years together, they always had each other's backs.

I also used to see a few of them about all the time, not just at football but also pubs and clubs in and around Croydon, Norwood and Beckenham, in places like Snifters and Bon Bonnies. Later on, they would be embroiled in a turf like war with other Croydon groups, people I knew as well, which would always have us in awkward situations when out and about. Fuck knows how it all started but people were being severely served up at the time. I remember one tear-up they were involved in with this Norbury Chelsea firm that I knew, they were rowing for a few years with this lot until acid house and the Es cooled them all down. Also another crew that Killa, Pete and Face knew, which was another longer drawn out war during the 90s which started over someone dating the wrong girl if memory serves me right. These were difficult times because it involved people we knew and liked but we were kind of stuck in the middle as they badmouthed each other. One incident left a pal that we knew fighting for his life in a shop doorway in Croydon. This was as a result of one of the main South Croydon lads getting attacked and given a good old kicking. It was tit for tat that went on over a few years and is probably still brewing to this day.

CHAPTER 8

NIFTY 50

hoo·li·gan/ hool g n/Noun: A violent young troublemaker,
typically one of a gang.
Synonyms: hoodlum - rowdy - ruffian - roughneck – rough.

Now people looking from the outside in would say that a bunch of lads fighting over a football match is ridiculous and I would 100% agree if it was as simple as that. I said it at the beginning of this book, that since I was a boy going from soul boy to rude-boy to casual to ragamuffin MCs, I was always in an environment of a crew or gang but not in the sense of a gang like today's youth that kill each other over postcodes, because that is ridiculous. It was more a camaraderie thing, to stand by your mates through thick and thin. When you're at school you have rivalries with other schools, you go to football and get one over on your rivals, even doing battles during bodypopping days where the best moves would blow the other dance crew away.

I don't know what it was that attracted me to the football firms. I remember discussions at school as an 11-year-old when a lad would show off about his big brother being a Chelsea Headhunter. There were schoolyard rumours about Man United's mighty Cockney Reds led by an 8 foot 3 giant called Banana Bob taking the Holmesdale end. Being fascinated while standing in the Holmesdale end and staring at the skinhead in his Doc Marten boots, trying to work out if it was red laces or white laces that said you were National Front.

Witnessing an impressive Chelsea mob arriving at South Norwood and looking the bollocks, many draped in Pringle, Lacoste, Tacchini and Fila and hearing stories of Arsenal and Birmingham with top black lads having rows at football in deerstalker hats and Burberry coats. Boys in school discussing threads and football firms, how we'd chat at parties about names and stories of notorious hooligans who were written in hooligan folklore, Tiny, Babs, Cass, Miller, Denton, Icky, Gregors. Watching the ICF documentary as cameras followed their every move, being frozen with fear as 100 Boro Frontline marched down Park road and throwing my first punch during a fight with a northern lad that tried to nick my Palace scarf.

You don't just wake up one morning and decide you want to be a hooligan, but as you begin to hang out with lads of a likeminded ideology and you go with them to games, you have a beer and a laugh and you bump into another bunch of likeminded individuals but they are different from you and this is your manor and there is another 60 lads behind you and they want to do something about it. I am no expert in human behaviour but the animal instinct in humans is to protect what is theirs and the football lad will act out of these instincts.

Are there rules? Supposedly there are. No bullying normal fans, no hitting women and children, no knives or tools etc (yeah righto), but as far as I know, there is no hooligan code of conduct or rules of behaviour treaty signed by Parliament in 1886. However, there are things that are frowned upon by lads up and down the country. Nevertheless, I cannot see how you can take a moral high ground when for instance, you are involved in smashing up a pub that your rival firm is in and the proprietor left out of pocket, then has to replace windows, furniture and having to lay off staff, left traumatised by the experience and cannot return to work.

In addition, I cannot explain why 49-year-old men are still arrested for football violence when they should know better, but they do. One thing I can explain though is that there is no buzz like it when the roar goes up.

My involvement has exposed me to some scary shit at times, for instance, when you are outnumbered and have to fight your way out until you're fucked but the adrenaline keeps you going. Being chased by 20 men screaming "get the nigger!" or "kill the coon!" and you are running for your life and miles away from home and all you can think about is your girlfriend who you left at home so you could attend this away trip and wishing you stayed in. Then if you asked me, if I were caught, whether them 20 or so Scousers would just have grabbed me, give me a couple of slaps and let me go? Who the fuck knows? because that night I was Linford Christie and was not going to hang about to find out because you live on your wits, you try to survive, you live to fight another day by making the right decisions.

The scraps I got into when with the boys that drank in the Wilton Arms was me fighting with my mates, that's me helping them out and it led me to becoming a member of CPFC Nifty 50. The fact that they were called Nifty 50 is irrelevant; it is just a badge if you like, to identify ourselves that we are the boys. It is the same if you are the Tonge Moor Slashers, Mongoose Cuckoo Boys or the Billy Whizz Fan Club from Bolton, or the Cardiff City Soul Crew, or the Lincoln Transit Elite. The fact that we all supported Crystal Palace was down to geography and it is as simple as that.

From as far back as my memory takes me, Pete and I would have had many conversation over the years about girls & football, girls, football, clothes, music, girls and of course football and would often discuss the topic of football violence and all the rumours and incidents we'd read or heard about. Pete was like me. He has always been around football lads from schooldays and he will be the first to say, it has always been about the camaraderie, the beer and the banter for him, but he also loves the clobber. He would have probably been in tear-ups when he was younger and amongst all the chaos and the bedlam that ensued during these skirmishes, I bet he would be able to tell you exactly what the other firm was wearing, so he is an example of many people who loved it and went to football for different reasons, but to have a good little firm you need people like me and like Reggie and Frankie, game cunts, that thrive on the buzz of violence and there were many of these in the Nifty 50.

But if anyone would have been reading any of the untold hooligan books about firms that never ever get done, and all the untold reports on football hooligan forums, you would have thought that Crystal Palace, since its inauguration, was like no other club out of the 92 in the football league and you might as well add the Scottish leagues as well, that never had a football firm.

Well let me fill you in now, all this 'Palarse no firm' crap, and all this stripy Nigel shit, let me tell you all now, BOLLOCKS! Suck my big black cock. First of all, Crystal Palace located in Selhurst, with neighbouring Thornton Heath, Croydon, South Croydon, Norbury, Addington & South Norwood nearby? Are you telling me that there are no naughty individuals that go to or ever went to watch Palace? I'll say it again, bollocks! Yes OK well done Millwall, You bring thousands of boys to us season after season and always make a song and dance about coming down and us never lifting a finger etc etc. Nice one, well done and as far as Charlton and Brighton are concerned, keep denying that we never brought anything to you, that's OK, if it makes you feel better.

Anyway enough of that shit because that was mainly directed at the clueless cunts, because during the early 80s especially, Palace had a number of mobs, Early Birds, Wilton Arms Boys, Woolpackers, Whitehorse, Nifty 50 and more recent times Dirty 30, Dirty 30 Youth, The HF-U5s and Holmesdale Fanatics (don't ask). Moreover, from my memory at first mainly with the Wilton arms lot, we have terrorised some clubs and have battled with good mobs as well.

As a club and as far as the violence went, I would say forget the main mobs like Yids and Pompey's 6:57. Although we had a nice boot off with them one year, 1986 I think, or maybe 87/88 season. It was the season they were playing for promotion and were pegged back minutes before full time. It went off inside the ground as we went toe to toe with them when main 657 got on the pitch at the end of the game. The main stand with Nifty 50, Wilton and various other lads emptied as we all got on the pitch to get at Pompey and pretty much had them backed off the way that they came. We were at it for a few minutes before order was restored. What I love the most when having these types of rows, is the organised chaos as you notice lads on both sides. Some are 'Queensberry rules' styling it, whilst others are flat out windmilling and a few just seem to bounce up and down on the spot. This would always have me laughing when I look back at it, as I'm giving out a few digs, backing off, flying in with kicks and backing off, grabbing a piece of fence or finding a bottle and launching it into the opposition and always remembering that unmistakeable roar of "CAAM ORN!"

Now my version of this event, after the game we had some good battles with them in and around the manor that evening. At the petrol station beside the ground they had mobbed up 100 handed easy, but this was a day when everyone and his dog was out for us and straight away we put them under a good bit of pressure, where Frankie would say, we pretty much ran them. We would never have it as us doing 6:57 because you will probably have people saying bollocks, but I was in the thick of it that day so what would people rather me say, that we got run?

As far as I'm concerned I saw pure fighting that evening, so any of the running wasn't done by my lot. People can talk what shit they want. We had it with them with a good Palace mob all down Whitehorse Road and outside the Prince George pub at the bottom and I'd even go as far as saying along Thornton Heath high street as well. With the pockets of violence going on in the middle of the road and in shop doorways we pretty much regrouped by the end of it all, but Pompey themselves, their numbers had dwindled. There was none of this 'Pompey came and we ran off' version, as some would have you believe.

I often get heated when hearing about things and other people's accounts. I understand you have to uphold a reputation but this is exactly how I saw it and it's not just my account, Frankie and others who I was with that day see it the same as I do. I'm even arguing as we write this book with Pete, who has heard different accounts from Portsmouth, which is fair enough but just because it's Pompey doesn't mean they can't come unstuck at Palace on home soil and that was one incident, that from what I had seen, where we done all right and had the result. Even early doors, Whitehorse boys were out mid-afternoon hitting a few minibuses as they come through past the Gloucester pub and by the end of it before and after the game, we was easy 80-100 handed and you can't say fairer than that. Anyway, Spurs, Pompey, Man United, Cardiff City, Chelsea, West Ham and Millwall and the other super firms aside, against similar-sized mobs we have been a match for anyone, so it baffles me why we get the snidey shit from these bigger mobs about us all the time. Not that we're arguing against elitism or anything, I'm just saying as far as I view it, this was a culture where you could go to any town with a football club and run into trouble at any given time.

Observing it from the outside when I began to see Palace's main firm getting involved, organising and having it during most of my days going down there, to get in with them in late 89 was a big thing for me because for years it was not just a case of "Yeah... I'm Palace, I'm gonna roll with this lot". I wanted to be accepted and was wary of pushing myself on them and driving them mad, but I was not alone, there were others that were also on the fringes like my pal Barry P. However, we were seen as lads from the Wilton Arms and no more. Maybe because we did not have the right clobber or the face did not fit, they would acknowledge you because you row at football but they were Nifty 50 and you were not (which also made you potential Old Bill) and that was that. So mainly with the Wilton lot I was making sure we were getting involved when most of the trouble would occur.

I remember the night game against Oldham in 1987. It was booting off from when we got off the train, when we bumped into similar sized groups of Oldham fans and were pretty much having a good old toe to toe with them before and after the game, it was a mental night. I was with Reggie, Barry P, Peter E, Robbie Kennett and the rest of the Wilton lot, mainly drinkers, but they were game as anything. I saw the main boys after the game and put myself about mingling amongst them. There were a few wounded amongst them, with one lad even served with a paving slab across his head, so I thought it would be a good opportunity to join in with them and seek some retribution. It seemed they had their own agenda that night and pretty much wanted it to stay amongst themselves, and I received the cold shoulder. I was later told that it was nothing personal, but a couple of the other Wilton with me they didn't want tagging along, especially Reggie, because they viewed him as the biggest liability. Although he was a good head, he just always brought the heat, which I thought was a little unfair, but he was a cranky fucker, I give them that.

The Nifty 50 was getting it on with Oldham alongside the rest of us Palace hooligans, during the skirmishes that seemed to be going off all over the place in town. Hearing that they all went to Manchester United v Chelsea the next day, with Chelsea and had it with Man U, I was a little bit put out that I wasn't able to tag along and many will admit at the time they were a right cliquey bunch.

It was not until an incident in Liverpool after Palace was humiliated nine nil at Anfield that I seemed to get my passage into their inner circle. It came well on top outside the Arkles Pub when a few Wilton boys and I were cornered by a baying Scouse mob, around 30 or so v 8 of us that looked as though they were extra hungry for some nigger carcass or something. With a big chiv I had grabbed off one of the other lads, who was not using it properly against the opposing blades waving about in our direction. I took a few enemy down, as I became the Anfield slasher (self-defence of course) before having to run for my life as we all eventually, have it on our toes, which was one of the scariest moments for me at football, I was very lucky to escape.

This in a perverse way impressed the top boys, but it was more a fact of standing firm with our back against the wall than escaping a possible lynching that opened the door. So I was in, at fucking last.

The makeup of the Nifty 50 firm was South Croydon and Whitehorse, who as I said, some were involved with the likes of Chelsea, Tottenham and Arsenal. I'm also reminded that after the Goathouse row with Charlton, you have heard some of them (well the few who at least admit to the incident) complain over the years that we were assisted by Croydon Yids, which is bollocks.

A couple of the top boys were involved with Yids and a main Yid lad is well documented as pals with the main firm, but they were mainly Nifty 50 and as I said before there was a hardcore group that followed other mobs and turned up anywhere there was a chance of a row, even a Sutton Utd v Middlesboro FA Cup game they turned out a 40-strong mob. This had the gavvers a little puzzled and in a flap when the ginger cunt that policed Palace games at the time identified them. Anyone that faced them or came up against them would have had a decent battle that's a certain, not that many mobs would confess to getting done by Palace, where it seems to be a way of life on the internet hooligan world.

Recollecting a few of many little incidents that would usually have been passed by over the years, Brighton especially may remember a nasty event, when a small firm of them got taxed of their clobber and tom by members of Nifty 50 at East Croydon. They knew who we were, we proper embarrassed them as well. That will probably be denied or rubbished as a non-event. Villa came down in 89 where we had a good old one-sided tear-up with them as 15 of their boys jumped out of a Mini bus, bouncing across at us as we headed back to our boozer, "Come on cockney cunts!"

The reports in the Croydon Advertiser the following week, describing the majority of them needing hospital treatment after the attack by Palace hooligans, told the story. Oh I see! Maybe we should have just had it on our toes then.

Another night this time up in the Midlands against Villa also saw Palace, mainly Nifty, up against Villa's Young mob this time in the pitch dark. We went head to head with them near an old church, it was a decent battle but as some of us got separated, the Old Bill had us and were marching us to the station. We could not help cracking up at the Villa making donkey noises as they singled out one of the main nifty boys and took the piss as they teased him about the size of his teeth.

The FEC (Forest Executive Crew) came from Nottingham, and we also had a nice welcome for them at the top of Whitehorse Road one snowy winter's evening when their minibus was attacked. From memory these Forest lads were doing a few Palace. One of the main South Croydon boys was clattered with a lump of wood as me Frankie and Barry P were struggling in the snow to catch up to the action. 20 more of us, mainly South Croydon, appear out of Park road with chivs out and duly had Forest on the run.

We pretty much had the windows in and occupants given a fair old slap after they showed for a bit, but we had the advantage number wise on them at that point and they were all soon back in the minibus attempting a hasty retreat. It was skidding and slipping around in the snow. My other memory of that evening was watching one of theirs with claret pissing out of his head, chasing after the mini bus after getting a bit left behind after the incident. It seemed that they had forgotten about him during their escape that would probably had been one cold journey home for them in the end. Here are some of the many stories I recollect and from listening to escapades they were involved in from Cambridge to Leicester and from QPR to Middlesbrough, when I was finally accepted as part of their inner circle.

Millwall Away 1986

That season the main group of Nifty 50, after an early meet, took the short journey to bandit country. Frankie described it, bowling from New Cross down to the Old Kent Road. Nifty 50 eventually came up against main Wall Casuals bouncing across the road to us. We were having it against them with even numbers, where Millwall would probably struggle to confess that we was doing OK up to that point. After the initial delight of bumping into them, no one really had the upper hand but this was Millwall and we were taking it to them, which was a feat in itself. However as more and more started to enter the fray the deeper we got down the Old Kent Road, it seemed as though everyone and his grandmother wanted to have a pop. Shopkeepers and other local tradesmen were running out of shops with tools trying to trip us up, and little crews were appearing from out of the estates and jumping off buses. By the time we got to Ilderton Road, it was described as nearly turning into a right pasting for us in the end because this was seen as Palace taking a liberty coming down there and Wall were baying for blood. Even the gavvers were enjoying seeing us getting digs, bullied and peppered with missiles from all angles as we tried to make a hasty retreat.

Our pride was restored when we acted out some retribution on the way back, after having our egos severely dented a little, bumping into another group of Millwall at New Cross after we had been split up. This resulted in an even 15 against 15 on the tube, which saw us proving that a bit of quality against similar numbers had this little skirmish end in our favour. However, you would still be hard pressed to find anyone to give us any credit for that. As most people would know, to take it to Millwall back then with the numbers we had, you needed some extra-large gonads to say the least. Admittedly we were a little hesitant to get the numbers over there in the first place, you have to take your hat off to them.

As I have got to know them after many years, they were a fucking game bunch and top lads as well. Anyhow, with what is expected at Millwall, 40 to 50 game cunts is no match for the mighty Millwall and their many pikey 'Keyboard Hooligan' followers that follow them nowadays with the comfortable fact of safety in numbers. Now I have nothing but admiration for main chaps at Millwall, like the proper Halfway Liners, Treatment or Bushwhackers. I would never in any way disrespect them, but the lairy little Bromley and Kent cunts that hide behind the name and the numbers grate my nuts. Palace came to

Millwall and had it with similar numbers before getting overwhelmed but we just continue to be laughed at over the years because we have never repeated it and were lucky to get out relatively unscathed. In some ways, it is our own fault because with everyone mobbed up, maybe we should have shown a bit more commitment to going over there if you want to split hairs about it, but then again how many mobs actually do?

Even as recently as 2001 or 2002, we mobbed up in the Porter and Sorter in East Croydon for Millwall and after various unsuccessful request to the Millwall contact we had that day to meet, we eventually landed at Norwood Junction with 100–120 lads only to be wrapped up by Old Bill as soon as we got onto the railway network. "Palace getting escorted to their own ground," was the sort of crap we got on internet forums, but they were wrapped up as well, so there is no pleasing some people but here is a suggestion... surely West Ham and Cardiff are more suited opponents eh?

Bournemouth 1988

We caused absolute mayhem down there when we travelled to the south coast that day. It was a good section of Wilton Boys and South Croydon on the train journey, where I remember Frankie playing up and he had been chased by train guards for trying to jib before sticking the nut on him. Well that was it. Gavvers had a welcoming committee for him and after throwing away the big bit of steel he had he was promptly arrested as we all left the train. Police were taking the absolute piss that day, I remember them giving us a few digs and knocking beer out of people's hands hoping to get a response, and they did. Near the end of the game it had all gone berserk, with pitch invasions and flares going off.

Frankie, released from custody after giving a moody name, was nicked again after a steward tried to throw him out and got his arse ironed out. We battled away inside and outside in the car parks. It was total madness that day and a proper giggle, people still say they remember me going nuts up and down the terraces that was actually captured on video that one of the lads had. A few weeks after that, Leeds came down and had their names tarred after they created mass disorder on a scale not seen on that part of the South Coast since Palace a few weeks before.

Birmingham City

I've always liked the Zulus, particularly the fact that they were a good firm with loads of blacks and in my eyes some deep northerners would have had the shock of their lives to be confronted by a top black firm like that. I remember seeing the news during their battle with Leeds at St Andrews and seeing the many casual dudes with afros giving it to the Old Bill and Leeds. Having already mentioned the end of season fancy dress battle we had with them in May 1989, where although we done OK, it came a little on top for us as we come up against the main bulk of their mob as they piled into the Arthur Waite.

A time before that I had come up against them in Feb 1988. We were 20 handed as we stepped out the Cherry Trees with a mixture of Nifty 50 and Wilton Arms boys, and we spotted a few Zulus getting on the train after the game. One of the lads suggested we tail them as we jog towards the London bound train and jumped onto an adjacent carriage hoping we weren't spotted. The eagle-eyed Zulus had already clocked us, when two large black fellas come through the carriage and were offering us a chance to dance with them. They saw our numbers and even though they were a few less than us, they were confident and were frothing for us to join them.

One of the Nifty 50 main lads that were with us at the time rallied all of us. "Let's stick together lads, c'mon, next stop!"

At the next stop, Penge West, we were off the train tapping on the open door button and straight into them in the carriage. This had them a little bit surprised at our bravery and on the back foot. There were some game lads amongst us and the main lad was impressed with the non-Nifty 50, like me, Gary and a few others from Wilton Arms and Addington that was giving as good as we got against this good Zulu firm, who were slightly taken aback at our response to their early offer. These proper rows really got the adrenalin going as we clumped each other inside.

Gary pointed out to us after that one of the Zulus was inviting us to meet them the following week where we were set to play West Brom. "Sandwell and Dudley, next week, get off at Sandwell and Dudley" I think he said, an odd request at the time but I gathered in hindsight it was the location for an ambush. 20 of us, mainly Wilton, alighted the train that following weekend. Exiting the station we were run ragged as Zulus laid in wait surrounding us with tools, iron bars, hammers, road signs the lot as we scattered in all directions. After the initial onslaught, survival mode has to kick in in situations like this. Me and Gary sprinting down the dual carriageway to escape the baying mob could have triggered off speed cameras, such was the speed we was travelling. This was not a very good look for us that afternoon as we made it to the ground in 2's and 3's, but it comes with the territory and after doing well against main Zulus the previous weekend we walked straight into their trap and got run.

Another unexpected tear-up with them was the weekend of the FA Cup semi-final in 1990 when we were facing Liverpool for the 4-3 thriller at Villa Park. Frankie described it that 25 Nifty 50 had jibbed the train up from London to New street and landed bang outside a pub with a few lads outside (we later learned were Zulus.) Immediately it kicked off and we proper had it with them backing them off into the pub before they come back at us with bottles and other missiles. The skirmish was at a lull when they have questioned us - "Who are yas?"

When we replied and said we were Palace, they were like, "Fock off loike, fockin Palace?"

My guess is initially they thought we were Yids or another London mob because this seemed to trigger them to respond. With the numbers they had they must have thought there was no way Palace were going to do a number on them and chased us up an alleyway. They caught one of ours and were duly giving him a shoeing before being backed off with a brick as Frankie has gone back into them down the narrow entrance. We eventually regrouped at the top of the alley as Old Bill arrived and moved us on, but Nifty had a right result on a good group of Zulu warriors.

Most of the lads that stayed out drinking in Brum that evening also reported to us at the game to have been 'booting off' with different sets of Brummies for most of the evening in the city centre.

Man United FA Cup Wembley 1990

You can't beat a good old FA Cup final day. After the semi-final we had, football wise that 4-3 win had us going mental and I must admit my voice was gone for the next few days after. The weeks leading up to Wembley, I had been with a few of the Nifty faces conducting a bit of business and socialising with them now, I was looking forward to the early meet at East Croydon.

There were a good 70 of us that travelled to Victoria. Frankie and a few of the other boys were on top form as they always were, planning and preparing, observing what we had, deciding where we were going to go and although it was a cup final against Man U, there were a few rumours of Brighton being about. As we reached Victoria, the only other mob we saw was the 30 or so lads with our older lad, Clive. Here we all decided to have a drink in Baker St, and by the time we were getting off the tube we were a good 120 strong mob.

It wasn't until we were getting back down to the tube that the action started. We bumped into 50 or so Reds and it all kicked off as they were getting off the tube. We flew into them as the others at the top of the escalator coming down were roaring us on. This was a good little tear-up and Man U were not backing off and stood. We all seemed to be having a lot of fun trading blows as bottles and beer cans were whizzing past. All of this was generating that unforgettable backdrop of acoustics on the underground platform which was halted after a few minutes when one of ours released a can of CS gas. This had everyone pretty much doing the off and exiting the station with our eyes all burning to fuck.

Reassembled back at Wembley, I've jokingly grabbed Frankie round the head. I was buzzing and he was none too pleased as he barked at me to fuck off. I didn't know at the time but during the kick off with Man Utd at Baker Street, one of them had done him in the side of head with a beer can and had perforated his eardrum. Later on after the game, his day didn't improve. As we tried to mob up we had 30 or so Cockney reds bounce across to us after they recognised the two of us from Baker Street. We had a good row with them for a few seconds, but it was like 200 more had appeared from out of nowhere. Due to the fact that we were too slow to mob up, we pretty much had to have it on our toes as me and Frankie seemed to be singled out by them, but we were too fucking fast and they weren't catching us.

Leeds United

It may be nothing of note as far as Palace having one over on Service Crew, as I'm quite sure they might actually have been playing Wimbledon that day. Pete and I were just leaving the Wilton arms one Sunday afternoon in 1991 after playing football and going for an afternoon pint with Gary Pitcher and the other Wilton FC boys. All of a Sudden, we were subjected to a volley of abuse from a passing Leeds minibus. In fairness I wasn't 100% that they were boys or not but I was enraged by their hostility towards us and their disrespect to our ethnic heritage, also the fact that they had thrown a bottle which smashed relatively close to us which I'm sure was a makeshift toilet they'd earlier relieved themselves in.

"Cunt, who you calling Nigger?" I've enquired. "Only my friends call me Nigger."

Gary suggested, "C'mon, let's go after the northern cunts."

Knowing the manor and guessing the fact that they'd be hitting the regular traffic congestion at the Whitehorse Lane Round-about, we jumped in the motor and hit a couple of back streets, then laid in wait in a side road off Whitehorse Lane. I was pleased with the fortune of having a skip with an old for sale sign on the end of a four be two slung into it. After breaking off a manageable piece, I attack the minibus Sir Lancelot style, sending it crashing through a side window before introducing them to the contents of a jiffy bottle. I would always carry one around during that time, after becoming targeted once too often in Brighton, and listened to them cry like babies when the freshly squeezed ammonia began to affect the personnel inside the vehicle, before doing the off down the side street. Like I said, I'm not sure if it was boys or not but fuck it they were a lairy group of lads going to football and deserved all they got.

There was another incident similar to this, when I was in the motor with one of the girls from the manor. I am sure it may have been Liverpool that were down, an incident at a crossing, the girl I was with got a bit of wog meat abuse from a small group of lads with deep Liverpudlian accents as they looked in on us. She's kicked off and next thing I'm chasing a couple of pricks up the road as I pull out a bat from under the seat, launching it after watching them fleeing and having shoppers and other match day fans ducking out the way, I mean, why bother give it?

I also remember during the mid-80s, when Palace used to meet at the Gloucester as mentioned before. Them days, Palace would gather there, mainly Whitehorse and South Croydon, the hardcore nifty 50 were often outside the boozer; four Leeds coaches came by and were absolutely smashed to pieces. There were a few Chelsea with us that day as we left the Yorkshire vehicles devastated as windows go in and the occupants are out and put up a show and got duly slapped.

Leicester - play-off final, Wembley 1996

This game at Wembley was always going to give us a proper turnout of lads. We got together early doors with all the main Nifty 50 lads, with the prospects of going up to the Premier League, every man and his dog was out. Reggie, Dee, Nifty and Killa, a few Wilton and myself, caught up with the 70-odd congregation of lads at East Croydon. Setting off that day all the main boys were catching up and having a laugh, confident today was going to be a good day.

We got to Wembley via a 2-leg semi-final against Charlton, where during the first leg and with roughly the same mob, we had taken a very impressive firm over there. On this occasion we had escaped the attention from the gavvers. 100 of us plotted up for most of the day at the Standard in Blackheath and a few other boozers around the area, another mark on us as far as Charlton were concerned as they keep harking on about when they say Blackheath not being in Charlton. They saw what we had but were slow out of the traps. Our main lad approached them and enquired, "Is this it, is this your boys?" We were also asking them whether the numbers they had were all they were going to bring to us that day. Interestingly, what was also embarrassing for them was the fella with this small mob of Charlton, who Frankie identified as a West Ham bod, was heard to have said to these lads that they had been mugged off by us and weren't impressed with them to say the least. Which must have motivated them, because they did get a decent sized mob together much later on, funnily enough, our numbers had dwindled by then because of the wait but it was all in vain. We were sussed out, put on a train and were fucked off by the Old Bill back to New Cross. I have heard their version of events, they thought there was a grass amongst us that called the Old Bill because we didn't want to have it with them, but I let you draw your own conclusion on what I think about that.

Anyway, back to the Leicester game. We were hoping on seeing more activity with the infamous Baby Squad, who were another top mob

I liked, another firm with a good mix of black and Asian lads. Getting on to the tube network, we split into smaller numbers to avoid getting harangued by Old Bill. We slowly mingled back amongst each other at Neasden and had a quiet drink in a pub, disappointed that there weren't any Babies seen as yet. As we left to head off to Wembley and having got to the bottom of the stairs and onto the platform, we were rubbing our hands with glee when a tube pulled up full with Leicester and even better, 40-50 Baby Squad, their main boys as well. At first we were inviting off the train those that were dressed in the usual clobber that we had identified, but the train was also full with meatheads and other Leicester boys who were grimacing and banging on the doors and seemed the keener of the two.

The doors opened and the unified roar went up to signal what felt like a mad 10 minutes as the two mobs clashed inside and outside the carriages. They weren't expecting the 60 or so lads behind us that came down. As they bounce across to us we surge and clamber over one another to get at them, this was a top mob and we were backing them off deeper and deeper into the carriage, all ignoring the Tannoy announcements to mind the closing doors. The doors are opening and closing while it is booting right off, the odd missile whizzes past me and the odd splash of claret can be seen as people are getting jooked. With a few fallen bodies scattered about the place, they still give a good account of themselves but the couple of times when the doors closed with me and a handful of Nifty 50 still inside, things became a little more on top as we pulled off some rudimentary windmill manoeuvres until the doors re-opened. Killa and a few others rushed back in to batter the oncoming Leicester and drag me and the others out as the warning over the public address system by London Underground staff signalled for us to get the fuck out of there before the gavvers came.

We were all buzzing after, me, Reggie, Nifty and Killa and a handful of others were away, then jumping a tube to Wembley with Killa cussing me and Reggie for getting trapped in the carriages when the doors first closed and questioning Mr Liability, Reggie, about where all the claret had come from before saying, "Forget it, I don't even want to know."

Getting to Wembley, me and Killa have had to walk all the way round to the Leicester end, because the box office to pick up our comps from Bruce Dyer was there and although trying to keep low key, it wasn't long before two big black lumps approached us.

"You remember Neasden? Have it with us now, come on" one offers.

"Neasden? What happened at Neasden?" was Killa's timely response as we glanced over at a few others heading towards us. This must have confused them a little bit, as they gave us a squeeze luckily, we also reminded them about the Old Bill, who were now looking over and now feeling the need to get busy at this little standoff. In the end, we were left happily to creep in an out and back up to the Palace end chuckling to ourselves.

CHAPTER 9

SUNRISING

By the summer of 1989, we all had regular girlfriends, well I say regular, as in went to pictures and go out for a bit of dinner from time to time type regular. We compromised some Saturday afternoons to go poncing around the Kings Road shopping or having picnics in the park. It was less hassle and it was worth keeping them sweet. I was seeing a girl called Carla at the time, a 5 foot 4 dynamite of a girl with a banging arse, she had long brown hair that flowed down to, round and about the length of her peach of all peachy arses. I was all over her when we first met at one of the Dance Wicked events but this relationship was like a train wreck as time went on, because she was always ready to go toe to toe with me at any opportunity. She was the first to get me doing Charlie, where together we'd get off our nuts and have amazing sex. She would almost have me cumming in my pants whenever she rode that derriere against me and would suck me off like a cock-hungry porn star and gaze into my eyes. She was pure filth, but she also had a fiery temper which would often see her going into a rage when we were out if she saw other birds around me.

This started to piss the other boys off because it was making other girls we knew a little paranoid, thinking they were going to get stabbed or something. They also pointed out how she always seemed to end up in the same clubs as us, as though she did not trust me and had a tracking device shoved up my arse to keep tabs on me. Especially when she'd appear out of the blue just as a bit of fanny was in close proximity and she'd just be all of a sudden in the bird's face and we always began rowing in clubs. The boys would all be cussing me when they weren't pissing themselves with laughter, whenever she flew into one of her jealous outbursts.

Do not get me wrong, I have been with unstable birds before and she was as unstable as they come but when everything was sweet, she was cute and cuddly as anything and could curl a toe like the best of them. What it was with her is that when we first met them in mid-88, Carla, along with a couple of her pals, was another set of girls that me and TJB and then me and Pete would go combo on. After linking up over a few weeks and fucking the brains out of each other, Pete then decided that her mate Susan was a little bit too clingy in the end and then totally blanked her. This sort of got Carla's back up at the way he had treated her.

Pete back then would always get to a point where he would get his hands too full, which was usually whenever Katrina was back on the scene, when he would drop a bird stone dead. He was in his own right to do so, but this triggered off all the jealousy and paranoia in Carla thinking I was going to do the same to her. This is something I never understood about women, they think you and your pals are identical twins and just because your mate treated the best friend like absolute toilet, we were all the same. Which would always happen, so from time to time one of us would be blamed for being the bad influence.

During that great summer the group of lads I mentioned earlier who drank in the Wilton, who I had now christened the Under 5s (not connected with football), would often go out on Monday nights down Camden Palace. One night following a quiet drink in the boozer, despite an already chaotic weekend and after another blazing row with Carla, I accepted their invite and went along for the ride. So together with Liam, Dee and two of their pals, Nifty and Roots, we drove up to Camden and had all popped an E and had a fucking blinding night and a further blinding early morning on the drive home as the tunes dropping on the car stereo had us rushing off our nuts. After getting to know these lads, they were often talking about Es. One of them suggested they might buy a bunch to sell and make a nice little change. It suddenly dawned on me, that whilst out in the previous months at these so-called acid house dos, very often, I mean ridiculously very often, we were stopped or approached by people asking, "E's mate, you got any E's?"

This would often piss Face off, as he would get offended and growl at people because he was being stereotyped by so many as a big lemonade with dreads and a bit of tom, so he must be a drug dealer. Pete wasn't fussed by it, he would just apologise nice & politely, as was his manner, for not being able to accommodate and then Killa would lecture them on the dangers of narcotics, where the irony would escape some people at an acid house event that he was being sarcastic. But hold on a minute, I began to suss, we're missing a trick here, if we had them, without even working for it we could be quids in. I suggested it when I next hooked up with the family on our way to another Sunrise do in White Waltham.

"We'd make a killing" I said excitedly. "What the fuck would we have to do to earn that money? absolutely fuck all, just stand about."

Pete was sceptical as he is with most things, but agreed that we were often approached for the little fellas but were still not sure.

"Where the fuck would you get them?" he came back. "We don't exactly know no one, and can't really go around asking moody-looking geezers who were serving up where they got their wares."

Interestingly though, when we had got to the door and were approaching the body search, it dawned on me when Pete nodded towards the black fella who was getting stringently shook down by the door stewards, "And how the fuck do you get past these fucking hulks?"

It was at this point we heard a bit of shouting and turned to see one of the doormen who was a big lump and a mixed race fella, who was another big lump, go toe to toe with each other as the other door staff looked on, assuring everyone that everything was OK. We were amazed, as the force of the punches rained with neither of them budging an inch and as quickly as it started, it was all over.

"What the fuck was all that about?" Killa quizzed as the two meatheads acknowledged each other and the mixed raced man carried on into the do. It was a really random incident that we always talk about when we mention this do.

As we entered the arena we completely forgot the conversation about becoming E dealers as we took in the full atmosphere. Having gone through the usual ritual, we had gone down the Swan and Sugarloaf beforehand. I bumped into a pal of mine in Croydon earlier who said there was a big meet there for the do, no need to go down the Windmill now. Face had earlier spoken to a girl he knew from Battersea and they said the Windmill would be rocking, so after we scoped out the Swan and Sugarloaf, the turnout wasn't impressive so we jumped back in the motor and headed for the Windmill, which was heaving with Motors. Jumping out, Face went to see if he could locate Sharon and her little lot and people were immediately approaching the car and asking if 1) We knew where the Venue was and 2) If we were selling any E's. We said negative to both enquiries.

Face came walking back over with Sharon and two other girls, Angelique and Jayne, and after a few minutes of pleasantries, horns started beeping as news of the venue was released to the masses. After saying "See ya later" to the girls, we followed the huge convoy towards the M4 and after a short drive down the motorway, which seemed to be filled with only Sunrise revellers, we were grinning, thinking out loud how mental this was. Sharon and her Girls also passed us in a BMW convertible, driven by some Michael Hutchins from INXS looking dude as we started to discuss the availability of Sharon's pals with Face.

"They look too stoosh for my liking," I said as Pete agreed. "But that Jayne looks quite hot, what d'ya reckon Face, she game or what?" he enquired.

Face had to remind him that he had already introduced her to him in Brixton Academy at a new year's eve party.

"Fuck me is that the same bird?" he said surprised, pausing, as he'd realised the fact that he'd seemed a bit too excited in front of us about her and styled it out changing the subject as he shouted "OI OI!" out of his window to another group of girls in a topless Golf, which switched all of our attention. We watched them speed alongside us blowing kisses as their hair blew sexily in the wind.

"This is fucking mental, fucking love it" TJ said.

In the venue, Lil Lois's *French kiss* and Shalor's *I'm in love* smashed the rave to shit. The crowd was going mad, we had ventured around to near a speaker stack piled up by the back near the exit to the fairground rides. There was a platform there where we saw Andy P, Keith Allsop, a lad named Bex and the rest of the group from the Swan and Sugar Loaf having it as *Strings of life* dropped. This part of the arena saw Croydon Borough having it large. Pete, Face and Killa knew a few more bodies in there from school and were embraced by many of them as though a long-lost brother was finally found.

What an absolute blinder we had, and this time I didn't even drop an E, I had one but for whatever reason I never took it. I was high on the buzz of this rave. This was the best thing I'd ever been too as we all at the same time raised our arms as the Lil Lois signature break drops where you hear the tempo drop almost to a standstill.

The Sun newspaper captured the moment beautifully the following Monday morning as the general public became aware of this underground phenomena. "SPACED OUT" was the headline, as everyone went fucking mental when the drop and tempo sped up sending the whole aircraft hangar off the scale. Whistles were blaring and fog horns sounded out, tune needed a rewind but the rave scene had not caught onto that yet. We danced furiously to the end of the track as the DJ was relentless, dropping tune after tune after tune until we were able to take a breather when that unmistakable riff from Kiraya's track *Baby let me love you for the night* bellowed out.

As we walked around the venue, through the mass of bodies, we bumped into Sharon, Jayne and Angelique again. It seemed as though Jayne and Pete had taken a little shine to each other, I can always tell with him, he had given it away in the car on the way up, now he was exposed as he done his trademark whisper into her lughole. My attention was immediately switched away when I saw Carla by the entrance with some black boys, so I mooched over. Seeing me approach, she seemed a little bit nervous. I said hello and began talking to her when I realised that the team of moody-looking spades were giving me evils.

"Who's this little lot, your new fellas?" I said, reversing the roles and giving her some of the shit she would often give me, then turning away before she could respond.

"You got a problem mate?" I enquired and fronted up the main one, who was screwing up his face. Face and Killa clocked this and nudging Pete and TJ, they said ta-ta to the girls and headed to where I was standing, but Carla's mate Susan defused the situation by telling one of the lads to leave it and Carla pleaded with me too to walk away. Face approached and was asking, "Is everything all right?"

By this time Susan and another girl were already walking the other lads away with Carla and Screwface close behind them and it left me wondering, if I had dropped my pill I might have been oblivious to them and might have got served up, who knows? I changed up the conversation and now started teasing Pete about Jayne as we headed back to the middle. He was now also cussing about the way Susan had looked at him with utter contempt during the little standoff.

"What's her fucking problem?" he enquired.

"Oh I don't know Pete, maybe you treated her like dog shit in a previous life or something" I thought. I chose to ignore him and continued digging at him, saying that he was about to become a lovesick puppy again.

"Fuck Susan, wha' happen with Jayne? You check it? Ya get digits bredrin?"

"No, I didn't get round to that bit, we got interrupted looking out for your black arse again," he laughed.

We then realised that there were 30-odd Croydon bods including football lads about in close vicinity that would have seen that boot off, so the moody cunts would have come well unstuck. But this wasn't the arena for booting off, this was a happy vibe and we were all in high spirits as we dance, as more melodic house beats had the hangar going mental. The rave went well on into the morning, it was getting on and without chemical assistance the boys began to wane and it took us another 45 minutes or so, hugging and saying good bye to people before we eventually left. Face suggested we go back to the Windmill as the girls might head back there and there was talk that the Windmill was usually busy with revellers returning from raves to chill out on the common.

Leaving the venue, the midday sun began to shimmer over the roof of the impressive 'ECSTASY AIRPORT' Aircraft Hangar at White Waltham. We sped up the M4 with shades on but still wide awake from the buzz of the night as we joked and took the piss. Killa and I had our regular cussing session as he tried to ridicule me about my clothing and other schoolboy cusses, a ritual which always had him go over the top as he made ridiculous suggestions that my mother and James Brown are the same person.

We never actually spent that long at the Windmill as it turned out, but having parked up and begun to cross the road to the common, some geezer approached us tailed by a cameraman. He asked if we would do a bit for a UK watered down music video for De La Soul's *Say No Go* track, which was rising the charts and was due to be broadcast on *Top of the Pops* within the next two weeks or even as soon as that coming Thursday. With a tape recorder blasting out the track, we were filmed making prats of ourselves dancing around on a street corner. It was quite a giggle and we had for a little while forgotten about it until it aired and we had all our phones ringing off the hook. People were calling us saying they'd seen us on *Top of the Pops,* which made 24th June 1989 a very memorable weekend for us all, concluding with our 15 seconds of fame.

I met with Carla again a few weeks after White Waltham. She rang me to apologise about her ex but to me it was not a big deal. We were on and off by then me and her, because of constant rows anyway, so she could see whoever she wanted. She told me they were out of Notting Hill and reckoned themselves as bad boys. I asked her if she was still seeing him and she said no and remembering the outstanding filthy sex, I began pursuing her for a mid-week meet for a bunk up. Putting up a good front at first, she told me I should go and find one of my other whores to mug off, which I thought was a bit strong but understandable. This was always part of the game with us, she was still smarting because she had already fucked me off a little while back, when she had discovered that I was still seeing Amanda.

At the time, I was working security at the ABC cinema in Croydon for a bit of extra money. One evening Amanda came to see me and asked for the key to my flat. I was surprised by the unannounced midweek visit but gave her the keys. She was looking tasty, stroking her thigh as she kissed me tenderly, telling me to hurry home. I could feel she was all tackled up under her work outfit. I loved it when she dressed like that, with her bins on completing the look.

As my loins began stirring, watching her walk away, I did find it a bit odd, her turning up like that. My instincts told me something wasn't right and was on the phone to Pete asking if Suzanne had called him about coming down.

"Nah mate" he said, "I won't be seeing her again."

I forgot, he was back with Katrina (Again!) so after explaining my suspicions he said, "Do you want me to drive round there and have a butchers?"

"Yeah" I replied.

"Come get me in half hour and we can drive around there."

"What you reckon? an ambush or something?" Pete said, before continuing, "No chance, you're just paranoid mate."

Pete pulls up in the BMW, it's 10 o'clock and he's a bit ratty now as he has to get up for work and he's had to leave Katrina in his bed.

"Come on, let's get this over with," he barked. We pulled up after the short drive, switching the headlights off and approached the car park like two hit men. Exiting the passenger door I left Pete in the car and said, "Come when I'm inside the front door".

I've knocked on my own door, Amanda's let me in and I enter with hesitation to be confronted by an angry Carla with her mate Susan and Amanda's mate Suzanne. They were all at the same time it seemed cunting me off with that 'ha-ha caught you out' look about them just as Pete walks in. "Fuck me, this looks all cosy" he said sarcastically.

On learning of the fact that Pete was banging Susan and Suzanne at the same time they tried to turn on him, but Pete went stone cold on them and was having none of it.

"As if I give a fuck, ain't fucking none of You'z now am I?"

He turned to me asking if I still needed him. "Nah! Go on home to your missus" I said with a grin, just to twist the knife in a bit more. Fuck it, I was bang to rights, so I switched all ignorantly and told them all to get the fuck out my flat. Surprisingly, when Carla & Susan had left, Suzanne said to Amanda "I'll leave you two to talk."

"Talk about what?" I said, this time angry that they had trapped me like this.

"You can all fuck off out, go on." I was trying not to laugh as I heard Pete drive off beeping his horn. "SHHHHHLAAAAAAAAAAGGGGGGGS!" he shouted, as they all gathered in the car park. With them all out the door I slammed it shut. I was thinking I was quite fortunate that Carla had gone reasonably without incident and was surprised she didn't launch a scathing attack on me. I realised how upset she would have been with the confirmation that she was right, I was just a lying cheating dog after all. Pete rang when he got in and was absolutely pissing his pants laughing.

"Sneaky little cunts, how the fuck did that come about?"

Later we learned that by a remarkable coincidence, they got chatting to one another in HQ's in Camden Lock. Of all the fucking luck, it could only happen to me, that two separate firms of girls could end up catching me out by general chin wagging whilst squatting for a piss in a nightclub toilet. That's the problem with birds - they fucking talk too much.

The year was progressing nicely for us on the going out front but personally we were still having relationship issues, mainly due to the fact that we couldn't keep our cocks in our pants. Pete and I especially had become a bit of a splinter group because we were mostly caught up with unstable birds and would often ring each other needing a cheer up or pep talk. A few of these occasions we'd end up venturing up to Croydon to go into a bar to pull an old slosh pot to take out our aggression on.

Pete always reminds me that on one occasion, I ended up pulling this bird called Melanie whilst he was chatting to a group of his old school friends in a bar near Surrey Street market. This bird had pins up to her ears, fucking drop dead pretty and she was game, or sounded game, from the innuendos she was responding with. The problem came when for me to take this one home, Pete would have to entertain her mate, and he almost vomited there and then when he saw the state of her. Being a true pal and the best wingman in the world, he took to his duty and took a bullet for his pal, but he has never let me forget it to this day.

What was also funny was learning that the ugly one was the on/off long-term girlfriend (she claimed) of this bod called T from North London. He was a dancer on the club circuit back in the day when we used to go Soul II Soul and most of the rare groove dos a few years before and was often in music videos. He and his boys did not take a shining to us and the feeling was mutual, as they always felt paranoid that we were laughing in their faces. There were a few girls we knew who were letting us know that he was often cunting us off to them and bitching about us. He was saying how we thought we were gangsters and god's gifts to women, which was half right, but we knew he was connected with one of the main DJs at the time so we often bit our tongues and wiped our mouths.

What a touch though meeting these two dorises. Pete after hearing this began to show a lot more interest in her, complimenting her on her massive breasts and other cheesy lines. In all fairness she had a cracking body, I would have fucked her myself. She just had a face like the back end of a moose that had been hit by a truck and reversed over. He continued to soften her up, and her mate at the same time also gave us dirt on a few of his boys which I won't repeat, I mean, each to their own, who am I to judge any man that enjoyed having dildos rammed up the jacksy? We had an interesting evening, having a few beers and ripping the poor fuckers to shreds, if only they knew the shit they had told us.

When it was lights out we took up position opposite ends of the room. Melanie's knickers were already juicy and wet by the time I was ready to smash the granny out of her as she buries her face into the pillow. With every stroke I made she was panting for me, observing and appreciating how wet I had made her. Pete had continued with his wooing, in between the "fuck me your tits are huge" comments. By the end of the evening, after teasing her about her man for the most part, comedy gold I must add, I had splashed my lot with Melanie, just at the time when Pete, suffering from carpet burns, took liberties after he bolted his and then quipped over a drag of a cigarette and said, "Be sure to tell your man T that that crew out of South London he always used to eyeball when we was out... you tell him that I came in your mouth when you kiss him next."

This had me choking on my beer as he continued, "And don't expect me to kiss ya now either."

She took it well by all accounts, but it was fucking hilarious at the time, a very funny night, whatever it was that either of us were down about around that time, that evening would have surely remedied it.

We had had a few combos like this that year, like a kind of summer of lust; Pete had become colder than Siberia during and after his breakups with Katrina, they were on and off, then on and then off again, in a somewhat turbulent relationship. She had a spell on him for sure and he couldn't get enough of her. He even confesses that the breakups always brought out the worst in him and the aftermath always made him so bitter that he wouldn't give a fuck about a bird's feeling any more. We were still young lads anyway but I always knew it would have to take a special girl to get us out of that mind-set but we did have some funny times.

When August approached, we had just gone through a very long hot summer and acid house fever was at its peak. After attending some more legendary raves like Energy, Genesis, Telepathy, Biology and World dance, we were all excited when the kings of the acid house parties, Sunrise, were hosting the next upcoming event. We all hooked up midweek and drove over to Battersea to see Face's pal Sharon, who was in with a connection that could get us the tickets at a good discount. We were all sitting round her gaff when in walk Jayne and Angelique, all tanned up and looking fit.

By now Pete and I had an instant telepathy which was similar to a hunting pack of lions on prey animal, because we had both clocked them as they glided in the room, walking in as though they had that effect they do in an American teen movie when the hot chick enters the scene, Angelique with her posh looks & Jayne with her curly hair, in figure-hugging Vivienne Westwood skimpy dresses and pins that would have done Daisy Duke proud. We gawped them up and down with a 'GAAAD DAAAMN' look on our faces that left us both with our jaws gaping, when TJB in hysterics said, "EASY NOW... HA-HA... You two wanna roll your tongues back in."

This had me telling him to fuck off, Pete blushing and Jayne and Angelique giggling.

On the car ride home after acquiring the sought-after tickets for Saturday's rave, Pete was it seemed now besotted with Jayne. He'd already met her earlier in the year at Brixton Academy and wasn't interested, then he was a little more interested when he'd seen her at White Waltham, but now after tonight... WOAH! That was it, he was giving Face the instructions to make it happen, he wanted her and would have probably made plans to marry her there and then given the opportunity. This had us in fits and ripping him to pieces about it.

On the Friday night we had all got together again in the Wilton Arms. We hadn't planned on any clubbing that night as we were saving resources for the big Sunrise do on the Saturday so we met for few drinks and I'd introduced the Family to the Young'uns, Jay, Nifty, Dee, Liam, Inch, Tony Roots, Wayne, Trippy & Mendez. They all wanted to go to the Sunrise do but the party was a complete sell out and tickets were now like gold dust. Sharon had already confirmed that we had the last lot she could get, so Pete put a call in to Brixton Dave, who surprisingly said some might be available and he should be getting some tonight but we'd have to get to him sharpish.

Pete jumped in the motor with Inch and Dee, whilst the rest of us stayed in the boozer. In the end, having driven there, it turned out to be a wasted journey. Pete was told that the mob that was bringing the ticket had sold them now. Whilst Pete was in the flat, his name was bellowed out to turn and recognise with a grin an old pal from back in the day called Raymond. Ray was another of the regular faces at parties back when we were younger who hung out with Paul and Danny, another couple of lads we knew from Streatham Vale. The significance of this meeting was no big deal; we'd known Ray and his boys for years, Killa and Fatman were team mates when they all played for Norwood and Redhugh Football Club and we'd often see them at the end of season presentations and disco where Ray would often show off his dance skills, at a time when he was considered as one of the best disco funk and jazz dancers.

Pete is having the conversation with him as they catch up on old times; Ray mentions that he does a bit of DJing now, confirming by handing him a flyer of an upcoming event. When he's revealed his handle Pete is going mental, because although he would have been relatively well known at this point, even as much as we raved, we never at first paid too much attention to the flyers, his name would have been on a few for some of these acid house and warehouse dos at the time, because for the most part we couldn't give a fuck what DJs were playing. However to us, Grooverider the disco kid was king during 1987 and 1988. On Phase 1 FM, his show was more or less the only time you'd hear the best funk and underground jazz on the radio, even before Giles Peterson. We also had a tape of his set that we would play in the car on the way to Babylon and the other clubs we were attending at the time. He was the first we heard play Norman Connor's *Mother of the future*, which if you spoke to Pete he considers the best jazz tune of all time and that particular tape even up to this day is one of Pete's proudly possessions because of the top tunes recorded from his shows.

Pete spent a further half an hour shooting the shit with him about Phase 1 days and saying how mad that all the time listening back the tape and not realising it was our very own Ray Bingham spinning them wicked tracks, before shaking off his hand with the offer of looking out for him in the future. After filling us all in when we were all back at the Wilton, we were feeling slightly proud because Ray was one of our own, but we could never have imagined from that random meeting that he would become the powerhouse he is today.

So that historic Saturday was upon us. We were excited about the rave and the Young'uns, who we knew were dying to come to the rave, were teased, flashing them with our tickets and Face dropped a line on them that was straight out the hooligan film the Firm - "You'z are under 5s and are not allowed to ride on the Acid house chuff chuff."

This only made them even more determined. I suggested they come to the Windmill and try their luck over there, even follow everyone once the Venue was announced and try and jib in. This I warned was risky and might end up with them taking a beating off Sunrise meatheads or set upon by Rottweilers but fair play to them, they were undeterred.

At the Party, after speeding down the M40 for Princes Risborough in Longwick, Buckinghamshire and parking up, we were in awe at the spectacle that lay before us. As I write this, I feel goose bumps and the hairs on the back of my neck stand up as I relive that unbelievable, incredible night. These Sunrise Promoters had surpassed themselves this time and if I'd have seen any of them I would have plastered them with kisses, of course I'd be hoping it would be Tony Colston-Hayter's Missus rather than the man himself. How fucking good was this? In the middle of the night we were jumping up and down to some smashers, Neil Howard's *To be or not to be* had us skanking with smiles all over everyone's boats like Cheshire cats but it was Sydney Young Blood, *If I only I could,* that dropped and would result in TJB hugging us all and saying, "I love you maan."

This had us all confessing our undying love for one another. All of a sudden, the Under 5s are jumping in all over us after jibbing in with grins all over their faces. The entire firm were now in the event, jumping around until the sun came up. To this day, this was one of the best nights of my life. It was a historic event and looking back at the amount of people we had bumped into throughout the night and the type of clientele these events were drawing, celebrities, football players, pop stars, football thugs and gangsters all having it. I scoped the thousands upon thousands of bodies thinking whoever the fuck is serving up in this gaff was killing it and what I would do for a piece of that action.

With the sunrise, came for most of us, after dancing non-stop, the struggle to keep on going. With most of the boys unassisted by any chemicals we chilled on the grass, observing the mass upon mass of bodies bouncing around. Imagine a beautiful scene as the sun comes up and the DJ begins to drop the intro to the spine-tingling Sueno Latino. That was the soundtrack to our night. Sharon, Jayne, Angelique and another bird we had not seen before came walking over and I could immediately see Pete's eyes light up. I walked up and intercepted her before she approached him, pretending I was going in for the kill. It was funny looking at the state of his boat as he gave me daggers.

"Just wanted to be the first to say hello to the bird my best pal is gonna marry" I joked, which made her look at me curiously as if I was a nutcase or something. Next thing the pair of them spend the next few hours chatting and giggling as my boy Pete delivered the lyrics.

"Won't be seeing him no more," I said to Killa, having him roar with laughter and taking the piss in a childish voice.

"Whaat, You sad? because you're gonna lose your best maate?"

"Big lip fucker" I said laughing back, "Yeah? You laugh mate, you'll see."

It was about 10-11 am before we drifted off home, as it took like forever to get Pete and TJB to leave Jayne and Angelique. There was also the West Ham v Palace pre-season game I was desperate to get to as well, which had me hastening everyone so we could get going.

The Under 5s, after driving round to find us, were all now out of the car and having a dance as a VW Golf with subwoofers sounding like a Jah Shaka four face was pumping out some LFO, which made our Natty shake in the breeze as we walked past. We were all fucked so said "laters" to the young'uns and shot off home down the M40. The ride home was relatively quiet for a change - it was as if the party was to all of us a life-changing experience.

I broke the silence. "Fuck me, imagine if we'd been on an E?"

Fact of the matter was, that we had been sold the concept of the acid house party when we met Trudy and Tracey 12 months beforehand, and in truth, it took some encouragement for us to leave behind our much-loved rare groove and venture into this cult. But we would never have imagined it would result in a moment in history like this, that would live in our memories for years to come. August the 12th 1989, Sunrise & Back to the Future, speak to anyone about that party and anyone who could admit to attending anything as mind blowing as this would struggle to find one. It bonded us as pals as we toasted each other with a couple of bottles of champagne courtesy of Brixton Dave, at a time when drinking champers was unheard of for us working class lads from the Heath.

We remember it and it topped off a vintage year of raving and music that the line-up of DJs had dropped over the 100K sound system stacked on massive lorry trailers. Pete and TJB have the extra romance about that time and continually bigged up the mood and the setting as they chirpsed the morning away with the two tanned beauties, so they will remember the rave for them as well. I shit you not. it was the best fucking thing in the world.

CHAPTER 10

EVERYTHING STARTS WITH AN E

With the introduction of the Under 5s came a period when music was the lower priority for going out at the weekends, and it all became about the MONEY, the CASH, the CHEDDAR. You see, these boys, all they were interested in was a pound note, every last one of them, but interestingly it was the quietest one that started the ball rolling. Liam was Dee's older brother, the same age as Face and me but he was classed an under 5 because of the rest of them, who were all mates who grew up and went to school together and were off the various estates within a stone's throw of Crystal Palace football ground.

It was me that introduced Liam to Clive, a Palace pal of mine who was one of their top boys. After bumping into the fella a few times at Camden Palace, he educated him with the knowledge that he could get them in the hundreds, so apparently they all clubbed together with cash from strokes they were pulling at the time, which predominantly were dodgy motors, and bought themselves a parcel.

At first, when I was going to Camden with them on a Monday night, we were just there to rave and to drop an E. I could drop it with them whereas with Pete, Face, and the others, I would not feel relaxed doing it as they would not have been on the same level. But it took me a while to notice Liam being cool as a cucumber when punters approached him. Liam and Nifty had a little routine going where when a punter approached, Liam would give a signal similar, but a little more subtle to those on a stock market trading floor, where Liam had worked for a couple of weeks before chinning some lairy cunt. Nifty would shuffle across, shake the punter's hand and move off whilst Liam, having already pocketed the dough, would smile and nod as with in agreement with the punter on a non-existent conversation. They were at it and by the end of the night they had cleaned up. They only held 10 at any one time, and the goods were held by each of the other under 5s and passed to Nifty when required. Overall, a good night would see them shift 100 Es at £20 a pop and that was without being greedy. By sheer craft and technique Liam was turning over a fair few bob within a few weeks and had cemented my notion that drugs was the way forward.

Inch was the only relatively legit one out of the Under 5s. He sold a bag of weed every now and then and was up to the usual bandulu (scams) that most of the Under 5s were up to back then, until he became the main provider of the main tool for any would be drug dealer - the mobile phone. Back then, your nearest thing to an I-phone was something a rasta man would refer to as a phone that belonged to him, eg "I and I phone." The phones back then were huge and bulky and to have one you were either a City bod, a telephone engineer or a hustler.

Inch provided our lot with three mobiles. Pete had the NEC 9A, which he bought because he was fed up with pagers and phone boxes, which due to his work had become a pain in the arse, I had the Motorola Micro Tac 9800 and Nifty opted for NEC P3. These phones you would often need a mortgage for phone line rental and call minutes but Inch was working as provider and maintainer for the London Carphone Warehouse. He would often get his hands on handsets and had the connections to get the phones live for us.

Liam, who now was the mister big, was doing business via the Under 5s and by the backend of 89 rolling into 1990, we were beginning to fatten our pockets as retailers of weekend pharmaceuticals. It was at the time a business worth doing and a period of opportunity. If you had asked anyone what your average drug dealer looked like back then, 90% would probably have said black, dreads, smart, wears a bit of tom, drives a BMW. So if 90% of people in the raves and clubs wanted an E, who'd they approach first? A mind-set that had the boys thinking fuck it, might as well make a bit of dough. Because in this capitalist society we live in, it is all about supply and demand. Moreover, before all the goody fucking two shoes start piping up when reading this thinking "Ooh but it's wrong to push drugs" well fuck that, you made us this way over the last year or so asking us for pills, I never pushed fuck all on anyone. In a way, we are the victims of an underlying racist view that because I am black, I can sell you a draw or a pill. I have even had crack requests whilst out clubbing, so like Tesco's I'm going to deliver customer satisfaction and get rich doing it and so we began, but we had to be clever about it because if punters thought it, then the Old Bill must think it too.

We adopt the nod and handshake strategy that Nifty and Liam used in Camden and at World Dance we split up into groups using our little crew of girls from the Wilton that we had nicknamed the Boo-Yah sisters, Charlotte, Tracey, Caroline and Maxine, to smuggle in the work and true to form we'd get approached.

"Es mate? you got any Es?"

We would nod in the direction of our dedicated under 5, who would slip the punter the E with a handshake and we would pocket the dough. Happy days. By the end of the night, we could all see the potential for expansion, which should have seen us move onto bigger and better things. However, after one night at a do in Shaftsbury's, it had dawned on us that we were not just filling our coffers but we were stepping on a few toes and it took some backhand tactics from our competitors that had us looking into renewing our strategy.

When a firm of East London bods demanded the doormen at Shaftsbury's pull up the Under 5s we ended up losing 75 pills and had to watch as the doormen passed on our work to these bods and explained, "No one serves up in London unless they are payroll, so next time, you'll lose more than your pills and by the way, we will only warn you the once." This left Nifty and the boys fuming and the firm out of pocket. We all got together at the Wilton the following afternoon and explaining it to Reggie he came up with the answer when he suggested, "Fuck London, you should hit the south coast, you boys would clean up down there."

He continued to explain that through Liam, he had bought a parcel of 500 but had struggled to shift them. He reckoned, our 'firm of blacks' as he put it, would get the pills rolling and us earning ourselves a packet. Liam, Nifty and Reggie then spend the next few hours discussing a strategy of serving the clubs in Brighton.

"So what about the toes we'll be stepping on down there?" Liam asked, Reggie replied...

"Fuck them cunts, they ain't gonna want to front a gang of spades are they? They're mugs."

We all reached an agreement that we'd give it a go the following weekend. This was around October 89 or there about, and unknown to us at that point, we'd end up attending the south coast on a regular basis for the next 3 years.

We attended many of the biggest raves in history, which also had me wondering whether we had missed the boat. Following Sunrise back to the future in Longwick, plus all the other parties on all the home counties and the headlines it brought to the mainstream, The government passed a bill through Parliament that made these acid house parties illegal. New policies came in that basically fucked with the freedom to party and over the next few months we were getting fucked off with parties we were due to attend getting cancelled due to the police.

The only last memorable do we attended was one in East Grinstead, which saw revellers having it with riot police before they eventually had to let the party continue. When the daylight came, every last raver was having it big time overlooked by police helicopters as we stuck up 2 fingers to Maggie's Blue Army.

We also had some good nights closer to home as loads of local faces bopped the night away in Chats wine bar in Croydon, all the fellas I knew from school and all the South Croydon Lot, Whitehorse, everyone who was anyone was in Chats on the few occasions we went down there. This in a way was important for us in the contacts we made in there. Pete, Face and Killa knew the boys running it. They were rumoured to be making big moves and were later embroiled in the war I mentioned earlier in the book with some of the Nifty 50 lads a few years after. They were good lads and they always seemed pleased whenever they saw Pete and the others.

Liam sorted bits and pieces out in there but we were not going to disrupt our mission of working the south coast. Instead, we saw it as a good way to meet with main faces to see if we could get better deals. It was kind of a networking environment for wheelers and dealers because it was no secret most of the boys in there was up to some kind of hustle or another. It was also a good chance for me to socialise with some Nifty 50 lads after only recently being accepted as one of their own. It was good sharing some class A and a jump up to the tunes or just having a beer and reliving some past skirmishes.

The truth is, the raids on Palace and the acid house era may have been responsible for most lads slowing down on the trouble at football, but it was not completely eradicated by all accounts. Moreover, it gave us as a relatively small firm decent combat with teams that for years had had bigger numbers over us, because if you really think about it the summer of love was over by late 89 and clubland was in truth beginning to become a lot more sinister.

As far as Chats was concerned, in hindsight, it was probably the worst place to conduct discussions on any business as everyone in there was more or less off their faces. Everyone was having it to the tunes, with DJs which included Garfield, Moon Man and our mate Andy P. We had some mad nights but it would only be a matter of time. With all the shit going on with raves up and down the country and the fact that it was no secret that the building was a den of criminality going by Croydon council's reports in the local rag. This described how there were underworld connections and the clientele all participating in recreational stimulants.

Luckily, for us, we already had our objective and that was the south coast, so we were not around when the place finally got spun. When the Old Bill moved in and finally had the place under wraps it was said that revellers in there at the time tried to hold them off by barricading the door.

O-Zone was another good place we frequented, again, another local do, held in Crystals Bar at Crystal Palace football ground. This had the same faces as Chats but a bigger venue and had Trevor Fung dropping the tunes in there. It also came as another wake-up call for us and a good call on our part that we wasn't going to fall out with local lads from earning their keep by stepping on their toes by even selling the odd pill. So for this reason we were often there just to socialise and have a party, and thank fuck we did too, because when the place got raided and seeing all the undercover gavvers who in hindsight stood out like a sore thumb when the lights went on, followed by all the shouting by them,

"POLIIICE...THIS IS A RAID, NO ONE MOOOVE, NO ONE TRY TO LEAVE!"

Seeing all the packets of sweets strewn all over the floor was impressive and would have had you believe everyone was serving up in there. We all had our shakedown by them and was fucked off with a warning some of us, as we only had a few sprinkles of puff and Rizla, the Es were already swallowed.

To see in the New Year, we opted to spend the festivities at a party in Brixton Academy. We were 20 handed when me, Pete, Killa, Face and TJB were now accompanied by Charlotte and the girls, Nifty and the Under 5s and the wives and girlfriends, which included Jayne, Dianne & Kay. Intentionally, any of us that were selling pills done it away from the main group, so there was no unnecessary heat on the girls who would be holding the main stash. Unlike our local nights out, it was a harder resist not to serve up that night, because just like with

120

previous nights throughout the last year, with the hundreds of requests we would get it would have been stupid not to.

When the acid house party was at its peak, many villains discovered the amount of money that was on offer, and it became common knowledge that many naughty firms would muscle the promoters, with the proposition of making them partners or get their party robbed and smashed up. The parties they controlled would result in them controlling the doors and he who controls the doors controls the drug traffic. This introduced a subnet of moody firms like my outfit hustling in the clubs. At 20 pounds an E there was money to be earned by everyone, but London seemed to be controlled by greedy cunts as I explained about the incident in Shaftsbury's, so throughout 1990 we were often down the South Coast.

Liam, Nifty, Dee, Inch, me and a few other bods worked our way into clubs, keeping it low and gradually getting the product shifted and building up our customer base. South coast was easy as we are more often than not cleaned out within hours. We increased the parcels steadily when it came apparent that during after parties that went well on into the hours, 24 hours plus in some instances, the demand for the E was greater than we often had in supply. Everybody wanted to be our friend and by the summer of 1990, it was 'happy days' for Reggie, me and the boys.

Pete came down on a few occasions but was well loved up now with Jayne, so was often missing at the weekends. I would regularly meet up with him down the Wilton or round my mum's house to have a chinwag over a pint of beer or a plate of curried goat and rice. Telling him about Brighton and the good bit of business that was going on reminded him that he had bumped into an old school pal who would clue him up on a massive parcel he was expecting. Pete asked if I thought Reggie would be interested in doing business, which had me a little puzzled because the operation was an equal partnership. With his knowledge of the crew, he knew we preferred the retail and the hustle in the clubs but with the worry lines of an 80-year-old farm worker who just lost his mule Pete was again advising me to leave that out and concentrate on controlling parcels.

"You could leave the 5s and that to do the clubs, have the rest of us as muscle or whatever, it's a better and less risky way to do business" he said with a concerned look. "I'll set the meeting with Gilly, get Reggie up, I reckon you'll get bail on it, you'll clean up."

We had the sit down a few days later in the Cherry Trees, and after Pete made the introductions he left us to discuss business. After Reggie explained his intention to smash Brighton to bits and be the main firm down there, Gilly agreed to deliver 10,000 pills to us the following week at £6.50 a pill and we would get 4 weeks on it. Reggie insisted that instead of 4 weeks he'd drive up and square up a fortnight Monday, such was his confidence in getting them banged out. We all shook on it before watching Gilly fuck off in his brand new Porsche 911 Carrera.

As we said ta-lah, we noticed the ginger cunt Bulldock, who was Palace's Football Intelligence Officer, eyeballing us. There was a midweek game on that evening, and most of the Nifty 50 was at the game. Only Reggie and me were left in the pub, which would lead you to believe that our mate Bulldock was seeing Reggie and me as the main threat and responsible for all the recent trouble at CPFC in recent weeks, which was bollocks of course.

"COME IN FOR A PINT YOU GINGER CUNT, YOU SITTING OUT THERE FOR?" Reggie shouted over to him. he ignored us and continued to read his imaginary report, gutted at the fact that we had clocked him,

A few weeks before, we'd had a major row with Brighton at East Croydon when 20 of us ambushed them on their way to Brentford. News of the event had reached Bulldock and rumours were circulating that he was going to give us surveillance up the arse, so to avoid police attention, me, Reggie and two other Palace lads, Peter E and Peter H, who were Wilton Arms boys, drove up to a cup game against Norwich. To cement our plan even further we took up our seats in the Norwich end, trying to be incognito. A Palace goal and the resulting complaints by stewards and Canaries fans had Bulldock gobsmacked that we had escaped his surveillance. After trying to eject us, we were flatly refusing to leave, as we had not caused any agg other than celebrate a goal. This led him to assign 15 odd Old Bill and a couple of stewards to keep an eye on us until the end of the game. With 5 minutes to go we all at once stood up and made our way out with an escort that was appropriate for a mob of 50, not the four law-abiding, hard-working lads who had made the car journey up there. After we blew them kisses goodbye, we decided to drive up to Great Yarmouth to get on the lash and maybe pull a few Dorises to have our fiendish ways with them.

Having parked up the motor, we plotted up in a Wetherspoons, making a few calls to Pete and the Under 5s. The Under 5s left with instructions to work Zap and the Escape and try and get a little team to check out a new club we'd heard about in Worthing called Sterns. We'd decided now we'd get B&B in Yarmouth after the landlady had clued us in on a guesthouse next door that would give us a cheap bed for the night and she was friends with the owner.

"We all right to bring brasses back?" was suggested but the proprietor did not hear.

So after a skin full of lager and the satisfaction that business was left in the capable hands of the Under 5s, we ventured out to find a night club. We came to a nightclub that was up a flight of stairs and making our way up, I just knew these door personnel were gonna be aggravation.

"Sorry lads not tonight" he said in a deep Suffolk accent.

"Why what's the problem?" I asked.

"No problem, we just ain't letting you in."

Puzzled and bemused I asked, "You're joking ain't ya?" At the same time, a group of mixed couples came up followed by a group of five men, and without a flinch or hassle from the door attendants in they went.

"Oh it's like that then is it?" I said.

"If you want mate, yeah!" replied this lairy looking lump who had remained schtum until now. "You ain't coming in, now fuck off!"

With this, Reggie turned and led us out. We'd not muttered a word to each other. Reggie picked up a lump of wood, which made us all grab whatever we could find. Reggie turned around and was back up the stairs, followed by the rest of us.

"CAAAM ON THEN CAAAANTS… LET'S HAVE EEET!" he screamed, unleashing the wood straight into the geezer's face who'd refused us the entry, sending him sprawling backwards. With all of us frothing now and showing no signs of backing down, we backed them off with an onslaught of fists, makeshift weapons and a tirade of abuse, resulting in them pulling shutters down, which gave us the signal to do one.

"Come outside you mugs, I'll carve you up you lairy cunt!" I shouted. Peter E pulled me away and we were out and up the road in a hurry before ducking into a kebab shop.

"All right boys?" said the owner. "Take a seat, I'll be right over."

Hello, this was nice, I thought as we walked over to the table where we saw a party of birds sitting down. "Oi oi, these look game," Reggie said with a nudge and we began to banter with them. After a nice chicken shish with chips, we were offering the birds a night out, the usual bollocks. Later on, we were walking along the sea front, when one of the girls (whose name was Donna if I remember rightly) and me became separated from the rest of the group. We passed a group of lads and as we pass I've heard one mutter 'wog meat' or 'coon cunt' or something along the lines.

Women have a natural instinct in the light of something about to boot off. She tightens the grip on my arm, as I've turned, almost swinging her off her feet. The red mist descends as the funny cunt is impersonating a monkey now.

"Yeah, you feeling strong tonight boys?" I raged at them.

Bang on cue, Reggie and the rest, recognising the square off are on them as I lay monkey boy out on his arse. The night's second boot off has the birds we have just met trying to calm us all down. The lairy lads, realising they had bitten off a bit too much, are now clambering over walls to escape the onslaught. Reggie pulls out a Stanley and is about to send one home with a nice souvenir to remind him of us. The girls start screaming and I've pulled him off before he sinks the steel into the fella's boat.

"Come on, let's get out of here" I said, pulling Reggie away by the sleeve of his Armani jacket, as he reminded me that it cost him £500.

By the end of the evening, only two of the girls came back with us. The others, nervous about our violent tendencies, jumped into a taxi and fucked off home, but I enjoyed the rest of the night tooting gear off Donna's bangers and watched Reggie winking at me as he got his cory polished off by the other bird. It turns out she was Donna's 40-year-old auntie. I fucking loved nights like this. They would soon become the norm, doing gear and getting our cocks sucked by dirty birds after a night of beer and violence.

Reggie and me were now full-time business partners, the Ben and Jerry of this lucrative enterprise, and under us the firm began to enjoy all the trappings that went with a pocket stuffed with cash. The maiden supply from Gilly was despatched in less than 3 weeks and we even stuck him an extra 5 grand to keep him sweet and the produce flowing in. But even better, through Reggie's girlfriend, who he was dating at the time, we made an Irish connect that gave us access to the high grade Love Dove tablets. This little firm were bringing in bundles straight back from Holland. The little white birdies were literally flying out of our hands and business was booming.

By the winter of 1990, we were having it proper, I mean PROPER, in the clubs on the south coast. A small fortune was pouring into our coffers. We hustled, wholesaled and distributed at the equivalent of £20 a pill and between £8 to £11.50 respectively, as you could imagine, these were exceptional times. With a few local boys on the firm now to help with the workload, we gained ourselves some good earners, who were also up for any bollocks that would come their way.

I was still mates with Pete, Face, Killa & TJB, but for whatever reason, they never really entered full on into the business side with me. They earned a bit of drink money acting as middle men on a few deals every now and then, but mainly because they had regular girlfriends and jobs and couldn't be arsed with the flying back and forth to Brighton every single day of the week. We would often be partying together still, with the full crew, and now, whenever we were out, the girls would all be out with us too.

I was still on and off with Carla but our relationship was as volatile as the Gaza Strip. It was really getting to me, the way she would pick an argument from out of nothing. Face always used to say to me that I should just dump her, even to her face. He couldn't even stand the sight of her by now, saying she was no good for me and she was fucking about with my head and our evenings were always getting fucked up because of her.

The icing on the cake came at Camden Palace one Monday night. I had been rowing with her (as usual) on the mezzanine floor. Her ex (Screwface), along with a team of his boys (the same moody spades from the White Waltham standoff) were all of a sudden wanting to get involved. They were all up in my face after she had done my head in and I shoved her out the way. They were all giving it, saying they were going to cut me and the usual shit. This was one of them situations when from nothing, animosity just builds up. After all, I had nothing to do with this firm, but it was noticeable from when we all walked in the gaff that this lot were offering themselves for a slap the way they were digging us out.

Must be the fact that Carla's ex just couldn't handle it, it must have been eating away at his insides, that I was sorting her out better than he was, or something, I just couldn't work out what his problem was. Face and Killa were watching the event unfold, analysing which one they wanted to attack first, Pete walks up and one of them had taken a swipe at him so I have nutted the geezer (Shhweet)and before you could even say "Let's have it then you mugs" we were backing them off down the stairs. The speed of The Family setting upon them had startled them into a hasty retreat. Pete Hong Kong Fooeyd a tall lanky one in the chest to help him down the spiral stairway. Face was raining blows on Screwface like George Foreman clubbing Ali in the rumble in the jungle. It was scrappy due to the restricted space on the stairway, but our attack on them was relentless, resulting in two of them sprawled out at the bottom of the steps with a couple of size 9 and a half Reebok classic in the rib and the chin for good luck.

The battle had led the rest of the Screwface gang to the bar area and straight into the Under 5s, who were now all over a couple of them, leaving one of them cornered at the bar bracing himself for a quality beating. Like a trapped animal he grabbed an ashtray and caught Killa square on the forehead with it just as security arrived and sent the kid sprawling across the table with a swift upper cut.

This immediately switched our tempers off as we all in unison nodded our appreciation of the knockout punch before we led Killa out. He was now stemming the claret with a bar towel that one of the other doormen had passed to him. We all returned to the cars, armed ourselves with tools, before heading back out to the main road and looked for the Notting Hill melts, excitedly looking about for them now to do them some real damage after they had drawn blood on Killa.

They must have had a secret trap door or something, because we stood around for around half hour but with no sign of them clowns anywhere. We decided to fuck off and get Killa some medical attention. Nifty was cursing that he was unable to christen Barry the axe and I spent the whole journey home being reprimanded, listening as Face and Killa bitched about Carla.

"You see, told you she's trouble. Every bloodclart time she's out it's agg, and now look, Killa gets his head lick up by ashtray."

By the new year (1991) Pete was now into relationship autopilot and had begun to drive down with me more and more to sample some of the high life and get that rock and roll experience with us. He was with me the night I first clapped my eyes on the girl that would become the love of my life, Helen. Now I started to mix business with pleasure.

She was only 17 when I first saw her but she had that look of sexiness on her. I bowled over to her in the Zap club one night, giving her the usual spiel I had mastered over the years of hunting birds in clubs. Dressed in a black mini skirt and long boots with curly hair, her bright glowing eyes stared at me every time I was around. She had the look of 'talk to me darling' all over her. Admittedly I just wanted to fuck her, I was high as an eagle and she was feeling the effects of a disco biscuit as well. Talking to her and smelling how sweet she smelt I had a bulge in my boxers. Acting like a meerkat on lookout, I spent the next few hours dancing with her, occasionally interrupted by customers wanting top-ups.

"I've heard so much about you" she said with an interesting sparkle in her eye as we chatted away. It suggested to me that she wanted a piece of the python that must have been obvious every time I was up close as we made convo.

"Yeah, like what?" I enquired cheekily, knowing that over the past year or so, we had been down there making a lot of noise as we capitalised on our new venture but also flown through a lot of the local fanny that had been throwing knickers at us in return for a mental night on class A and champagne. "Oh, quite a lot, being a hairdresser a lot of women love to talk" she replied.

This had me chuckling to myself at the fact that depending on who she had spoken to, with some of the shit we had done you would have thought she would have run a mile. The chemistry was definitely there from the off and something about her had me turned on. As young as she was, she gave the persona of someone a lot older than her 17 years, which was something that I have had to defend for years since the boys were now calling me Rodney the nonce, but age is nothing but a number, as the song goes. After taking her number, I was begging her to meet me for lunch in the week, where we could have a proper talk while we were not flying off our faces on drugs.

I was on the phone to her the Sunday afternoon, having half recovered from another mad weekend back at my mum's house. I had driven back to London with Inch, Nifty and Dee and ended up at a warehouse do in Nathan Way in Terry Waite country. I was quick to point out to Helen that she should have taken up my offer to come with me because Nathan Way was rocking and that she was missing a cosy up in my bed right now. It was strange to explain how I was already besotted with her, but in my life of violence and chaos I suppose I wanted to be a bit more like Pete, who very often hints about the need for me to calm it down a bit. In a way I was expecting his approval.

I'm on the phone later telling him, "I think I have met the one." I held the phone away from my ear as he roared at me with laughter, not the reaction I expected. He continued to take the piss because Nifty and the others had already been in his ear about her age but he's disputing this even more, despite the fact he'd seen and conversed with her and knew how she gwarn, but he was in full flow going along with the Under 5s.

"Seriously Flux? A man told me she was 15, bruv."

I told him to fuck off in the end and left him laughing along to the dial tone.

My first date with Helen was a quiet spot of lunch down the lanes in Brighton. We conversed about music, the rave scene and life in general, and she was amazing, we spent the whole afternoon together. It had been a very long while since I had courted a lady the old-fashioned way. Eventually on the 6th or 7th date with her (what's that all about?) I take a gamble on a room at the Grand and I work my way into the most unbelievable evening of sex with her.

Throughout the book I've explained the effects a real toe curler can have on a man's head and mine was gone. I'm laid out on my back with the stupidest goofy look on my boat as we snuggle up in bed.

My expression soon changes though, when my mind switches to Carla upon seeing the mobile phone flashing away on the other side of the room. Even after the battle with them shit outs from Notting Hill, I still couldn't leave her alone, she was break-up sex, make-up sex and fucking nothing else around, booty-call sex, with the impression it would continue like that forever, but this seemed like the best time to make a clean break. Although breaking it off with her will set off a Gaza strip turnout I can bet.

I already felt the backlash of her scorn recently after a row about some crazy rumour she had received third hand, about me with a stripper from the Wilton. She'd clocked me on the back of my head with a vase when I've actually corrected her that it wasn't a stripper, it was a brass, but now I'm actually quite worn out from the constant rows with her.

By the 16th repeat call she made, I answered, asking "what the fuck?"

"When you've finished with your fucking little slut, can you meet me at Brighton train station with my fucking money?" was the angry response down the phone. I'm not sure whether she had clocked me or just used a Jedi mind trick. She had done this on another occasion, arriving in Brighton unannounced, but I'm sure she wouldn't have just sat in silence watching if she had seen me, as I'm now responding in a manner to make Helen think it's a business call.

"I've had enough of this, I'll send someone down" I replied "And after this, don't fucking ring my number again, talking to me like that you cunt." Followed by the click of the phone hanging up.

I don't know whether it was because I had just had my toes curled or what, but after having such a lovely chilled day out with Helen, Carla's voice on the phone just irked me no end. I tapped the number of one of the local boys and called Sasha and instructed him to get down there with a monkey (£500) and a message.

"Tell them this is us done now, so much so I couldn't even be fucked to see 'em face to face" I said. Sasha understood and delivered. Funny, when I see Sasha the next day, he said she just shrugged her shoulder and fucked off on the next train back to London, which made it seem as though I had escaped unscathed, but I know her too well.

I never clocked it at the time because I did not own a vehicle. The wife of one of our suppliers had come to Reggie's one evening to deliver a weekly parcel. She stayed for a couple of drinks and a few lines with us and returned to her car to discover the tyres all slashed to fuck and

CUNT carved onto the bonnet. I never questioned it at the time, as she explained that someone must have identified the motor incorrectly and left it at that.

A couple of weeks later, I received a lift with Tony's bird (one of the local lads) after a night in the Escape. She came in to collect a bit of dough I had for Tony to take home. She was in there for half-hour or so as I counted up. A commotion outside drew my attention away and I was out the door in time to see a car's rear lights speeding off and Tony's missus' car with a burning rag hanging out of the petrol cap. I was stunned for a few seconds, but Tony's bird sprang into action, pulling the rag out as we both stomped the flames out.

At first I was thinking enemy, but remembering the other incident a couple of weeks ago, I was muttering, "That dirty fucking cunt" under my breath, as my thoughts trailed onto Carla. There had been plenty of opportunities to put one on me if someone had a real problem, I was always out in the open and it was not as though the address was common to all and sundry, only the firm, the odd bit of fanny and of course, Carla. Knowing her, her jealous impulses and reactions over the years it could only be her, and I was fuming. I calmed Tony's girl down as she was beside herself with fear thinking what she'd been caught up in. I told her to be cool, it was a jealous ex and nothing to worry about. I half fobbed her off with a ton to cover the little damage that was caused by the fiery rag.

Nifty, Reggie and Sasha turned up just as she was pulling away and I explained the events. Reggie instructed me, "Tell her, this fucking Carla, she's gonna end up in the Thames if she keeps coming around here fucking about with guests of mine outside my house. Why can't she just get hold of you and cut your Hampton off like normal women, instead of being all sneaky? I'll help her hold you down, ya cunt" he continued with a smirk.

Problem is, with her doing our suppliers wife's 30 grand BMW, this could leave us liable, so I spent the next few days trying to track Carla down since she refused to answer my calls. I ended up threatening her parents and two of her close pals that if anything like this carried on I'd be up there and they could suffer the consequences, as I was getting more and more livid by the day.

By a sheer stroke of luck, she was spotted by Pete one day when he was at work, hanging out of one of them green roadside telephone junction boxes in the city somewhere. Although with all the altercations and aggro Carla caused over the years, Pete still got along with her. After their long conversation, he's telling her all she's doing is mugging herself off. He's basically just given her a friendly warning, that I was ready to have something bad happen to her and hers and had a couple of skagheads ready to go medieval, with the promise of a large lump of brown as reward.

"Listen girl, you and him weren't supposed to be. All that sneaky shit you've been pulling, all you've done is target the wrong people. And if the Irish fella whose wife's car you damaged gets wind, he'll turn the place upside down to get ya. As far as he's concerned it was mistaken identity, which suits us knowing the fallout. So do yourself a favour, leave it the fuck alone."

Pete was good at getting his message across when needed, as he will always pacify, with the understanding that she wasn't all to blame. He himself gets annoyed enough with me that it often leads him to criminal damage, but enough was enough and the shit had to stop. He explained to me after that it had her repentant after the conversation. She gave him a kiss and a big hug and thanked him for understanding and that she would speak to me.

Her words came in a letter. A five-page double-sided apology landed on my mum's doorstep. She had propounded her undying love for me, that we will always remember the good times (This probably amounted to no more than 4 weekends of Class A taking and filthy sex.) She continued that she no longer had any more bitterness towards me. I was not convinced at first, not until Face bumped into her at a party in Notting Hill soon after, where she was even more repentant and apologetic to him. Face did not have any time for her whatsoever in retrospect, but he believed she was genuine as he repeated what she already knew and said it was for the best. I could now finally tell the skagheads to stand down.

How ya like me now?

My Local Team with the Wilton Arms, Nifty 50 & Dirty 30

Palace fans upset before losing to Liverpool 2000

Palace at Q.P.R circa 1982

Zulus want it, we obliged but superior numbers prevailed

Zulus in Tu Tuís, Selhurst Park 1989

Good old pitch invasion. Palace v Blackburn 1989

Palace on way to Liverpool 2000

Dirty 30 v Cardiff 2002

Dirty 30 Youth, Luton 2004

"He sleeps in his ca-a-r..." Elmer getting some stick from the lads

D-D-D-30! CPFC Youth on the move

Mic check. Young Senator T.J.B and Daddy Fluxie combination 1985

T.J.B, Me & Pete, 1986

With The Face 1987, Janet Street Porter Bins?

Boys London, with TJ 'Galton' and Face

Killa, Pete Nice & Face winter of 1987, Funky Dreads coming through

Pete, Flux, Killa, TJB and Face, from boys to men (1989)

Flyers from back in the day, bless the funk

shout!

"IT'S A BRAND NEW EXPERIENCE"

shout!

AT THE SANCTUARY
HUNGERFORD LANE
OFF CRAVEN ST. WC2 (Charing Cross)

EVERY TUESDAY
10p.m. — 3a.m.

TURN ON & TUNE IN
70's RADICAL CHIC ESSENTIAL

★

SHAKE & FINGERPOP
"IT'S A BRAND NEW EXPERIENCE"

£3

RIGHT OF ADMISSION RESERVED

Cleopat
Needle

Embankment
Charing Cross

CHARING CROSS
Hungerf

TURN LEFT OUT OF CHARING CROSS
THEN LEFT AT .. DOWN ALLEY TO
THE SANCTUARY BENEATH THE STATION

OBSESSIONS

FUNKI DREDS
AITCH 'B' + JAZZIE 'B'
"Throwing down Raw dancehall Justice"

2 ROOMS

TICKETS AVAILABLE AT:
Soul II Soul Shop
162 Camden High St
NW1 One (Basement of
Great Company Store)
☎ 01-267 3995
☎ 01-482 2697

"OBSESSIONS
HOT LINE"
☎ 01-858-8184
☎ 01-674 0205

S
E
P
T
30
FRI

10 Til 3.am

JASPER
THE VINYL JUNKIE
ADMINISTERING "LIVE" HOT ACID
ON THE DANCEFLOOR

2 GROOVE

Buses:
22, 25, 8

Holborn
Chancery
Lane
St Pauls

121 HOLBORN CIRCUS Opp Daily Mirror

ADVANCE TICKETS ONLY: SEE ABOVE
PRICE :- £6.50. / NO TICKETS AT DOOR

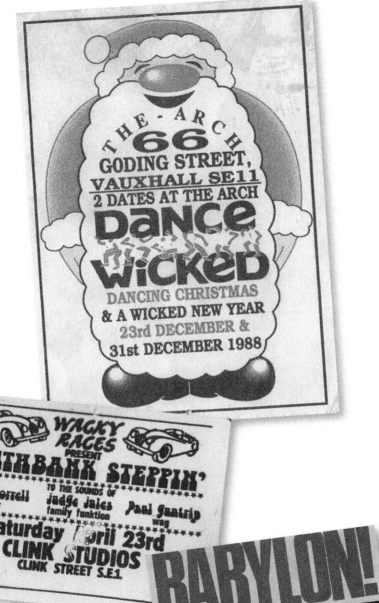

A Thursday night regular
for me and the boys

The Funky
Dread, We pay
homage to you,
Soul II Soul

Sunday nights, Africa Centre was church, praise the funk

you are cordially invited to

A MIDSUMMER NIGHTS DREAM

on *MIDSUMMER NIGHT*, SAT 24th JUNE

THE MOST SPECTACULAR EVER

Supernatural
Suspense
 S U N R I S E
Magical
Mystery

WORLD WIDE PRODUCTIONS CORDIALLY INVITE YOU TO THE

SUNRISE

SUNRISE
&
BACK TO THE FUTURE

1989
Dance Music Festival

Saturday 12th August
12 Noon - 12 Noon (24 Hours)

Entertainment

◦ Sunrise Video Premier ◦
· 12 of London & New York's finest DJ's ·
· 3 Live PA's · Walk in video game ·
· 10 Bouncey castles · Go-Karts ·
· Fairground · 100K Turbo sound ·
· Multi colour Lasers · Fireworks display ·
and for the first time
CINITRON ON DIAMOND VISION featuring
Video scratching and sampling

Blinders,
The 2 best
nights we
ever had

The Sun headline after White Waltham

Me, Pete, TJB, Face & Killa (the Family, 1991)

The Family and Under 5s, 1991

You wouldn't want to fuck around with this lot

Sterns 1991 after that unbelievable vitamin Es night

Helen and Tina, Bang club 1993

Helen with the girls, Charlotte, Mandy & Debbie

Only a tenner?

Voodoo Magic with Micky Finn, GQ and Fabio

Back Row =   Fluxie,Juicey Johns,Grooverider,Face,JJ Frost,Killer
Front Row =   Dezzie,Pete Nice,Diesel,Danny B and Benny

Inta Natty line up to play De Underground boys

Inta Natty
Logo

INTA older, with Face, Killa, Grooverider & Fabio

The front cover Shadow (Playboy mag) Playford you rascal!

More from Playboy… I mean Playford

INTA Warriors hard step anthem

Volume 2 Dreams of INTA

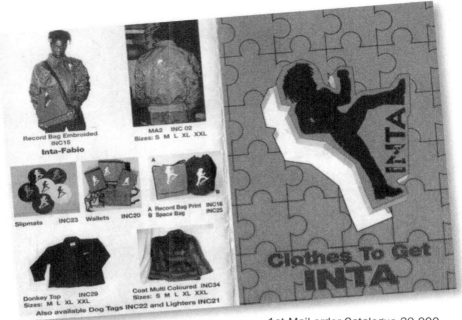

1st Mail order Catalogue 20,000 distributed to spread the word.

On Page 3 the late Mickey Lynas R.I.P.
Danny talked him into it.

We invited Terry Turbo down
for a few pints and a chin wag

INTA NATTY Merchandise. Clothes to get INTA

Inta Natty Style, Oxford dropping the 'Ain't yer babe' label

No reason for this other than the fact that they looked so damn good

MC FLUX and DJ Bailey Representing Inta Natty, Black Sheep Bar 2010.

DJ Bailey (right) with the INTA crew

Full Inta. The original Hardstep crew

Best men. My Wedding day 2001

THE FAMILY & UNDER 5's.
My home coming 2010

On a social one with Pete and the boys

Working with DJ Verdict at Mastermind records

2010 with D.J Rap

On Stage 2012

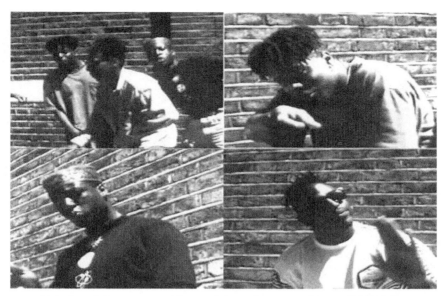

Nah, I can't have none of that, tell 'em what to say Mace - SAY NO GO

Sir Radics: Original 80s Soundman

Jiouxie Nice: Sir Radics MC

Me and David Rodiagan 2012

Flux on the Mic

Palace 2013 Last day of the season missed out again due to banning orders

DJ Rap, Oxford Sarah, Juice and Pete Nice Modeling for Inta natty & Ain't yer babe.

Me & Fabio (Family) (© Trevali Photography)

2014 Me, GrooveRider Pete Nice & Killa

1992 Me and Colin Dale, Golden Hill   Gyal dem still love me! Me and my Pal
Fortress rave Isle of White   Zoe been a rock for me since my release

On stage again 2014

Me, Pete Nice, Face, Dan & Killa Laying my brothers Mother to rest

Me My brother Howard, my sisters Allison and Sonia, circa 1971

Me, MC Fats & Pete Nice. 2014

Me, My brother & Sisters Love my Family

Mum & Dad Wedding day 1963 I was just a glint in my fathers eye

Me and the Legendary MC GQ

Rocking the Stage at Sundance festival 2014

Under the spot light

Me

THE GUVNORS

By mid-1991, I was more or less a Brighton resident with Helen, tucked up out the way in Peacehaven. I now had a nice little escape away from all the madness as I enjoyed some quiet nights in with her and her family. Amongst all this, Reggie was getting wind of people bad mouthing us and he would get increasingly wound up whenever, whilst out, Sasha and Tony, two of the locals who were on the firm, would report back that some locals where giving it the big'un. Reggie was now becoming more and more unstable, at football and now at work. He had the names of the people who were baiting us, calling us pussies and a 'London wog outfit'. The main gob was a fella named Birthmark Barry.

One night Reggie and me were in a restaurant with Helen and some sort he was regularly banging named Carly. We clocked the motor creeping up outside with four bodies sitting inside it and immediately got on the phone to another young Brighton lad called George, who was starting to emerge on the scene with our firm. I asked him to drive over to us. "Bring the tool bag, we're gonna do these cunts" Reggie barked.

George parked around the corner and entered the restaurant, confirming a motor full of meatheads were outside scoping the gaff. We instructed him to take the girls out the back and drop them at the cab shop, then to meet us at the end of the road. Unsure of what we were going to do, as we didn't know whether they had shooters or not, Reggie, in the way that he does, gee'd me up as he took a can of CS and a large chiv, then carefully slipped it up his sleeve and kicked the bag under the table towards me.

"Arm yourself and let's go" he said.

Dropping a wad of notes to cover the meal and the drink tab, we made our move to the door. The lad George slowly drove past us as we walked amongst the traffic towards the motor parked on the other side. Having recognised Birthmark Barry, Reggie was straight at the driver's door, at the same time trying to ram the knife in the window and almost severing the fellas head. With this unexpected response, panic set in and he and his boys screamed, "GO... FUCKING GO!"

I was right on top of the passenger door and managed to put the window in with the hammer before catching the spoiler on the boot. The car sped off, sending a few dustbins into the road and oncoming cars screeched to a halt as they hotfooted it away from two crazy mad men armed with a samurai sword and a sledgehammer. This was how it was described when the rumour of the incident spread around Brighton, but it still never stopped them badmouthing us at every opportunity.

We even put the word about that we'd meet them for a straightener, to confirm who were the guvnors once and for all. When we all came down 20-handed one Friday night and plotted outside the Zippedy Doo Dah Bar waiting to meet them, we weren't surprised at the no show. This had the rumour mill in overdrive with the notion that it was an off organised between Palace and Arsenal, because Birthmark Barry, Zarkhof and their boys were all Gooners. It still carried on after with Zarkhof, Samson and Microdot Mark and another fella called Darren, who were still putting it about that we were in over our heads. One occasion when I was out with Helen one night, I was attacked by them. I suffered a couple of digs but escaped getting properly served up, doing the off before they sunk blades into me. Don't get me wrong, they were good heads and no mugs but whenever we fronted them firm handed, the bad mouthing was as far as it went.

People would find it hard to believe that a firm like ours would be running shit in Brighton without anyone lifting a finger and no real threats to our lives as you would expect nowadays. Pete even to this day finds it hard to believe, but as I've said before, sometimes a reputation can make you twice the power that you really are. Also, back in them days, there weren't many mad Yardie or evil Albanians about pretty much and you don't fuck about with them cunts.

The fact is, it came to a point when many people knew that Reggie was a game cunt, sorry let me rephrase, a fucking raving psychopath and did not give a fuck. Then people realised that I never gave a fuck, adding that to the Under 5s who could attack you like a pack of hungry wolves and add to that two big dreads and one mad African and the Wades family, who were well renowned in Brighton at the time, it was no wonder that no one fucked with us and those that did got a rude awakening.

Like the time when a silly wannabe hard man called Sam found out when he tried to test us. Our firm of hustlers now consisted of local dealers who controlled the clubs and were watched over by the Under 5s and the Wades, so no one would fuck with the trade. Doormen were also taken care of by Reggie, who kept them all sweet. One of the new boys on the firm was being introduced and doing all right for us for the few weeks we had him working. Midweek, whilst back on the manor and drinking in the Wilton, it was end of season and no football was on but Nifty 50 lad Frankie was in the boozer with us. By the way Nifty is nothing to do with Nifty 50, we named him that because we used to take the piss saying he was shifty, and for some reason or other it got shifted to Nifty or Shifty Nifty or something along the lines.

Anyway, he received a phone call from the lad we had named Blocker (due to the shape of his head) saying he'd been taken by this Sam fella and his pals, slapped about, robbed and told to tell his coon mates that this was their manor before being fucked off with a boot up the arse. Nifty proceeded to repeat what he'd heard on the blower. We then made a call to Brighton George to go on a reconnaissance mission to locate this prick.

"We're doing this tonight" I said, seething at the audacity of this fella. Nifty, Dee, Frankie, me and the other Under 5s loaded up into 2 separate motors. Before speeding off, we told Tony Roots, Dee and the others to go to one address and wait as we went to check out the address that we'd been informed of from the dozen odd phone calls we made to our people in and around Brighton. Reggie at the time was on remand over an alleged firearms offence. He was nicked after a row with staff of the Frog and Jacket bar, and he left there pissed before returning, smashing his hand through a window and firing four shots into the ceiling, sending the staff and patrons cowering under the tables, so for now Reggie was out of the picture. The Wades however, had offered to grab the kid and 'disappear him', but I declined that offer, advising a scar is a better reminder for people than to make him disappear.

Arriving in Brighton in world record time, we approached the address. Frankie suggested that it was best that he approached the door, then us to steam in when it opened. We parked up around the corner, walked back to the house behind Frankie and on the Rory behind a wall. Frankie knocks the door and we could hear him explain to the occupant just like an esteemed gentleman out of the ICF ITV documentary *A Knocker's Tale*.

He began to explain to the homeowner that he was doing door to door on behalf of blah blah blah etc. Just as (as he would explain it to us later) he saw the man turn ghost white as his door was rushed by me and Nifty, who was inches from burying an axe into his forehead before we all collided with the closing door. We fight our way in the house and Sam is chucking everything but the kitchen sink as we scream "Kill the cunt!" A kid's tricycle, Action Men and Transformer toys are aimed at our heads, he escapes out the back door and over a fence just as I launch a large knife in his direction that sticks into the fence with that twanging noise like a Robin Hood arrow.

"Fuck! no one is covering the back" I thought, as Frankie scales the fence in hot pursuit. Nifty heads back out the front door trying to head him off and I struggle to retrieve the steel that was embedded into the fence. Turning and leaving the way I came, I was confronted by some doris with a screaming dustbin lid in her arms. She was bawling out, "Leave him alone, what has he done? He has kids!"

"Fucking sit down and sort your fucking baby out!" I screamed back at her. "And clean up this shithole."

I then leave mother of the year to her chores and find Nifty and Frankie bewildered that the cunt has escaped their grasp. By now the street is alive to the commotion. I signal to Inch, who screeches up to us and we drive round in one last attempt to locate him before steaming round to George's house to dump the weapons. A reluctant Nifty is not best pleased, having to leave his beloved Barry the Axe behind, but 3 angry fellas attacking a family man's house is a sure nicking as police cars fly past us in all directions after the event. Cunts like this Sam fella should know better than to fuck with people pretending to be all gangster and bringing that shit on his family. He was lucky not to receive any further consequence for his actions.

It wasn't until we were half way back up the M23 that Nifty lifted his silence and laughed out loud, "Gwarn Frankie! Working on behalf of the men crippled and maimed by naughty cunts society."

This had the car laughing at Frankie's patter to Sam when he opened the door to him and the axe almost opened him up. It was the last we ever saw of the prick; he must have followed Lord Lucan's route or something. Although during one of Reggie's prison terms he did see the fella, who even tried to give it the big'un in front of the other inmates, but Reggie put it right on him and he shat himself again and backed down. Following Sam's lucky escape act, we ended up back on the manor just before closing time, but with the adrenaline still in our bloods we ended up round Inch's house and hit the cherry.

This had followed more fights and attacks that I could ever remember. At Palace we were having it big time with Nifty 50 as we had some major tear-ups, with Reggie (when he was about) and me usually going in and trying to cause as much harm as possible to opposing fans. On one occasion, following an away match, some of us would end up in bars around Central London for a booze. Reggie and me were in a pub one afternoon which was full of scarfers mainly. Palace fans were singing *Glad All Over* and other songs from the terraces.

In the pub were these two meatheads, proper Phil and Grant Mitchell turnouts, giving it that they were Chelsea and taking the piss out of some Nigels in there. Reggie had been at the bar and was giving them daggers whenever they looked over, and one approached him asking if he had a problem...

"Nah mate, I'm just having a quiet drink with me pal."

From that the fella said with veins popping out of his neck, "You better fuck off back to your boyfriend then eh? Palace mug."

Reggie, as cool as you like, walks back over to me, shaking his head in disbelief.

"'Ere, you'll never guess what, that meathead just called you a nigger," he said.

Well as you know, they never actually said that, but Reggie thought it was a good chuckle to wind me up and set me off.

"Fuckin what? Who?" I snarled. With that we both walked over to Phil and Grant. The chubbier of the two fat cunts removed his coat and the pair of them were pushing out their chests now. I asked them politely, "Why you calling me a nigger for? What have I ever done to you?"

Without waiting for any answer, I sent a Budweiser bottle smashing into the face of Grant (or Phil) and proceeded to jab Phil (or Grant) with the remains of the glass in my hand. Reggie was on his pal and before we knew it claret was everywhere. Blood was pissing out of the fella like a fountain all over Reggie's £400 Hugo Boss jacket. Again emphasising the cost of the jacket because the prick has never let up on it even up to this day.

We calmly walked out before people realised the commotion (we were subtle like that). Escaping on the first train out of Dodge, we then jumped a taxi from Charing Cross to the Wilton. We were told that Bulldock had already been in looking for the pair of us with reasons to believe that it was us that had attacked a pub full of Chelsea fans (do you see the problem here with Old Bill now?) We swiftly jumped another cab to Reggie's car, which was parked up in Purley, and fucked off down to Brighton, where we spent the next few days panicking.

A few days later we finally got word that there was no fatalities after the incident, which was a huge relief as I make promises to myself that I'm quitting all this forever now and was going to keep out of trouble.

Unlucky for me though, it was not as easy to follow through as it became a weekly event. Some cunt would try it and we'd end up serving them up. Brighton lads would often try to attack us as well, referring to an incident when Paul C (who we are good mates with now by all accounts) and a few of his Irish Celtic cronies bounced over at us one afternoon. It was always a Palace v Brighton/Celtic v Rangers animosity between us that saw a few standoffs and skirmishes over a few years. During this incident we were only six handed, me, Reggie, Nifty and a couple of others, and as they came bouncing across I tried to gas them but due to the wind direction, ended up gassing my lot, then having to back off as Reggie and Nifty were half blinded by friendly fire. Reggie still has a go at me about it to this day.

Through our dealings in Brighton we did get on all right with some of Brighton's firms, the ones that were genuine and put all their rivalries aside when it came to business. Even on one occasion when Wolves were down on a Friday night, while we were out and about working. I was impressed at the amount of Stone Island clad black lads that Wolves had in their mob. Anyway Brighton were well under the cosh that night against this impressive Wolves firm. It was kicking off all over the place from what I can remember, but Brighton were doing OK and stood firm against good numbers. Witnessing this, and loving a tear-up ourselves, we stood and had it with Wolves. We received a fair few digs from these big Wolves lumps and it was a very eventful evening as Brighton had several running battles with the Yam Yams in and around West Street.

Another incident, this one was quite funny, was when Reggie was in Zippedy Doo Dahs with Liam when some sand monkey called Ashad, along with the Eubank twins and few of their mates, were in there enjoying the hospitality of the bar owner. Reggie made a remark to a lady they were with which they took offence to. They made sure he heard them say that he would struggle to leave the gaff that evening and they were gonna teach him a lesson. Ashad, being a little brave in front of his crew, was put in his place after Reggie fronted him, saying "See you, you little paki cunt, best you fuck off before I stick some steel in ya!"

One of the door staff has now pleaded with Reggie to leave out the back, but Reggie, as Reggie was back then, was saying, "Fuck 'em, I ain't scared of them."

The doorman said, "I know, I just don't want our establishment to be in the publicity because the Eubank family get injured in a knife attack by some psycho, so please do me a favour, fuck off out the back door."

Reggie has reluctantly gone out the back, and they are all outside about 15-handed now waiting for him. He manages to slip away and gets into Liam's motor, returning to the bar a short time after to get a closer look at them. This Ashad geezer was now stopping cars as he weaved in and out the traffic looking for Reggie. He walked up beside Liam's motor with Reggie in it.

"What's going on bruv?" Reggie asked.

Peering into the car, Ashad begins hollering about the outrage that had taken place inside the bar and is now looking for some geezer who had upset the Eubanks and the ladies that they were with. Reggie replied, "Yeah that was me" before gassing him in the face and leaving him squealing in the middle of the road as Reggie and Liam drove off.

This fella was incensed and soon let everyone who would listen know that Reggie was a marked man now. In the gym weeks later this Ashad was telling the gym owner, who was actually a pal of Reggie's, that he should bar Reggie from the gym and that he was bang in trouble. However the gym owner in the end told him to leave it and just to walk away. Instead, the sand monkey continued with his rant. The gym owner then had to school him on the modus operandi of our illustrious friend, ending with the statement, "You see if you carry on with this with him, you'll be bench pressing one day and he'll come along and drop it on your fucking head, you cunt."

The next time he saw Reggie, he was quick to go over to him and apologise, hoping for an assurance that there was not a problem between them, that he was of Iranian and not Pakistani origin, and also to ask whether he was safe to continue with his weight training. It was stories like this that were starting to make people aware that we weren't people to fuck around with and it was not uncommon to see people being chased up the road after giving it to us.

This fella called Darren and his pals, one of them a West Ham/Brighton hybrid called Fat Matt, were found out when they saw me again and thought I was alone one evening and were giving me the usual, "Come on Palace, come on you black cunt!" After I produced a small but very shiny axe blade from my jacket pocket, and they realised Reggie and Nifty were in close proximity drawing out big chivs, they were off up the road in no time leaving us pissing ourselves watching the fat cunts wobble up the road after chasing them for a couple of blocks. "WHERE YOU GOING? IM RIGHT HERE YOU MUGS" I shouted, laughing my bollocks off.

Things got a bit more serious when two fellas doing things properly and quietly put word to us that they wanted a sit down to discuss business. We knew of them but pretty much had avoided any involvement with them. More to the point was that they saw us as an irritation but not worth the hassle of going to war with. Big John and Little John were two older gentlemen in essence. Looking at them, they were your stereotypical diamond geezers with fingers in every pie that you would see summed up by Hollywood's portrayal of English gangsters. They were very understated but had an air of seriousness about them as Reggie, Nifty and I pulled up chairs and accepted their offer of drinks and cigars (obviously they were watching too many movies).

"You boys have been making a lot of noise down here and we know for the most part there has been retaliations and what not" said Little John. "We would like to offer you some work that will benefit us all, if you can hold off from the nonsense and the aggro, including that football lark."

Reggie appears to be narked by this implication. He takes his football hooliganism very seriously, but he sat quietly as they ran through a history of drug trafficking and other wheeling and dealing. Their main game was puff, and tons of the shit, with a distribution network from here to Glasgow, but they saw us as their carve up to the lucrative local Ecstasy market and the little network we had already established in Brighton. I can see Nifty's brain is going into overdrive when he asked, "So why do we get this privilege?"

"It's simple" came his response. "We have the finance and the network to make your money grow, to organise things properly and not end up having the south coast as a free for all, I mean proper lock it down."

My thought was that we are nicking money off them. They were old school and didn't have the sharpness or the street savvy to have it in the clubs, but also they were more business and I was thinking they could probably put our money to good use, instead of the reckless spending we were doing.

"Look, all we are asking is for yous to have a think about it. If it ain't for you so be it, we'll just go our own ways."

If I was a paranoid man, that statement could have sounded a bit like Virgil Sollozzo out of the Godfather, a kind of take it or go to war offer.

"It sounds good" said Nifty, who by now had stubbed the cigar out after only four puffs. "But what numbers are we talking about? We are already getting packages for next to nothing and shifting 7k more or less every week, just by doing the few clubs in and around Brighton."

Reggie interrupts, "Not being funny, but if you are talking parcels bigger than that, we would have to put ourselves more in the open and smash the whole lot from Hastings to Portsmouth, that's more ticked out, more collections, more headache."

We all shook hands at the end of the meeting, and Reggie insisted that we would get back to them. This could have been our opportunity to earn some big time dollars, but we would have to get our act together as our finances were all over the place and we were already playing catch-up with our Irish supplier. The car journey home had Reggie letting paranoia cloud his judgement about the sit down.

"You wanna trust them with our money?" was his response. "All we know, they might be planning to get us out the way, who the fuck knows?"

After getting back to Reggie's flat and having a few lines and brandies, Reggie said he would try and get some background info on them. He said we would stall them for a bit and try and get our house in order and to make sure there was not any whiff of Old Bill or any other underhand plots going on. This included speaking to our Irish supplier, who was well connected.

A couple of days later, I was down the lanes with Helen tucking into a bit of lunch when I bumped into Big John. Exchanging a few pleasantries, he recommended that the steaks in the establishment were the best and instructed the proprietor to give us a bottle of wine on the house. Dropping me a business card, he offered an invite for Helen and me round his house up in Saltdean at the weekend, where we could discuss business a bit further.

The invite became more promising after an altercation on the Friday night in the Frog and Jacket resulted in Reggie in nick on a threats to kill charge. This was after he had instructed me to "take care of the witnesses", which resulted in me having a bar manager over the bar with a seven-inch knife pressed against his throat telling him if he goes to court he's dead. A little subtlety goes a long way, but what the fuck do I know? Because it came right on top with Reggie serving a short bit of time on remand. By the weekend I was chomping Big John's hand off to do business with him and we toasted with a few glasses of champagne the dawning of a new day.

Then came the headaches. Reggie already had his fears from the off and had even warned me to leave it alone until he at least made bail. Too late, work was already underway. Me and Nifty called all the workers, bumping up a few like Sasha, Tony, Trevor Wades, Becky The Bag, a kid named Alfie and Liam, instructing them that we were going to be getting some major parcels and everyone had to step up, that we needed more leaders on the firm to control the south coast properly. Everything went to plan initially and every Sunday night George's and Reggie's flat were piled up with notes. We counted up and divvied up the takings and over the space of 4 months, 4 large suitcases were collected in return for more large parcels of Es, puff and Charlie.

We got an update on our (unskimmed!) money and had already banked 40 large into Helen's and Reggie's other half Mo's accounts as we got money dripped back to us. Brighton George splashed out on a brand new BMW convertible paid in cash, and Reggie's other half threw down part payment on a new apartment with a view to setting up a new and healthy environment for their expected baby. Me, well, I splashed out on garms and treats for Helen and paid top dollar rental on a posh flat in Peacehaven overlooking the beach. Helen went to town with it, furnishing it with TVs, leather sofas and B&O hi-tech.

Our network of clubs spread along the south coast and we even took the precarious step of dipping our feet back in the London market. Regular Moondance raves in Barking, Utopia at the Tasco Warehouse in Nathan Way, Telepathy, along with World Dance and Fantasia's organised large events, had us rattling away Es like bags of Skittles. To lighten the load we had connections through football and had lads collecting large parcels from us for cash, and life was sweet. Unfortunately for me, I love the cherry, the Es and the coke as we partied like it was 1999. I started to hand over my responsibilities to other people because I was having a good time, and of course, I was the Guvnor, the Don, and money runs uphill, shit runs down.

It was no surprise, with my luck and total lack of concentration, on a par with an ADHD victim on cherry cola, that things would eventually go pear shaped. First it was the £18,000 that went missing from the count up, then raids at the Escape, the Zap, and the Star Pub in East Grinstead. One of the biggest earning bank holiday weekends saw 4 of our workers lifted and 2000 Es thrown away, but wait for it, the worse was to come. Rumour had it that Big John and Little John had been under surveillance by major crimes for 2 years. As careful as they were, the major crimes unit of Met Police had a line to their whole operation. It turned out that one of their most trusted partners was an undercover officer out of Scotland Yard, so they also had a line on the money, their money, our money, so all that bollocks about putting our money to work was going straight to the law and not the overseas investments I was hoping.

They came through our doors as well, the places we had for counting and sorting, but we had nothing worthy of major crimes in there other than a few tools. That was a stroke of luck really because the Wades had nicked most of the heavy stuff to sort out some fellas that were giving them a bit of aggro. All we really done was make the case against them two more watertight as suitcases and holdalls of loose bills was more evidence for them to throw away the key. Lucky for me, eh? I was back down in London after a mad night in Nathan Way with all the boys, so Tony and Sasha's late afternoon visit to the Wilton arms had me speechless at the fallout. "Well that worked out lovely then!" Inch said in disbelief.

The news was travelling down fast, with more of the firm entering the pub. There was more bad news regarding Liam and Alfie. Terry Blocker gave me the heads up that they had had the Irish fella over for 30 large and I was getting the impression that that would be falling on my head. The pub was full with our so-called staff by the evening, no one wanted to be anywhere near Brighton at that moment in time. Remember that lovely posh flat near Peacehaven? I actually spent 2 weeks in it tops before having to abandon it during the fallout. So all I wanted right now was a big fat toke, a taste of that insatiable blend of washed cocaine, infused with one part baking soda, slowly flamed by lighter. So that's where I went for the next few days.

CHAPTER 12

MC FLUX THAT'S WHO

**No Matter where you come from respect due all crew,
MC Flux is passing thru.**

The 90s drafted in years of my life which leaves me looking back thinking, how the fuck am I still alive? Because with success comes excess, where I was personally succeeding and exceeding a fair amount. It's the point where with the stress of the game and all the bullshit that came with it, the crack pipe began to be a nice escape but it was also to become the source of my troubles. Throughout 1991 and the most part of 92 the money was in and out of our hands faster than a rat up a whore's snatch. Pete had come down at the weekends more regularly and we had many blinding nights in Sterns. While the lads served up, we started getting in with a few promoters, like Brian from Pure, Slinger, who was a promoter from Portsmouth and Mensa who was the main man at Interdance, the promoter of Sterns, who was always hospitable to us with a bit of VIP.

It was one of these nights when Pete had me to one side asking about my general well-being and making sure if I needed to talk that I know he is always there for me. Fucking top bloke, everyone else was so busy with earning it was difficult to gauge if anyone was really stressed or under the cosh. We'd ask each other occasionally 'Are you all right mate?' Or 'how the fuck are you?' etc, but it was more in passing, it was never meant as a 'come on son and have a little cry on my shoulder'. Pete I could talk to about almost anything but he'd got wind of my new relationship with the crack pipe after being informed by one of the lads that people were getting away with outstanding debts. But the last thing I needed was him doing my head in with it.

"You sure there's nothing you want to share with me?" he quizzed. I was relieved when Helen and her friend Rachel approached, which had distracted Pete's attention.

"Have you met Helen's mate Rachel?" I interjected and was relieved that I had managed to swerve his questions as he turned his full attention on Rachel. She was a good looking sort by all accounts but a bit complicated, which I thought should keep Pete occupied and away from prying any further into my habits. At the end of the night, we all met back at George's house with all the girls and the entire firm, where we would probably watch the film *Warriors* or the film about football hooligans - *The Firm* - for the 100th time.

Me and Helen would be chilling on the sofa as George entertained us on the decks. Charlie, Es, marijuana and champagne flowed, and every so often people were disappearing to either smash some fanny or bang out on some rocks as the cherry was forbidden for certain prying eyes. We carried on well into Sundays and on a few occasions birds tweeting on a Monday morning would signal the end of the celebrations. All courtesy of George, who was impressing and out in front as his gaff was now headquarters.

To say the time we all spent in Brighton was eventful would be an understatement. Looking back over the last few chapters, it is almost as though my life was one big two and a half year blur. I was hitting the crack heavily by now and shovelling pills and trips as though they were going out of fashion. We were party animals in a party town and in the end, business was affected as we began to lose control. It got so bad one night I was a bit wired and I am told I had a black kid called Kay pressed up against the wall threatening to cut him because he owed me money. Helen was shouting at me to let him go, and I was getting deeper into the red mist. After everyone's pleas, I released him. I was reminded he'd already paid Nifty the dough and was straight with us.

We were also becoming ever more paranoid, with people having a pop. Perceived missing money resulted in me ordering Nifty and Inch to look for properties and heavy-duty tools - we were going to the mattresses. It was in my head that people were watching and plotting against us, so we needed to be ready. The spat with Kay was one of many isolated incidents. It was still not clear why I grabbed him up, but I was a pretty loose cannon at the time and after word had got to Pete, he advised me that I should come back to the manor and stay out of Brighton for a few weeks to sort my head out.

By the end of 1992, the whole operation started seeing a downturn. Most businesses go through these boom and bust periods, for many reasons, mainly economic and the state of the market. Our decline was part self-inflicted by total and utter carelessness and piss-poor management, because me and the Under 5s lost parcels, swallowed and sniffed all the profits. Reggie was in nick again, this time over some bullshit drink driving offence, where he failed to stop and crashed into a shop following a high-speed car chase. People were owing money left right and centre. Even Dee's brother Liam went underground after getting nicked in Camden with a bag of E's. He had it on his toes, first to Ireland and soon after... who the fuck knows? Even Dee hadn't a clue.

The word we received weeks later was that it was not just the nicking, it pans out that he had bailed a few big batches off a face we knew and had been fucked over by some black firm in Tooting. Had he come to us he might have had some backing, but he had gone independent after all the troubles in Brighton we had and was then into this fella for some serious dough. This added to the bird time he would face for the pills, so off he flew. The young lad George was the only sensible one and he had pugged his earnings away. He offered to step up and said we could eat with him whilst we tried and recoup our losses, which was near on impossible, as people owing 75% of our dough had vanished off the face of the earth.

Along with the bad and the mad situations hanging around us at the time, we still were having a good time in between, when we were out raving. Pete, Face, Killa, TJB all the Under 5s and the WAGs were all coming down the coast and having it at the Sterns all-nighters, where Mensa and his Inter-dance organisation were putting on the best parties, with all the top DJs there week in, week out. With guest list sorted for all the crew, we would spend many weekends down there for the next few years, which would eventually lead to the return of the Ragamuffin, Lyrical Don, MC Flux on the microphone.

Pete and me were always having conversations about MCing, as it was still in our blood from our sound days, and listening back sometimes to old Young Senator mic check session, we would mainly be discussing about how gutted we were at what could have been following the collapse of the sound. Also around that time, making his own way back with the microphone, Pete was doing some music projects with Fuzzy Dee, who was an old LWR Deejay. Pete explained it was funny when he was on a job at BT when this other BT engineer walks in and begins to talk to him and Pete was like "I fucking recognise that voice," but could not put his finger on it. He starts a conversation with him then the fella confirmed that he was Fuzzy Dee from LWR.

Fuzzy Dee had a studio at his house where Pete had done a couple of rap vocal tracks with him, culminating in a performance at a talent contest at the Hackney Empire. We all went down to support him. We were about 30 handed with all his family there as well and all the girls making sure he got good votes by screaming for him at the top of their voices. He came second in the contest behind a very funny comedian, and we took exception to one of the judges, who tried to say Pete was just basically copying Jazzy B and Rebel MC. Everyone else was looking on in disgust, and our lot let football songs ring out as we sing the terrace classic, "You'll never make the station!" and "You're going home in a fucking ambulance!" Pete, on stage, was signalling for us to pipe down, trying to hold back laughter as the judge looked on bewildered at the abuse.

Over time I was always suggesting to Pete that he should MC at raves over the DJs. He was in my opinion a better MC than I was during our sound days, but he never wanted to do it, saying it's a different game in raves. MCs need to hype the crowd where he saw himself more as a lyrics man, which brings me back to my earlier reference about our old Young Senator pal Beaver Banton. He was a vibey crowd entertainer for sure and would have been an ideal rave MC.

Going back a little bit, there was a time when Inch, Dee, Nifty, Mendez and myself used to go down Slammers in Gravesend occasionally around 1990. Out of all the firms we were regulars down there, at first trying to drum up some business but it soon became a venue to just have a rave and a relax to and pop a disco biscuit or two.

I'm remembering as well that it was here one night we met Kelly and Jo in there, two Ipswich girls we got chatting to. We saw them down there often, and the pair of them later on became celebrities on the scene, when they became dancers for Slipmatt and Lime's SL2 outfit. They were good sorts who always had me impressed with their moves on the dance floor. Without a doubt, I bet the pair of them could pull out a few manoeuvres in the sack, not that I personally ever had the privilege. From memory, both had boyfriends at the time but Inch was seeing one for a short period and the other had a little fling with Pete later on when she was SL2.

There is a funny story about that little fling of theirs. I won't go into it too much detail, but a couple years after, she turned up at Rage on the arm of a DJ friend of ours, who told us that she denied seeing him on an intimate level and made Pete out to be some kind of liar, which we thought was a bit weird at the time, there was never reason for us to lie about fanny that was certain and seeing that she used to be all over him, begging him to take her home when we were out. Childish I know and I'm not trying to turn this into a kiss and tell story, but we found it quite funny when discussing it writing this book. I just wanted to put it right back on her, the truth right here, in writing, if she's reading it, because she knows. And fair play, 9 out of 10 I've been told, a squirting, toe-curling nympho that growls like a tiger.

Anyways, digressing a little bit, we were in Slammers one night and nicely buzzing on an E when I just all of a sudden took up the mic and began to hype the crowd over a Jumping Jack Frost set. It was something I never planned but just saw the mic sitting there when I was skinning up and sharing the spliff with the legendary Frost, who had been acknowledging us over the few weeks we were down there. I just picked it up and off I went and that saw the beginning of my career as MC Flux, more or less. Soon after that, when we were all in the upstairs room in Sterns and DJ Pig Bag was on the decks, we had all necked the legendary love doves and I had Nifty, Inch, all the boys and also the Sterns crowd going mental when I stepped up to the mic over 4 Hero's Mr Kirks Nightmare and bellowed...

I, I, I, I, I, I, I, I'm Rushing
wha' me do !
wha' me do !
I, I, I, I, I, I, I, I'm Rushiiiing.

And it was a rush, that's the part I enjoyed, being the centre of attention, but it wasn't all down to self-absorption. Back when I started MCing on sound systems, as I said earlier in the book a lot of inspiration to 'chat the mic' came to me from listening to the Saxon, Jamdown Rockers and Sir Coxson sound tapes. You could also say that the same thing came about when we received a copy of a Grooverider tape in 1991 recorded at Central Park in Portsmouth, that featured MC Cool and Deadly. I'm not kidding when I say that TDK C-90 cassette could have easily have been played over 100 times en route to wherever we were going at that time. We absolutely rinsed that tape out the amount of times we listened to it back then. So if anyone was to ask me who my biggest influence was to become an MC I'd definitely have to say that it was MC Cool and Deadly, but at the time I had no idea how big it would become as eventually, on the South Coast at least, MC Flux would become top billing for many rave promoters.

So now with Pete, Face, Inch & the Boys as my entourage, Under 5s doing what the Under 5s do best and that was to earn a pound note, we enjoyed a few successful years of indulgence on the south coast. With our connections with Mensa in Sterns, I made a point of doing a bit of networking and we would often find ourselves back at our old stomping ground, Heaven nightclub, the home of Babylon, where now Rage was the resident pre-weekend rave. Everyone who was anyone was at Rage on Thursday nights, where often Pete, Inch and me would be in VIP sipping champers with the main DJs and promoters of the time. Pete also started doing a bit of flying for Pure, who were the promoters of Rage, to ensure we had guest list for the huge Dance 90-91 etc raves.

I remember us having it right off at the Dance 91 event in the Brighton centre and cleared over 300 pills. The under 5s rinsed the place out with over £1000 worth of moody fivers. It was really funny leaving the rave in the morning and seeing the venue owners going ballistic and almost in tears to the gavvers after realising their take was awash with these crappy-looking notes. From what I can remember they were so bad the Queen looked like Dame Edna Everage.

By now most of the boys were already out of the building with their pockets jangling with pound coins. The scam was crude as well as simple in the fact that you would just send anyone up to buy a bottle of water or a can of fizzy pop and pocket the loose change. This was one of many scams they would pull off over the years, where this time as I started to get busy being an entertainer the Under 5s under the employment of Brighton George they were pulling off some unbelievable capers.

Like the time we had all gone down to Raindance and had a blinding night in Peterborough, the first time Pete had taken an E. I had offered him half a disco biscuit on a weekend where he had had a stressful time sorting out some Portsmouth boys we knew with a parcel and had some bollocks with the count coming up short. He was also under the cosh with his girlfriend Jayne because he was back out raving

154

all the time. I guess with every relationship, when the honeymoon is over you wanted to get back out with the boys as was with the case with Pete.

A few weeks later we were going to another Raindance which left George passing on a parcel of 2000 Es as none of the Under 5s would be around to work the clubs. Last minute we had a change of plan, after getting a call from Mensa that afternoon to work the main floor in Sterns with Colin Dale, Dr S Gachet and HMS. When we got down to Brighton that evening George was none too pleased that we were going to a Sterns all-nighter with no tablets to sell. In Steps Nifty, brain in overdrive and unknown to me Pete and the others at the time, had popped into the chemist on the way to Sterns and cleared the shelves of vitamin tablets.

Sterns was exceptionally busy that night and the tablet trade was not peaking to say the least by the time they arrived. A couple of lads we knew, Mickey and Troy, had already cleared out their one hundred, which they were going via Pete's connections. Bob and his Portsmouth lot, who were another business connection we had, were cleaned out as well but surprisingly there was still a demand for Ecstasy. In step George and the Under 5s, supplemented by the 50 or so legit tablets they were holding that evening, somehow managed to retail 150 vitamin E tablets with an 85% mark up.

They were marketed as exclusive and recently-imported splits and slow jams (fuck knows). You would get more of a rush from a sniff off a crack whore's knickers than the moody pills they had sold. You had to have understood that many people who bought them were the same punters who would have bought a legit Love Dove from either Mickey, Troy or Bob and his crew. We often found with Love Doves that the rush on these was smooth to full on in stages. Many a time previously whilst driving home we would get an unexpected rush from a pill we had necked hours before. This is the only explanation why they got away with the vitamin trade and even had people shaking off their hands and complimenting them on an A+++ product. That night will always live in our memories as we captured the moment, equivalent to a Facebook 1000 'likes' moment, when we artistically placed the money that was made on the bonnet of Pete's BMW.

We could actually have written a whole chapter about Sterns, which was a very memorable place at that time for us. This was not just for business, which was not as enjoyable any more and more of a must do. It was a needs must situation due to the fallout I described earlier and because the music around this period was immense. We had so many laughs going there and many a night rushing off our nuts. It always used to make me giggle watching the boys, after a couple of hours grafting, necking Es and having it right off for the rest of the night.

Those fond memories and the images of Pete, Ray Bans on, jaw going off like a pussycat on space dust. Forget about having a convo with him when it's dark and the bins are on because he was on planet Neptune. The tunes are banging, it's lights out and head down, as he describes, "When it's time for lift off on a Love Dove... I'm gone."

He was often for hours on the same spot doing the Nifty shuffle (a dance style created by Nifty when he was on Es). I can even remember one incident when two fit as fuck blonde Pompey sorts, who were regulars down there in their tight all-in-one cat suits, eased up on him on the dance floor. While I am rocking the crowd I catch a quick joke with Colin Dale as we have been clocking them two sorts all night as they gyrate away all over the fella and Pete has not even noticed they are there. The disappointment on their faces was hilarious - it was such a funny thing to witness believe me. A lot of business connections were made in Sterns during this time and I would not have been surprised if every single pill swallowed in there would have directly or indirectly been provided by us. This makes me wonder a bit whether I was craving the limelight to be an MC just for the love of it, it could not have been for the money, that's for sure.

At our heights during this period in 1991, our appetite for partying would see us earlier that year, on the May bank holiday, hire motors and go into Brighton, smashing it on a Thursday. In Eastbourne we were smashing it on the Friday. The regular Saturday night was in Sterns, then a freshen up and a livener round George's and Helen's house, then up the M1 & M6 for the big Time and Underground do at the Rag Market in Birmingham on the Sunday afternoon.

Parking up near Birmingham New Street and walking to the venue, we would act out our favourite scene from the film *The Firm* and have locals looking on at us play fighting and trying to make out what the fuck we were doing. It was funny going up to the event 15 handed and having security deliver us the disappointing news that the rave was locked down as the place was rammo-jammo. Well fuck that, a bag of 20 Es saw them lighten up and in we went. More Es and some heavy one-foot skanking, as everyone is proper having it.

If you ask any one of us, any of the boys, no one would even remember the journey home as we all woke up as a pile of bodies round Reggie's house. Later on though, it was only the hardcore that were left still standing, which was now only Pete, Inch and me with Helen also coming along for the ride, then it's off to Central Park in Portsmouth. We lasted about an hour in there, which wasn't too bad by all accounts. I still managed to tie up a nice deal for a 5K parcel for the next day with a pal of mine who I had lost contact with. All in all that was a hardcore weekend that we have tried to emulate on many occasions since, but failed miserably. It was such a wrench on our bodies, causing havoc with some of our emotions on the come down from it, that the following weekend I think was the only period in about 5 years where I do not think there was a single complaint from any of our girlfriends as we all stayed in.

Another memorable weekend for us was in August that same year, starting off in Sterns. It was packed to the rafters with the two blacks and a bubble outfit, Top Buzz, headlining and smashing the place with Mad P ringing out...

Monte, Monte, Monte, Monte Christo
You don't know how the story goes
There were 2 blacks and a bubble
On the decks they were trouble
Jungle techno on the double
Know the score dig the scene

I was impressed with that and their little set, with him (Mad P) especially, he inspired me to say the least. By now we were regular with Colin Dale on the Road at most gigs as my legitimate bread and butter was now almost confirming us as a 2 man team on most events on the south coast. He wasn't scheduled at Sterns that night but we left around 1am to catch the ferry to the Isle of Wight for the Golden Hill Fort Treasure Island Party, where a few hours spent partying in there saw Pete, Inch and me again cocktailing narcotics and swishing champagne.

At one point we were spinning off our nuts in a private back room with a pal of ours called Helen from North London, who was giving us an unofficial but very impressive private dance show. She was a good crack who we'd got friendly with over the years as she was a regular in Sterns and Rage. She had the build and dance movements of a gymnast, with a peach of an arse that was always showing through the skin-tight outfits she always wore.

There were also rumours we overheard that Mensa had done an audacious flyer drop from a helicopter during the rave, but I think we missed that stunt. By late afternoon when we were finally leaving we were delayed with a few moments of banter with Grooverider, Fabio, Paul and Danny. All of us were teasing Pete about the 2 Pompey sorts that were also at the rave (looking good as usual I might add) that he'd blanked and had missed out on a possible gang bang while spinning off his nut a few weeks back.

Most places we went we would bump into Groove, Paul and Danny and it was always good bumping into that lot. They were really loud and just used to crack us up with some hilarious shit they used to tell us. I know me and Pete were often the target for some of their humour but they were good pals of ours and often took us back to the discos at the Norwood and Redhugh FC end of season parties where we was always entertained by them back in the early 80s.

Another thing that makes me chuckle as well about that Treasure Island party is MC Lucky. He was the MC that night, but we had no idea where he was doing it from as he was on walkabouts with a cordless microphone. Listening back on the tape the noises he makes on there always brings a smile to my face, "BRRRRRR HAA HAR HAAAR" he would shout out and for some reason it sounded really good.

While on the road with Colin Dale, we think back and remember that he was an OG, another legend we already were dancing off to during the rare groove–acid house crossover period and he was also one of our own as he was off the manor as well, a Croydon Boy. We'd hit clubs regularly from mid-91 from Brighton to Bournemouth and Southampton to Plymouth as we racked the miles up.

Colin Dale, Colin Dale, Colin Dale
putting your body right into a spell

was one of many lyrics I would drop announcing the bad boy on the decks and getting the crowd jumping. Someone at one of these events when me, Inch & Pete and Colin Dale strolled in, would say, "Yeah! Colin Dale and the Techno dreads." I started to use that on the sets and we would get the shout from Colin on Kiss FM on his weekly show. He dropped the bad ass Techno dread anthems Lenny D Ice's *We are I, E* & Cool hand flex's P*ump up the set with flavour* which had me Pete and Inch going nuts the previous weekend when he dropped it. *We R IE* was another of the definitive tunes at the time that we had first heard when Grooverider smashed it at an outdoor event in Northampton.

We were having it right off after me, Pete, Inch and Brighton George bumped into some of our old pals from the old Moped Crew from back in The Young Senator Days. Little T, Otis & Jason, who was with another face from the manor, Roger Deans. That was another wicked night although at the time we were mixing business with pleasure. Having sold out the 80 or so tabs George was holding, we necked a Dove each and was proper having it until well into the morning.

It was one of these nights on the road, must be 1992. We were at a rave in Hastings I was booked on, hosted by the world famous dance DJ John Digweed, called Storm & Unity on Hastings pier. This was one of the main events I was headlining that elevated my career back then, so big props John I haven't forgotten. Brighton George was with us again that night but was light on product as he had accidentally crushed a bag full of Es in the gear stick sleeve where he used to pug up in case of a tug from the gavvers.

In the rave he had the great idea of sprinkling some into a spliff which we all smoked. The end result was us spinning off our nuts so badly paramedics were almost called when Pete was sat for an hour rushing his tits off sitting on a pool table. No one could budge him. Colin and me, who had to perform that night, were absolutely struggling and on the tape of the event, you could hear the exact point where you knew he was struggling when he got his mix and levels all wrong. A funny night in the end but we never smoked an E Spliff in a hurry ever again. Brighton George, when we saw him last in 2009, still believes he had a conversation with Jimi Hendrix that night.

These were happy and exciting times for me and I was milking every minute of it, not even giving a second thought to the fact that I was probably taking liberties. Surely the DJs are the main focus? But I must be a star in my own right, that's the swagger instilled since my Young senator days as my popularity was getting broader the more exposure I got on the road. My agent Caroline was doing excellent work, she had me billing main events for Pure, Innersense at the Lazerdrome and Fantasia amongst others.

When the Hertfordshire based hardcore group 2 Bad Mice were let down moments before a PA at the Sanctuary Milton Keynes one night, I was called up as a last minute stand in, which culminated in me signing with the Moving Shadow organisation and touring with them. Looking back this was possibly the pinnacle for me at the time, because apart from being the most talented individuals I had met Simon, Sean and Rob were a fucking good crack as well, and I had many great nights on the road with them. The most memorable was the trip to LA, probably my first trip to the US of A at the time and the Moving Shadow lot were always nervous about my timekeeping. During our tour in Los Angeles, some random fella we met at one of the events had a team of lap dancers and brasses wrapped around him. I'm sure they were brasses because we recognised them from the strip gaff down a few blocks. He also had a big parcel of this yellow cocaine that culminated in me going missing for a day and a half and living the life of Snoop Doggy Dog. It was that kind of get-together, with all kinds of fanny with their tits out and excessively loud music.

After a frantic few hours of panic assuming I would not turn up for our performance, they were quietly impressed, especially Sean and Simon, who were shaking their heads in pure admiration when I rolled up to our next gig with minutes to spare in a convertible Mercedes driven by one of the fittest sluts I've ever laid my eyes on. It's true, there is no business like show business and I certainly enjoyed my stay with Hernandez or whatever the fuck his name was. All I know is, he was a blinding host and I don't know where he gets his shit from but it was some badass gear and I'm sure I was dribbling Jack Daniels all down my shirt because my boat was so numb. Fucked if I can remember what went on the past 24 hours. Rob Playford had a right old go at me about my professionalism, but he was high-fiving me at the quality of the sort.

CHAPTER 13

RAGE

As I said in the last chapter, on a Thursday night at Rage it was the who's who of the Rave Scene. We would often bump into Grooverider, who was at the top of his game now, and we would have a great evening laughing and joking about with Paul and Danny and enjoy lots of attention from star-struck rave scene girls. Pete always jokes of this period when you'd be in VIP and some of the sorts would always come up asking if he was a DJ, MC or Promoter. Pete would always answer, "I work as a telephone engineer at British Telecom but I could still plate your fanny and fuck you up the arse if you're up for it." Then he'd walk off in fits of laughter.

As time went on, it did become a bit jarring for him I think. It's bad enough people asking you for drugs all the time because of what you look like, now you've got these birds on the scene who seem to be always sniffing about for guest list and free champagne talking to you just to work their way up to an A lister. Funnily enough thinking back, we would discover that a few of these girls were all right once you got to know them properly.

Pete seemed to always have time for them and listen to them when they got lagging and started bitching on about how used and abused they'd been by one rave scene celebrity or another. I am not sure whether he was all that sympathetic but he would listen all the same and I think that's where he got the tag 'Pete Nice' because I remember Grooverider and Danny always asking why Pete was wasting his time listening to their bullshit. He'd reply that he heard some funny shit and in some cases it led to a bunk up on the odd occasion when he had a few Grant Mitchell from East Enders moments; the ones when you'd drop that line "You're too good for them babe," and you got that "ah you're such a nice bloke" response. That's when you were IN and before you know it, she's all over you and then you're together in the spoon position the following morning. Grooverider, Danny and, Paul would be in stitches at his long-winded game and would laugh at him and say, "You too nice. Just feel dem up and show dem your teeth, You don't have to converse with dem, you too nice to dem Pete Nice."

Over the years, we would discover that that lot had a name for almost everyone, so that's how he became Pete Nice and has been Pete Nice ever since.

With Rage came a few momentous occasions. The raving history books would show you that it was where Goldie first fell in love with Drum and Bass when he was the boyfriend of DJ Kemistry and she brought him down there for the first time. Many people would remember the star struck graffiti artist face pressed up against the cage watching Grooverider and Fabio hold mass with amazing sets. Some say these nights inspired him to write his *Terminator* track under the guise of the Ruffige, which had us all kicking some hard steps to this hi tech break-beat sound.

Many of these new tunes the boys were dropping, without a doubt, were ideal for the venue, and like most people I believe Groove and Fabio's careers took off into overdrive. Their influence and the type of beats they were playing swerved the whole dance scene into the jungle and drum and bass era, such was their pioneering power at that time. Me, Pete, Inch and many other people would find ourselves one-foot skanking on the dance floor as though we were re-living a Jah Shaka dance from the early 80s.

Rage was a place where I forged many friendships with faces on the scene like the famous Rapido crew, with Timmy Ram Jam, Les, Food Junkie and the Boys. Hardcore General and many of the prominent faces I met and got to know through Rage nights. It's also here where

I met my agent Caroline Kakoo of Unique Artist, who was only just finding her feet on the scene at the time but she would go on to manage Andy C, DJ Hype and Mampy Swift to name a few on her books. It was also where Inta-Natty was conceived, but I will divulge more on that a bit later.

I was half a celebrity by now so attending Rage was more business than pleasure. I was networking with the social leaders on the scene and having a smoke and a good laugh with People like Top Buzz, Mikey B, Mickey Finn, S Gachet, Ray Keith, Fabio, Jumping Jack Frost, the Ragga Twins, Randall and all the East London De-Underground crew. I was also socialising with people from the pharmaceutical business who like me were having a night off and sharing a few beers and lines of coke while discussing the plummeting prices of Es and the effect it was having on our economy.

One of these nights I was with Pete, Nifty, Brighton George, Blocker and Inch in there when someone said to me that they had heard that Grooverider had died. Rumours were of a car accident and also that he had been shot. After a few minutes of panic as I repeated what I had heard to Pete, in he walks with Paul and Danny. Meanwhile people who had also heard these rumours stopped and quizzed him as he made his way up to the cage where the decks were. After we sank a few beers Paul would eventually put an end to the mystery as he filled us in and sketched over the events.

The previous week in Rage there was an altercation between Grooverider and a member of this North London outfit. At the end of that night, tooled up, he confronted Groove, surrounding the DJ booth with some of his boys. A fracas ensued and Grooverider offered a sweet left hook, cracking the fella on the nose and spreading it across his face like a bit of Plasticine. The heavies on the doors were quick to intervene as threats and insults were directed towards Grooverider and Fabio, who had stood their ground during the attack. After hearing Paul explain the sequence of events and his concern about the firm involved, the rest of the night seemed a little tense to say the least, as I was expecting a bit more aggro from these gentlemen. The night passed without incident, but we later learned that the outlaw and his crew had had a hit squad out. They followed Grooverider, Danny and Paul through the cover of night from Rage, over the bridge and into South London and Grooverider watched his rear view mirror, at the time rebuffing the thoughts in his head that he was being tailed. As they approached a set of traffic lights at the Elephant and Castle, the trap was sprung, with three cars boxing them in. Occupants emerged from the cars all tooled up with chivs, machetes and baseball bats. Paul (as he explained later) had a rush of blood and leapt from the car to confront them, but soon retreated after Groove screamed at him to get back in, then floored his 325i BMW, mounting the pavement and escaping the imminent attack.

Now Groove is no slouch and can have it with the best of them, but he was lucky to have escaped as we began to learn more about that north side crew. They were not averse to a bit of killing and maiming. That incident signalled a declaration of war. Danny was now on the blower to Mitcham gypsy pals of his demanding firearms from them and was ready to go to war. Countdown to the next Rage attendance following the 2 consecutive acts of aggression and all kinds of messages were coming back to me during the week. "Soldier up... Firm up... Are you sure you and the boys will be there?" It became apparent that Grooverider was not going on the lam and would be playing his usual set and totally focused on slamming some killer vinyl.

Personally I was hoping the fella would have swerved the gaff, but maybe it was a case of 'the show must go on' or 'we don't bow down to terrorists'. Either way, I've now had to have the Family, the under 5s and a few other thugs that I could trust all ready. Given the situation and assessing the possible fallout, a few game cunts were probably no match for seasoned gangsters but it's the main reason why I love these boys, the call that there might be a spot of bother went up and my boys were willing to go in.

Now in hindsight it was none of our business, but he was our mate and that's what we do. Whether Groove was aware that there was a posse of us tooled up and expecting bother is unclear, as it turned out it wasn't him that even called it on, it was Danny and Paul, incensed by the lucky escape from the machete-wielding mob that summoned our little firm together. It makes sense now because when Grooverider entered Rage that night he seemed his usual bubbly self and did not look that concerned in the slightest, but in all honesty, I was touching cloth at the thought of going head on with this bunch. Even through our warring with mouthy rivals while serving up Brighton, it never ever called for a full-blown gun fight. It was never required, as our show of force and numbers was enough to rebuff any opposition, so this to us was a step up because we knew these bods were the real deal.

The impending night out at rage was going to be the first time we would be hitting that venue without the entertainment joys our usual visits had experienced. We were in there all moody faced, wondering whether this could be our last swan song in Heaven nightclub. Faces in the crowd that were unknown to us were a potential enemy as me, Face, Killa, Pete Nice, Juice, Nifty, Danny and everyone were on our guard thinking it was going to go at any moment. Even when the playlist from Groove and Fabio was stomping I was so on edge I could not even bust a hard step to the beats.

It's funny when you recall events like this, as I remember at the time rumours floating about over the few days that it was a North v South London thing. No matter how many times you try to underplay these things there are always the Chinese whispers that have these events spiral out of control. Now with football and the E trade in Brighton I was already constantly in a wartime state but this situation seemed to escalate very quickly from DEFCON 5 to DEFCON 1. Gladly it would take a United Nations intervention to end it, when Top Buzz front man Mad P's older brother intervened and war was averted and in hindsight the reason why our main man looked so relaxed that evening while the rest of us were developing ulcers, I guess the reality of it was, Grooverider probably had everything under control and was possibly more influential than what he made out.

We swerved Rage for a couple of weeks after that. Conveniently for me a booking at one of Slinger's promotions in Switzerland got me out the country for a few days so I had a breather from all the bollocks back home. However, running away never solves anything and I still had to come home to more shit. By the middle of 1992, after Pete, Nifty and me had sat down and worked out the amount of work we had gone through, it turned out at a guesstimate that we had amassed or rather lost an enterprise that had racked up possibly 6 figure earnings. I remember Pete being gobsmacked and yelling, "And what the fuck have youz lot got to show for it exactly? Absolutely fuck all!"

In hindsight and in an ideal world I could have done with Pete or someone like him being around from the start to handle the money side, because he was pragmatic and the most level-headed out of all of us. We were all 100 miles an hour, earning bundles, and with the mind-set that this would last forever. We had partied and gone through money as if we were rock stars with a platinum selling album that included a popular Easter, summer holiday and Xmas song included in the track list that would see royalty cheques land on the door mat until I was old and grey with wrinkly nuts. How we had gone through all that dough is unimaginable without a single property or a legal cash front to show for it. I should have at least have bought myself a Porsche or something, even without a driving licence, just to look at it. Reggie languishing in prison also didn't help as we began losing many parcels to unreliable workers. We were too busy partying to collect the debts and had got too careless in protecting our reputation.

A good scenario would have seen Pete monitoring and keeping an eye out for any discrepancies, then ordering and delegating us for any Tom, Dick or Harry to get fucked up because the count was short - after all we were always good at collecting when we knew when we had to. Instead we had anarchy and chaos, in addition to the business ideas and deals that all went to shit, like Nifty's E factory venture costing a massive 15 thousand pounds to design and develop a tablet-making machine to make our own Es and maximise profits. He grinned and came out with the Del boy catchphrase, "This time next year Rodnee, we'll be millionaires!"

Setting the wheels in motion, he received the required investment in an Adidas sports bag stuffed with notes and had the press made up by some moody engineering firm in Old Coulsdon, the ingredients imported courtesy of some mad Bulgarian he met in the Wilton that Terry Blocker had introduced him to. It only took the first 10 tabs to fall apart before we realised the shit was not going to hold. Just like Willie Wonka's chocolate bars there was a secret ingredient, and we had no Mr Slugworth to try and discover the secret recipe, it's funny because you can Google all that shit nowadays, so now guess what? We send boys out to chemists, Boots, Superdrug, off licences, petrol stations, with the simple instructions - go and buy Lemsip, Beechams, shit stoppers and any other pharmaceutical that is supplied in capsule form. We then spent a week and a half working flat out creating our very own Dennis the Menace, which looked more like rhubarb and custard tablets. End of the day, with snowballs, Mitsubishis and other variants on the market we could hardly give them away, compounded by the fact that with the mix of low grade MDMA & speed concoction in them we were basically fucked. Still, resilient as ever, the Under 5s used their initiative and went out and robbed some rival dealers to minimise our losses. Then this became a regular occurrence, but who gives a fuck, money is money isn't it?

Business was left to Brighton George and members of the Under 5s and while I jetted off to Ibiza and Switzerland with the Interdance organisation and up and down the UK shores with Moving Shadow having a major good time and partying like it was 1999, a chain of events kicked off which left our activities on the south coast well and truly over. Brighton George under our supervision was a superb earner and very skilful at spotting opportunities. When we all became enthralled in getting smashed off our faces and partying the whole weekend, George assured us he would take care of business and make sure money was still being earned. So he could be in pretty much any club or party we were at and work with no hassle or threat of robbery, because by now we had the whole place locked down and had pretty much smacked most of our rivals into shape.

Nevertheless, he was only responsible for his parcels and none of the other five parcels we ticked out to sneaky fuckers that ended up disappearing with the majority of the firm's work. I must have missed that call to inform me the weekend's payment was not collected. Where the fuck were all the 5s when I was missing with the cherry or partying for the whole weekend and spending the following week in bed trying to shake off fatigue? They were back in London of course; it was down to me and the Wades to collect the money. We used to hang people out of windows in the beginning to set an example, but we had not had to do that for months now as we all thought collections were made, everything sweet. In the end, we fucked up.

Eventually this left George as the only one with any real capital that could provide parcels at weekends which helped us breakeven and as I got busier being an entertainer, he became the main man. But he was also a greedy little shit and if he could sell you a parcel of wood resin or solidified dog shite as Lebanese black to earn an extra grand or 2 then that is what he would do.

Midweek he called Pete, who was up in Harrogate for work for a few days at the time. By now, he was living a relatively quiet life with Jayne. He had a little side venture with Portsmouth Bob and his Portsmouth outfit, not earning bundles but seeing him by. So he gets a call that day from George asking if Tony Roots could borrow his new BMW just to look the part on a little deal he had put together, assuring him it was kosher and he'd pay him a grand for his troubles.

Now I had to think back to a conversation I had with George a couple of weekends ago in Sterns, when apparently he had been approached by one of Portsmouth Bob's boys, asking if he could provide them with 4 kilos of cannabis resin. I had known the previous week that Nifty had a load of hash that landed on him that turned out to be shit and unable to shift. George said perfect, that would do. but

Nifty had already binned it. This is when George implemented his plan to deliver Bob's crew with the kilos they wanted.

It was mid-afternoon on the Saturday when Inch rang me and said some deal had gone pear shaped and to meet him, George and the others down the Wilton. I then get a call from Pete, screwing. "What the fuck?" he shouted. He had received a call from Portsmouth Bob, who told him his boys were on the manor sorting some business out and apparently some geezer had just fucked off with 15 grand of their money. Pete now started to think after putting the events together that George was involved and they had used his car, which he was starting to get livid about. I told him to hold it down, jump in a cab to the Wilton and we'd sort something out.

Arriving at the Wilton I acknowledged Bob's number 2, who was a lad called Sean, there with George and Inch, and when Pete's turned up he's had to keep schtum as he now knows that if this situation isn't handled right there could be big trouble. A concerned Sean was happy to see Pete and hoped he could resolve this problem, get his money back and they would say thank you very much. While Pete was trying his best to pacify Sean, I was clued in on the truth and then told, convinced by George, that they don't need to pay the money back, instead, just drive them up to some black area and tell them the people they want are plotted there to go in and get it. If we gave it back they would know it was a skank. Foolishly I went along with it. At the end of the day, this was my firm and 15 grand is 15 grand. It would at worst help pull back some of the dough we had lost in the first place. So in the end I jumped in with Sean and one of his boys and told them to follow Inch as we took a moody drive to Railton Road in Brixton. Pete was fucked off back home, but not before he assured Sean that they would get their money back no problem. He was probably ready to smash George's face in for baiting him up like that, but more so for fucking with his little bit of income. He told me to get everyone back for a sit down later to talk about it.

Meanwhile Tony Roots and Dee were back at Inch's Flat counting out 15 large. Going through the motions, Inch returned out of some random building we pulled into, which I recognised as one of the locations to buy a nice piece of crack cocaine. "Them cunts are taking the piss," he said' "Let's just tool up and go through them. Come on."

Looking at Sean, he was now white with fear at the prospect of going to war with black crack dealers in the heart of Brixton and just wanted to get the fuck out of there. We told him we had to make an example of them for taking liberties, and Sean was then saying, "Look, this is a bit too heavy, let's just leave."

So that's what we did and as per the original plan for Brighton George's scam of the century successfully concluded with the notion that they had been ripped off by some moody Brixton spades and that was the end of it. Later that evening it was party time. George split £8,000 with the Under 5s and paid me £1,000 and gave £1,000 to Pete as promised for using his car, plus another monkey for compensation. Well that was that, but not before Pete made a beeline for George and left a few words ringing in his ear before leaving with a right hump.

The rest of us remained to hit the cherry and get out of it, while some of the boys got their cocks sucked by brasses as we drank champagne all night. However it was far from over, because George, as well as greedy, was a mouthy little shit as well. The next day Bob rang Pete and told him that basically, the Portsmouth boys had got wind of the fact that George had mouthed off to people that he was planning to do this to them.

I said to Pete "Fuck 'em, that's George's problem now." I told him not to worry, but as far as Pete was concerned, there goes his little weekly cash cow with Portsmouth. Two o'clock on the Monday morning I get a distressed voice on the phone like you would not believe. It was George, who had now been taken by Portsmouth boys. They snuck up on him outside his house, coshed him and bundled him into the back of a van, where they slapped him about from Brighton to Portsmouth

171

and after some hours of torture he was pleading with me to round up the money to get him out. What the fuck could I do, and why the fuck is he ringing me baiting me up now?

"This is your fucking problem, going about mouthing it off to all and sundry, what the fuck did you expect? and I'm telling you now, you better not have told them our addresses, you cunt."

Slamming down the phone I was in a panic, as there is no way this prick had not given us all up. I rang Pete on his mobile: "Pete, I think it's gonna come on top, they've taken George and I'd be surprised if he's hadn't bubbled us all up."

When I heard Pete being calm it relaxed me a little bit. I knew he was never deep in most of our illegal activities but he knew the score and said, "Why the fuck is he ringing us anyway? We haven't got their money, he has." This still resulted in spending the rest of the early hours with no sleep. Pete, when I spoke to him at lunchtime after having Bob on the blower, told him "Look mate, this deal is fuck all to do with me either but you better do yourselves a favour and sort it out."

So a tired Pete (and when he's tired he's a miserable cunt at the best of times) is proper narked now he's been threatened about something he had never done. This infuriated him no end and it takes a hell of a lot to get him going, because all the time he had known Bob, done business with Bob, drank and socialised with Bob. The prick was basically telling Pete Nice that he does not give a fuck if he had nothing to do with it; it is his firm so he will feel the backlash as a result.

"Mate, it's up to you, but if it was up to me, I'm saying lets go war with them, if that's what they want" was the suggestion I made. After a brief pause, he said, "Fuck it."

I made plans and called all the heads I could to meet at Inch's house at seven. With a full crew all tooled up and ready I made phone calls to George, who was now back in Brighton and now told in no uncertain terms, "Call them, tell them you have their dough and to meet you in Sterns car park."

Pete was surprised to hear his phone ring with some fella on the end making threats. He was screaming his response. "Don't worry, you'll get your fuckin' money. Meet us in Sterns car park at 9 o'clock yeah? but don't come on here making threats to me son 'cos we're ready if you want some."

Hearing this, I was furious and grabbed the phone off him before he could finish. "Listen here you cunt we ain't no mugs here, come and meet us and get your money we'll have George with us he'll pay ya but if you carry on and if you want to have it with us you are welcome."

I gave the phone back to Pete but the tempo has changed surprisingly as Pete is now being told, "No need for the heavy stuff mate, we're only a small little outfit blah, blah, blah, blah."

We still insisted on meeting, but it seems as though they were not too keen now. Still, we set the wheels in motion and made our way to Brighton to meet George, who was now with Reggie, who had recently been released after another stretch. A sorry-looking George was now battered and bruised and on the wrong side of the crew, because basically, with his own greed, he had abused the fact that he had Under 5s in his corner. He could no longer be trusted as I was 100% he had given up addresses. He was still none the wiser to the Portsmouth boys' retreat but I told him he best get them back their money, which he handed over. I used it to pay some of the heads I'd drafted in following the threats and told him that he was on his own from now on.

A few more weekends were spent on the south coast, although we were mainly partying. The E trade, with the millions upon millions of variations available, market saturation saw business totally eroded and our profit margin bottomed out. It was not the end of the world for me though, because MC Flux was blowing up and this saw me perform and work alongside some stellar names. I had to pinch myself at the time.

Although we were clubbers and had been raving for years and years now, it was nothing compared to being on the same platform with the likes of Carl Cox, Judge Jules and John Digweed and others I mentioned before. Even the likes of Grooverider, Fabio, Micky Finn were superstar household names, big hitters that I was working with both here and abroad. My passport was also in constant use, which would eventually see my bank account finally accruing a generous legit balance for the first time in years (tax-free wages back then as well).

When I was home, I made sure I had quality time with Helen, who was my main squeeze, my baby love. Because we all had mobile phones by now, everyone was in regular contact and I enjoyed meeting up with Pete and Jayne, going for drinks and meals and doing adult stuff. On one of these occasions I can remember Jayne being happy at the prospect that she was going away on a girls' holiday to Cyprus with her pals Angelique and Sharon. Helen and I were smooching away having missed each other so much, and Pete and Jayne spent a lovely evening smooching away saying how much they were going to miss each other, all very sweet and touching.

But then after the 2 weeks passed Jayne called him to say she was staying out there for the summer and that he should start to live with the prospect that she might not return at all. He was absolutely in pieces. Now I have known Pete for a very long time, he has a manner about him that is very passive and like I've said before, it takes one hell of a lot to get him to lose the plot, but I jumped on the first train from Brighton on hearing the news, to see him shaking with rage. If he had turned green I would not have been at all surprised, and as we headed into Croydon for a few beers, his anger turned to sorrow.

At the end of the day, I do not remember him being anything but a gentleman to her, but I would say that, he is my best pal. Sure they had their rows and game sorts in his face all wanting a piece of 'The Pete Nice' and this didn't help but as far as I knew, she was his one and only. I suppose maybe he neglected her a bit as with our thing of fucking off out every weekend having a party but mainly chasing paper. I also have to take some responsibility too, because I never drove and always had Pete to rely on if I needed a lift to anywhere to do deals or to MC. He was my roadie and I was truly grateful. It would be almost 6 months before she returned and I think Pete had entertained a couple of rave scene girls, but other than a girl called Melissa from the south coast, he might as well have been with blow up dolls such was their worth to him.

I think by the time she returned it seemed like he just wanted things to go back to normal or something, but he took her back. Helen was a diamond for him as well, she had tried to set him up on a few dates with mates of hers and really done her best to gee him up. When I asked him to look after her while I was away and make sure she was sweet for money or guest list for anywhere, he did it and they became good friends because of it. She was a good girl was Helen, a heart of gold and I was bang in love with her.

Anyway, in between all this soppy Mills and Boon stuff, during the Inter-dance tour of Ibiza, I met and became good friends with a promoter called Robin, who wanted to book me to headline his Mantra events at the Event in Brighton. We began travelling down to the seaside town again, en masse from the Wilton Arms, with the crew and all the girls. Face and Killa would be absolutely pissing themselves as we approached the door when ravers would rush 'MC Flux' as if I was Michael Jackson. They play on this and take the piss even more. pretending to be minders. They shove people out the way as I am herded into the building. "COMING THROUGH - OUT THE WAY - VIP" Face would shout, keeping a straight face and holding his ear like secret service ushering the president, really funny at the time but Helen didn't find it amusing having him barge her out the way with Pete in tears and taking the mickey out of her.

It was always a good crack at the Mantra dos where the attention from local girls was getting to fever pitch and would often see someone blatantly flirting with me even though Helen was by my side. On the Mic, it seemed the crowd were hanging off the lyrics as the DJ smashed all the dance floor favourites. We turned out a few good weekends at Mantra which became an event we always looked forward to. We forged more relationships, most of the boys helped themselves to a few of the local seaside sorts who were flittering about in VIP like kids in a candy shop, especially for Pete, who was now attracting a lot of sympathetic female attention after Jayne fucked off during the summer.

After a cat fight broke out one night between Lisa and Melissa, two of the local VIP crumpet floating about, if I remember right, it had centred around Brighton George, who was good at negotiating and pulling a bit of poke but shit at keeping his birds in check. Pete eventually broke it up after pulling Melissa away from throttling the other poor girl and popping an E in her mouth to calm her down. This led him to another Grant Mitchell turnout, after they hooked up a few days later, which he explained was another toe curler worthy of many a mid-week silent journey from Croydon to Eastbourne to visit her.

For a few of us, there were girls flying about all over the place and "I want to fuck you!" was their regular chat up line. I have to admit, I had to be Jedi on most occasions as often I would get propositioned for a taste of honey from many star-struck females unfortunately (wink, wink). There was one girl, named after a flower, who was just to fit to resist. This also now reminds me that along with the notoriety that had befallen us during the last few years, a funny little pattern of events came about.

Inch, or Inch High - The Dirty One Foot Skanker, to quote his full name - at the time, like the majority of us, was accustomed to getting off his face. I always had a good time watching him smashed on an E and 'having it' to the tunes and often he would introduce us to this girl and that girl that he had got friendly with when he had been spinning off his nut on the dance floor. On one occasion in Mantra, he introduced us to a cute and curvy young 17-year-old sort called Tina. She became his main squeeze and enjoyed getting to know us and partying with us. Even my Helen took a shine to her and always looked after her. She became, you could say, a part of our little clique and she would more often than not be out with us on the south coast and also in London as we attended more of the clubs in the smoke.

Tina's 18th birthday was approaching and she was making plans to celebrate with a party at her house or maybe in a pub or hall of some sort in Burgess Hill. Remember earlier in the book, how I wrote how a reputation can sometimes give people a distorted view? Here is my point.

Tina's mother was surprised one afternoon to get a visit from the local constabulary. They advised that under no circumstance would her daughter be able to hold any form of birthday celebrations on their patch, where her 'unsavoury friends from South London' would be attending and flooding the place with drugs and taxpayers' money wasted on our police force, which would be on standby, based on the risk of an outbreak of violence as a result of these London hooligans. Following up, he said, "continue, and we will take action and break it up and arrest everyone for drug possession and breach of the peace."

It wasn't surprising; exaggerated words in Burgess Hill had spread like wildfire. Inch said that on his few visits to the neighbourhood to see her, there were a few curtain twitches and rumours spreading around the town about Tina dating a London gangster. Inch, like the rest of us, was just a regular guy, not an angel may I add but definitely not the underboss to Carlo Gambino from the Gambino crime family, as some locals would have had you believe back then.

The truth of the matter was, between me, Reggie, Nifty, Dee, George and Blocker plus additional muscle from the Wades family we were the only ones really who were heavily involved with the real heavy stuff. The others occasionally dabbled when the opportunity to make a quick dollar was about, but when we were out with Pete Nice, Face, Killa and the full crew which was very often and all of us ready to stand up to any of the shit that would have come about whether affecting Reggie or me or anything to do with our trade, my boys were tight and everybody knew this. Who gives a fuck what conclusion they drew? You could fuck with us if you wanted but those that did got served up and our reputation went before us, culminating in Sussex police getting their G strings in a tangle.

But hey ho, we had great enjoyment pissing ourselves about it and Tina had her celebrations at the next Mantra do, but I would like to just take this opportunity to apologize to Tina's family if we caused any embarrassment back then and to let them know that we all thought the world of their daughter and always looked after her, so they needn't have worried.

1992 drew to a close, apart from the Mantra parties. We had pretty much avoided the south coast for a little while as the London scene was where it was at, at that particular moment in time. Many Saturdays were spent on the road or at Lazerdrome in Peckham or AWOL at The Paradise club. We bumped into Portsmouth Bob in Rage one Thursday night and Pete spent a good few minutes assuring him that he had nothing to do with the scam, after all, why would he? he was doing good enough business with them in the first place.

I guess he was acrimonious in the end but it was not the same around them any more. Which was a shame, because they were good people and good company. I even had a good chat with his Mrs as well and she explained that they were devastated by the fact that we had been involved with it, but even with our reassurance that Pete and me had not set up the scam, I suppose guilty by association didn't make things any better.

It was no surprise then, when we were at another Mantra do in the Event in Brighton a few weeks later, that there were some Portsmouth lads we knew inside the place and one of the Under 5s had warned me about one of them making the 'cut throat gesture' towards Pete when he walked past them. I said not to worry about it, the matter was dead now. One of the fellas there was a face on the scene called Slinger. He had done some promotions in conjunction with Mensa of Inter-dance, I had worked for him at his event in Switzerland and I had done business with him on a couple of occasions too, but their business was separate, or so we thought, from Pete's main Portsmouth lot's business so I was not sure what his problem was.

We were all standing about as the party was coming to an end. Slinger seemed as though he had had a few cocktails too many and was being a pest around the DJ set that was headlining Grooverider and Fabio there that night. Pete with Jayne again was backstage and

178

everyone was there, all the boys, the Family, the Under 5s, the Girls, Promoters, DJs, Paul and Danny, when all of a sudden he's made a sly comment to me which I can't recall, but it was enough as the red mist descended.

"Who's this cunt talking to?" I thought trying to hold it down. I'm half frothing, half trying to realise that this is Robin's event and I don't want to give him any agg for doing this cunt on the stage, but now Slinger has just launched himself at Pete and they are now rolling about wrestling on the floor and the whole backstage just goes up.

I see the lad Sean (acting a little bit braver since the visit to Brixton with us, where he nearly shat himself) flexed as if he wanted some, so I quickly turned a can of gas onto his boat and put one on his nut as everyone now is worried about this cunt rolling on the floor with Pete. Groove and Fabio are also getting stuck in. In the melee some innocents are mistaken for enemies and now it seemingly appears as if Pete is getting his head kicked in as everyone starts wading in.

Even Robin the promoter is wading in. I've then got this sensation that I've tooted a big line of larger - my nose feels all bubbly and my eyes are beginning to sting. Face and Killa get Pete up off the floor and Slinger is left sparked out on the deck as he shoes him in the boat and the rest of his crew are toeing it out the front door.

"CS! CS!" people are shouting and I've realised I've fucked up with the gas again because even though I done the cunt and he's out the game, Mr Gas Happy has struck again and I've fucked everyone up with friendly fire - again.

As everyone bundles into the toilets, we are frantically rubbing our eyes with cold water to soothe the effects of the gas. Reappearing out the bogs we can see the cut throat gesturing boy struggling to get out of the building when wham, he receives an uppercut and is sprawled out on the deck and security shaking their heads in disapproval. It's still kicking off by the looks of it, but it turns out it was Groove and everyone else having a laugh and a joke about the incident as the effects of the gas die down, but not knowing what had happened and were curious to know what had kicked it all off. "Long story" I explained, but the consensus in the end was that it was all my fault, that I had started it and have now cleared the building with CS Gas.

Listening to everyone's account on the way home most of the boys had panicked because they thought Pete Nice had been chivved and were wading into the fella trying to get him off when instead they were both getting a kicking when he was on the floor rolling about with Slinger. We look back now and absolutely piss ourselves about it, but it definitely signalled the end of our empire down there for good, an eventful 3 years to say the least which looking back seemed like an eternity.

In fairness to Brighton George, after his kidnapping by the Pompey lads he never gave in and would go on to make himself a fortune in different lines of businesses, although some would argue that he fucked a few more people over by grassing. These could have been rumours started by haters of course, but let's just say he's not short of a few bob and making a very tidy living in the diamond trade.

The following week in Rage, after the boot off with Slinger and his Portsmouth boys, Brian came over to us when he saw us enter the VIP area and told me and Pete that we had to leave because we were barred due to the trouble at Mantra. Bemused and thinking he was joking we continued to the bar, but as we necked a couple of beers we realised he was being serious and things became very heated as we try and make him see sense, as well as trying to understand what the fuck it had to do with him anyway.

Grooverider eventually got wind of this after Danny was over pointing out the fact that we were with them. Grooverider was enraged because he was trying to get his mates to accept a one-week ban. In no uncertain terms, he informed Brian, that if we get barred this would mean he (Grooverider) is barred too and the whole dance will get locked off.

Therefore, with the prospect of losing his headline DJ and the fact that Groove would have taken Fabio with him, Brian backed down and apologised by buying us a beer each. Danny, as Danny was back then, was being loud and obnoxious in Brian's face following this, cracking up laughing and started shouting out, "Stand Firm, Natty Stand Firm, INTA NATTY FIRM!"

The reference to 'Natty' was because me, Pete, Paul and Danny all had dreadlocks and the 'Inta' was an abbreviated hooligan reference to the Inter City Firm. So from that night on and a few weekends later we are invited to follow Grooverider on the road and while he's dropping the beats, Pete Nice, Danny, Paul and me were often on the dance floor shouting INTA-INTA and INC and also other football-inspired chants to go along with our Yobbish behaviour. And that was the birth of the INTA NATTY CREW.

CHAPTER 14

IBIZA

1993 was banging because now we were having it again, Thursday until Sunday as I partied and worked the main dos all over the country. It was constant in a pleasant way because for the first time in a while I was not looking over my shoulder or having to teach people a violent lesson. Legitimate work rocking the raves was my only graft. My diary was fully booked as promoters sought after my services.

On weekends that I was not working, we were on the road with Grooverider. On some weekends if he was booked to work the far reaches of the north or the deep south of England, after an early start to begin the long trek on the motorways it would sometimes lead to a marathon session. We would often get to Paradise Club for AWOL as the sun came up, then moving onto the garage and house do at the Elephant and Castle before we finally made it home at some point in the late afternoon, making it on most occasions a 24-hour stint.

As well as all this, I dipped my toes for the first time into club promotion, first with a night I hosted in the downstairs pool room of the Wilton Arms, which I named the Tomb. This is where I had TJB on the decks spinning house and garage, although by now he was not about with us as much after he shacked up with some bird in Kentish Town. He also went from being a non-smoker and relatively teetotal and apparently began to smoke weed and drink vodka. This would later lead to him having a breakdown as something in his head snapped when he split up from the bird.

The Tomb was also where, after hearing a demo tape he had sent me, a fresh-faced DJ Bailey was released onto the scene, performing excellent sets for me on most nights along with Garfield, aka DJ Love Buzz. I also got my hands on another club, which was attached to the Norbury pub, where I promoted a Friday night session called Club Extreme. I was lucky enough to know a fella called MG who had a piece of the gaff and was also top boy of a little Chelsea firm off that manor that included some pals I went to school with.

This night became very successful for me. I had the young rising star DJ Bailey headlining it and had most of the main DJs like Kemistry & Storm, Kenny Ken, Randall, Grooverider and Fabio played. We had many good nights in there and I was enjoying this period of relative legitimacy, but I still had Reggie in my ear, always having to play catch up following consecutive prison terms and always getting me at it to shift a kilo of puff here or a parcel of Es there. It wasn't a surprise that that side of me started to reappear again as I put work out on the streets, but I still ended up getting fucked by unreliable people.

Pete was by my side even more now as he and Inch shared the driving whenever I was booked to entertain the dos, and during this period I was called upon again to gee him up after Jayne fucked off once again and left him for the sun and sands of Cyprus. This time it turned out it was for good, leaving Pete absolutely devastated. It turned him, as far as women were concerned, into an out-and-out stone cold bastard.

From what I can recall, we had had a few conversations over the last few weeks and Pete seemed intent on slowing down and putting his full attention into his relationship with Jayne. Having taken her back after the last time she went out there the previous summer they were back together and happy, it seemed. It took a lot of bollocks for him to do this, after Groove, Danny and everyone was in his ear about it. I knew he felt she had taken a liberty and mugged him off in my eyes, but I was behind him 100% in the end, even though I was surprised that he took her back, knowing of the many sorts on his case at the time. In all fairness, it was nice because everyone then was in settled

183

relationships. Weekends we were all out together with the girls partying and having a laugh and a good time. All the girls were nice and friendly and all getting along with each other and during the Club Extreme nights and the after parties at either mine, Charlotte's or Nifty's, we were like one big happy family.

The alarm bells were ringing when Pete told me about discussions they had, saying that Jayne was going back to Cyprus to work for 2 months, kind of like a last blowout before settling down with him and getting married with kids and a dog and a life in the country. He even bought a ring, from what I recall. It was a conversation she even repeated to my Helen. Fuck knows what was in this girl's head. She had sold the idea to Pete at a time when in his head, he didn't want to hold her back, then resenting him for it. She made a promise, but I guess she had her own good reasons for staying out there. I don't believe she had that malice in her to purposely fuck him over. However it was hearing that her two pals had returned in mid-August and then Angelique calling him to deliver the bad news that was the cherry on the icing on the cupcake. Nice one darling, a fucking telegram would have been better.

Anyway fuck that shit, September came and couldn't have come soon enough. A couple of the others had become dejected with relationship issues, so me, Pete and the boys decided we too needed some sun and sand and packed our bags for Ibiza. Having been there the previous year with Inter-dance, which was more of an all-expenses paid busman's holiday, I was invited out by Mensa. I was more looking at it as an opportunity for making contacts than getting paid.

I met some important people during that time, people that helped my MC career take off, but it was not without incident either, including a few alcohol-fuelled orgies and raids on bars and nightclubs by the police after Nifty, Tony and Sasha flooded the island with moody currency. The Old Bill wasn't happy and it got to a point where they just felt the need to slap any English they could come across, so it was an eventful holiday to say the least.

The trip with the Family - Pete Nice, Face & Killa and all the Under 5s Nifty, Dee, Inch High, Mendez and Tony Roots - was a different trip altogether that always triggers fond memories. It was such a blast as we partied for 10 days as part of a Kiss 100 holiday and party package where we met loads of people, girls especially, having started the party going by getting on it since Gatwick. Many first time fliers like Pete, Tony Roots and Mendez sank brandies to get the old Dutch courage going. With the flight itself and the many lagging passengers, you would have thought there were many on their maiden voyage.

The first few nights, as with most lads' holidays, was chaos as we binged on San Miguel lager and class A and held court in the apartment during our recovery during the day. 'Holding Court' is when we pull up members of the firm on any recent wrongdoings or anything we were suspicious of in the past that we all had to account for, which includes any discrepancies or scandalous actions. It was hilarious some of the confessions that we, especially Killa, forced out of the Under 5s like Tony Roots, Inch and Mendez. We were absolutely crying with laughter.

Each of us had to quiz one another about something they had any inkling about and would have to present the evidence and cross-examine to force anyone that was not forth coming with the required info. In the end we were all sworn to secrecy that nothing that was revealed would ever leave the room, ever, you know the one: "what happens in Ibiza, stays in Ibiza."

It sounds pathetic now but it was hilarious at the time as a truce was born under oath of the newly formed Suck Pussy Massive. This was a name of the splinter group Pete and Dee (who were struggling with breakups) conjured up. After a few days 'holding court', if you gave allegiance to it, whenever shenanigans went on, there would be this hand gesture declaring you were flying the flag for The SPM. It's a little funny thinking about it now, for example being at the bar and cracking on to a good sort or leaving a club with a Doris the SPM member would signal to his mate from the other side of the club that he was on it with two thumps to the chest with the left hand, then a Nazi-type salute.

This would result in queries by many curious people throughout the holiday wherever we went, asking what the fuck the gesture meant as more and more of us joined the elitist group.

It was also a holiday where I witnessed Pete turn into a monster. We used to enjoy our time during the rare groove and early acid house days as we combined with one another to pick up birds but having been deep into my relationship with Helen I now kind of restrained my sharkish instinct. It was weird as it was no longer the fun of the chase any more. It wasn't uncommon for girls to be throwing themselves at MC Flux, but I'm not saying I was an angel either. You know how it is, as hard as you try to be Jedi there will always be one or two moments of weakness that forced me into the dark side to suffer a few lapses.

Pete on the other hand turned brutal when it came to prey, because instead of drowning his sorrows with booze and drugs like most people do, Pete with his heart full of resentment, was drowning his sorrow with pussy - and drugs, oh and booze as well, and rebounding as he drank with, chatted up and snogged birds in the night clubs. On a couple of occasions, he left me locked out of the room I was supposed to have been sharing with him. "NO ROOM AT THE INN!" he would shout from behind the locked door after hearing me knocking and rattling the door handle.

At the time he was like Jekyll and Hyde. I console him over Jayne by day, then he was hunting like a wolf at night, which had me worried that he might go and do something silly. Me, Face and Killa had to keep a very close eye on him, although Face was confident that he wasn't that weak and told me to just let him blow his steam off. "Fuck me" I thought, "he must have enough steam for the Orient express the way he's going."

Confident as Face and Killa were about his state of mind, I on the other hand was more tuned to how he really was feeling because of that close connection we had - with everyone else he would put on a front. I even remember one conversation with him during the holiday when he was pondering the idea of staying out there because the girl he truly wanted back home was out of his reach. That was a statement I really quizzed him on that made me realise his behaviour wasn't purely about Jayne. It had me turning the table on him a bit because after all our time together, it was usually me with an over-reaction of emotion and the fucked up thinking of doing things like that, not Pete, he was a creature of comfort. Maybe he was thinking if Jayne could do that shit so could he. Who the fuck knows what was going through his head? His reasoning for an extended escape on foreign shores just wasn't like him at all, but as I expected, him pulling some large-breasted sort from Essex later that evening seemed to put pay to that idea after I was locked out of our room again, but it was cool, he seemed a little bit more at peace after that night, which was a huge fucking relief I can tell you.

All in all it was one of the funniest holidays I've had in my life. The joking and the piss taking was having me in tears, you just had to have been there. The very first night as we got into our apartments Killa made his way to the balcony in a hurry but never realised the door was shut. He ran and smacked his face into the glass, leaving a heavy print of his massive lips tattooed onto the glass and Killa on the floor in pain. Like I said you had to have been there. It still has me in tears just thinking about it.

The antics were stepped up even more when midway through the holiday Grooverider and Paul decided to fly over and party with us. This ended up with the crew having fanny all over us for the remainder of the holiday. Inch and the Young 'uns were themselves causing a bit of havoc as they terrorised the streets on mopeds while they were off their heads on Es, Ya-Yo and beer, narcotics brought from home and smuggled in tubs of talcum powder or cocoa butter.

One night in Club Esparadise we got chatting to a group of girls from Manchester. There were a few of them if I remember rightly and they seemed to be star struck that we were connected with Grooverider. Pete of course was in fanny magnet autopilot and straight into one of the girls, while most of us tried a little bit of decorum. Pete in the mood he was in was probably just asking outright if she was up for a bunk up or not. If that's what he was actually saying I couldn't really tell but he'd have his tongue down her throat without even buying her so much as a drink.

We later on left San Antonio and jumped into motors, cabs and onto scooters and headed to Ibiza town, to a little club over there that Groove mentioned about some fella he knew would be there. It was one of these plush clubs which looked to be full of millionaires, which made us look well out of place because a few of us were lagging drunk. Groove's mate must have been a heavy hitter to have us all bowl in there unchallenged. Most of us being flush at the time, we were acting like Balearic playboys and sneakily give it large to bar staff that the main man said we was sweet and blag a few bottles of champers, but rowdy as the Under 5s were and not afraid to front anyone, the snatch in there were icier than Norway in winter.

Don't get me wrong, I am not saying that we can't show a bit of etiquette now and then, but this was a lads' holiday and rather than have Grooverider suffer any embarrassment from our loutish behaviour we decided to fuck off back to San Antonio strip. A good thing in the end, because I'm sure Dee either used some inappropriate words to a couple of ladies in there or their fellas just didn't like the look of him. These two Adonis-looking dudes that looked like they come straight off a Chippendales calendar were hollering at him in Spanish. It's funny because in any language that tipping point for when it's about to kick off seems to be universal. Nifty, in his deepest (South London) Spanish accent and his Tony Montana 'Fuck Casper Gomez' facial expression, defused the situation by saying he would smash an empty champagne bottle into one of their faces, which definitely put paid to any more trips to that nice part of town.

The 10 days absolutely flew by. Everyone smashed the island to bits as we had it night and day boozing and partying and knee deep in debauchery, I remember everyone returning back to England and having to spend 3 or 4 days in bed recovering from all kinds of bugs and fatigue. Mendez especially fell short while out there having had seizures and all sorts of problems but thankfully recovered. We really pushed the boat out, and all in all a good time was had by all, but now for me it was back to business as all the bookings continued to fly in. My popularity rose and I became one of the main MCs on the circuit.

CHAPTER 15

INTA NATTY STYLE

Are you ready for this ?
Cos this one's cris'
You want it ?
Come, come, come get it
All move and groovers
All body movers
(MC Flux circa 1992)

Having people, or I suppose I should refer to them as fans really, in my ear repeating my lyrics back to me when I'm out, is a surreal experience. When people are giving me so much love as an entertainer it really makes you appreciate your worth. I had something I could control now, a job which should set me up good and proper, and I was touring all over the world as the time flew through 1994 and 1995 where I was headlining in Germany, Japan and the States. The only down side to this was that I was leaving Helen, left at home as I was away so often and also because infidelity started creeping into our relationship as I could no longer resist the power some females have when they bind their spell on me.

Moving Shadow have taken up residence at Equinox in Leicester Square with the Voodoo Magic night and more often than not we have a full crew out and I have nightmares sorting the guest list as the crew accompanied by the Boo Yah girls Tracey, Charlotte, Caroline, Maxine and Lisa, plus Helen & Tina, Nifty's girl Mandy, then there was my sister

Alison and her pals all wanting guest list and all accommodated as the Voodoo Magic nights were one of the best promotions at the time. Everyone who was anyone was there. It was great fun and I was getting paid too.

Most of the crew were settling down now with their girls. Some were rekindling old love conquests but mainly new girls were on the firm now, even Pete after his few months of madness had hooked up with a really nice girl called Nadine who he had met at one of my Club Extreme nights. She was a leggy blonde who had caught his eye when he was assigned to taking money and signing off the guest list at the club. We nicknamed her 'Red Boots' after the red boots she was wearing that night and I was relieved to see him calmed down, after he told me that he'd hooked up with Katrina again. I was fearing the worst, but he was over it all now as he explained that she was married with kids now. She had contacted him out of the blue and they spent a couple of nights rekindling the old flame again. He knew he'd always have a thing for her but he had closure with both her, Jayne and whoever else it was that his heart was pining for over the past months for that matter as the Inta Natty project was about to take his focus away from all that. He'd resigned from BT with a nice big lump of money as he began to vision that it was time to step up. When the time is right the time is right, that's what our mums have always told us anyway.

So as the year progressed people were learning of the Inta Natty Crew as I, as the ever more popular MC Flux on this ever-expanding rave scene and the rest of us made it known in every club we went that we were about. Grooverider encouraged this as well and brought out a dub plate one weekend "INTA WARRIORS". He was totally bought into it as his Inta Warriors bussed a skank on stage. We were out with him most weekends and travelled the whole country on the road, which was a real eye opener for me and Pete at the scale of his fame as he was worshipped by promoters and ravers alike. On the scene at that time Grooverider was king. The scene determined what was 'in' according to the standards set by him as we witnessed the respect, sold-out event after sold-out event where he was headlining. When we attended a rave in Newcastle, even some teenage girls and grown women seemed to be swooning as if he was out of the Back Street Boys or Take That. Together, we as his 'entourage' enjoyed all the perks that came with travelling with a superstar DJ and surprisingly the most we ever saw him demand was orange juice and Rizla, but we were always generously accommodated. Paul and Danny did well too as they stalked the clubs in predatory fashion and would often disappear to get "shine" or a bunk up behind speakers or wherever the fuck.

Those days we attended many legendary club nights like the Quest nights in Wolverhampton, Shelly's in Stoke, The Eclipse in Coventry. The hospitality at all these clubs were impeccable, we necked Es and washed them down with bottles of champagne. I would often use these opportunities to enhance my own career and make sure people got to know me, but it wasn't all business, they were good people as well. We were meeting the Coventry lads, Mickey Lynas, Bam-Bam and Neville, who were really good company. They were the promoters for one of the biggest and most enjoyable raves in 1992, the Amnesia House book of love.

I always enjoyed going to Coventry, having spent many weekends in the Midlands, like Birmingham, where I met people like Zulu top boy Walton and the Starlight lads, also Lenny, Bassman and Luton Terry. We smoked a spliff or two with them and a few Zulu lads. I was a bit wary of them at first but Danny knew the main lad, Big Ginger, who was a top geezer by all accounts.

We had regular attendance as well at the main promotions on the London scene along with AWOL and my weekly residency at Lazerdrome in Peckham. The music was again now getting us all interested as Helicopter and DJ SS's lighter tune were the classic anthems and Inta Natty were running wild. The Sunday Roast was run by Everton and Kingsley, 2 brothers from out of South London but fronted by a Tooting Lad called Paul, and Jungle Fever events had us observing the scene heading into a new direction. The hybrid beats played in Rage had led to a more bass lead genre. Tunes like Studio 2 *Who Jah Bless* typified the type of bass lines and into the Jungle we went.

Jungle music sort of brought us back to our sound system days. Classic reggae lead riffs ripped the speakers with bass lines that tore off your chest. One Roast event had us thinking we were at a blues party in Thornton Heath back in 1985. MC after MC grabbed the mic and toasted over the tunes and rewound for the next MC to step up. It was funny to witness, but MC Moose had to bring it back into perspective as he announced that this scene was about the tunes and had the Microphone switched off and let the DJ spin the tracks out.

It was roughly around this time as our reputation and recognition grew, culminating in us behaving like a UK version of the Wu Tang Clan. People knew us as the Inta Natty Crew and knew we were Grooverider's boys. We would have journeyed up and down the country with him to many clubs, meeting many, many people and having some right old shenanigans. There also seemed to be an air of mystery about us with many questions asked about what Inta meant. Danny had made up a connotation that it stood for I'm Not Telling Anyone and it was even rumoured that there was this dark secret bonding us together which had something to do with women. I'd like to set the record straight on that, in as far as there was no roasting going on.

We even had a bit of friendly rivalry with other crews on the scene, like DJ Randall and the De-underground lot, which would eventually lead to a showdown on football pitches in East and South London, a challenge that saw us defeated home and away but we still steward the 'ringer' goalkeeper they played in the first game who we believe was one of West Ham United's.

They were really fun times and me and the boys had a lot of laughs at the expense of a few unfortunate individuals. Especially with Groove about, people seemed a little bit intimidated if we were all out at an event anywhere. It wasn't uncommon for one of us, usually Paul, Danny or Groove, to crack a joke or make an observation about someone then

193

all of a sudden you would hear us in fits of laughter banging tables and basically just going nuts.

Pete now confesses that at times it would make him cringe a little, although trying to hold back laughter - all the furore and people looking round at us made him a little bit uncomfortable but then he also began to identify that it seemed he was getting approached by people enquiring what we were all in pieces over, which had me wondering how the dynamics of the group was viewed by our peers on the circuit back then.

Pete Nice. My best pal, cool temperament, as passive as they come, a little bit reserved, who would give anyone the time of day

Danny B. Loud and aggressive, a joker who to me at times seemed like he could intimidate a woman into the sack and have her act like a porn star.

Paul Juicey Johns. More laid back in fact so laid back you could probably use him as a table and eat your Sunday roast, but he was a smooth operator when it came to the women.

Flux. That's me, kind of in between Paul and Danny with a touch of arrogance thrown into the mix.

Then came the next level of Inta, where you have Face, Killa, Bailey & Inch High who were a mixed bag ranging from loud and also full of it to shy and reserved. It was also considered at the time that Jumping Jack Frost, Fabio, HiJak to name a few were also seen as Inta Natty members. Then there was **Grooverider,** the king of the dance music scene. It was amazing but not surprising how much respect everyone on the circuit showed for him, after all he was exceptionally good at what he did and an even bigger character with charisma to go with it, so when it came to women all of us, well Inta Natty Crew anyway, was aware of a state of mind that would befall some of the fairer sex on the scene at any given time, called 'Riderism'. Now just for a giggle I will explain, because we had many jokes back then about it. Whether Groove himself was aware of such a thing is unclear, but it did exist. I have been witness to it and Pete Nice has fallen victim to it on a couple of occasions, but in fairness Riderism is not an exclusive 'ism' because Pete also fell victim to GQ-ism, but that's another story. Riderism - you won't find this in a dictionary and it doesn't reflect on all women around at the time, but it would always sneak up and feel like one of them 'you've been tangoed' moments.

So imagine you was working on a sort, a good sort, fuck it, let's just say that you had an interest and your objective was to have it off with her. She's fit as fuck or maybe just has a slutty look and you can't wait to get your leg over. So you put in all the ground work, maybe babes it out a little bit with a bit of wining and dining or you may have shared a glass of champers or two, or even just bought her a Ribena and a packet of fags. Remember not all sorts are the same and you can't just turn up expecting to get a bunk up on the first night, you will have to graft a little bit from time to time.

Now you have done all of that, then you show her a bit of VIP and everyone's about. The king of the dance music scene walks into the room after finishing his graft, sometimes he wouldn't pay them any mind or may occasionally, point out if she was fit, or point out any flaws in her shape or attire or whatever. Being who he is, there were plenty ladies about who were upfront when they wanted to jump the bones of a superstar, that was similar to Riderism but most will argue and have that down to being a dirty old shit bag and nothing more. Crucially, at the end of the day, what might be a good sort to you, maybe a pig to him, but even if it was a good sort or even on the odd occasion he fancied a bit of bacon for whatever reason, my point is this - if she is in his lug hole after you've introduced her, don't be surprised that without even so much as a "fuck you and have a nice day," to see her fuck you off for the bigger fish. Now this is no reflection on him, we were often in stitches joking about it. I'm just summing up the type of birds that were about at the time, that is what we at Inta called Riderism. But it's also fair to say that there is also rebound Riderism or any other ism, when after being shunned, you play the role, the shoulder to cry on, to a discarded ism victim and end up with a bonus bunk up as I explained a few chapters back with some of the girls at Rage nights, which as I explained is known as doing a Grant Mitchell.

Anyway enough of that as there was more serious stuff to delve into concerning Inta Natty. One morning in the middle of 1993 as we chilled out in the car whilst Grooverider was playing a monster set at a Roast do in Notting Hill, me, Pete Nice, Danny B and Paul Juice began to discuss the prospects of developing Inta Natty as a brand. Danny, having discussed merchandise with current merchandisers at that time, people like Murray of Dreamscape and Mickey Lynas of Amnesia house and Dance Trance, were already playing with the idea of designing a logo to represent Inta.

By the end of discussions that morning, we were excited by the prospect that we could rule the world, but after being persuaded by Paul and Danny we agreed to keep it quiet until we had a business plan in place to be able to sell the idea to Grooverider. The only thing was, me and Pete were on the assumption that we'd get the plans in place and would present it to Grooverider Dragons' Den style and get his full backing.

As the planning progressed it was becoming clearer to me from my perspective that for my part of the plan, promoting Inta Natty events and raves, it seemed as though I was being pushed out and that the plan was to produce merchandise first, as this was the more secure way of marketing the Inta Brand. I suggested surely the music side of it was more important and with Groove doing the music side with Inta Natty record label, raves would follow suit and the global brand would take off. It was an argument outvoted 3-1 that we go with the clothing.

I remember it to this day and I hold nothing against Paul and Danny. I knew it was a mistake then and so did Pete, but he went along with it anyway, when they said we should produce the merchandise first and leave Groove out of it so we would be independent and reduce the risk of him taking full control of the whole thing. After all it was ours to do what we wanted, which would be a decision Pete to this day kicks himself about. Their argument was put forward and they gave a very strong point to consider.

Hindsight is a wonderful thing and with all due respect on all sides, for me, an Inta Natty Brand with the scenes number 1 DJ behind it is a marketing man's dream and for them to continue to progress without him would bring dire consequences. Pete Nice was undecided but a vote of 2-1 decided the motion.

When I got the call that Thursday afternoon, this was early 1994, I will never forget the complete and utter rage and at times the sadness I heard in Grooverider's voice that day. Understandably it was a betrayal, but it took me a while to get my head around the reaction from him I was hearing. I knew there would be some kind of reaction but not one of biblical proportions. It must have really cut deep as he vented it all out during that phone conversation. I mean I don't remember word for word, but to say Grooverider was upset by it would be the understatement of all understatements.

He had been filled in by Mickey Lynas because he was "helping out the Inta boys" produce some sample garments for the merchandise venture after Danny had reached out to him. Mickey felt guilty knowing the secrecy they were holding from Groove, but understood that Inta wanted to branch out on their own. It still was a conflict of interest on Mickey's behalf. He held Grooverider in the highest esteem, he was his best man at his wedding witnessed by 16,000 people at the Amnesia House Book of Love rave, so Mickey felt it was only right to tell him after he had invested in the first batch and had also tried to talk them round that it would be better to go with Groove's blessing than not to and thought maybe if he forced the issue, everyone would come around and everything would be sweet.

Danny and Paul were always from the off adamant that we should crack on without him, but Mickey was not alone in his scepticism and I could not see any advantage in doing so. Pete at least considered that at worst, it would be a disadvantage to begin with, but thought with himself at the helm also putting up money there would at least be opportunity later on down the line to bring Grooverider in to develop the rest of the business after the initial start-up, and it wouldn't be such a big deal. However, we would get a rude awakening when a sit down was called, after I let Pete know and he let Danny know that it was going to kick off big time.

We sat down at Grooverider's house with Paul, Danny, Pete, myself, Sarah Sandy from Groove connection & Fabio, who I guess, were summoned to act as UN envoys. They done a very good job by all accounts because the conversation was getting very heated at one stage as me and Pete looked on in a daze and listened to all sides of the argument.

Personally I could see Groove's point - why would they feel he would try and take over? This was never really explained other than a couple of examples, which to me were all about trusting people with money. The fact of the matter was that it was only an assumption, because Groove is very cautious when it comes to business and is very headstrong in his opinions. Maybe that would have led to arguments and disagreements along the way, but life is about compromise, remember this is only assumed, what the fuck did we know? They knew him better than Pete and myself but I struggle to this day to understand why we just couldn't have taken the opportunity to use it as a clean sheet, put all differences aside and moved on for the sake of Inta Natty and world domination, everyone deserves a chance don't they?

Again, I mean no disrespect to anyone but I think by the end of the meeting it was clear to me that it was more to do with personal issues and personalities and nothing to do with business. That was the real reason why that call was made to leave Groove out of it but by then, everything was in motion. Pete had accepted voluntary redundancy from BT and funded the venture and would eventually plough in near on £20,000 on the project, so there was no turning back, but the damage was already done in my opinion, as for me, with no vision of any part to play or contribute to the Inta Natty world conquest, I was left with only a cheerleader role by representing on the mic.

Fair play to Grooverider, a lesser man could have (if he really wanted too) squashed them like a bug, but he did not maliciously set out to harm the Inta Natty project in anyway. However I noticed after a while that he wasn't wearing any piece of the attire like the rest of us was, instead he opted for Jarvis Sandy's Desert Storm if my memory serves me right and I really feel that when he released his record label Prototype, in a way it was as though it was an afterthought and he really wanted it to be INTA NATTY or INTA WARRIORS instead, but that's just my personal opinion.

It was also my opinion that the boys would now be up against it to create the global brand that the inclusion of Grooverider would have become and by the end of day, they were working extremely hard promoting it and getting it out to the masses, but Pete confesses, "We never really had it planned out properly from start to finish... you can have a good idea and a half inkling about business but to run a business, you need a strategy and I don't believe there was one."

It would take a marketing course he attended later on to realise that to create a global brand without even a SWOT (strengths, weaknesses, opportunities, threats) analysis was a big risk in itself and that their business plan was fundamentally flawed.

They cracked on regardless and done quite well getting a general buzz going, but competition started to spring up from all angles. Every rave organisation from here to Timbuktu was selling rave gear including the likes of NASA (Nice And Safe Attitude) run by Warren Knight's Melodic Distribution company, who Pete holds in high regards and gives props to, because even though they were competitors, Warren helped Pete out with advice, shop contacts and manufacturing resources.

So along with Jungle Fever, Roast, Desert Storm, Lucky Spin and AWOL, to name a few of the endless list selling rave gear to strengthen their brand, all Inta Natty had was a name, with nothing really solid behind it backing it up. Even Moving Shadow brought out a line of Shadow ladies' wear and the flyer/catalogue they distributed you could easily have mistaken for a Playboy mag when it was officially launched on a Voodoo Magic night. Grooverider saw this and was looking at it impressively, but then wasn't slow to point out to Pete, Paul and Danny that Rob Playford was looking to blow every man out the water with this, a statement which I thought was like when my mum would say to us as kids, "If you can't hear, then you must feel", a message meaning a lesson was learned after an error of judgement had been made. It had me a little concerned that they were going to have their work cut out to compete with this set up.

Driving home after Voodoo Magic with Pete, he was looking at the booklet for half hour with a blank look on his face just staring through the pages. Helen asked if he was worried about the Competition...

"Fuck the competition." he replied. "I'm checking out the fanny in here, they're gorgeous."

This would give you the impression that Pete could find positivity in the face of adversity in any situation, but I knew otherwise because if it wasn't clear before, it was definitely clear now. The competition out there was fierce and it would need more than reputation to keep on top. Despite all that, they grafted and lived and breathed it trying to make it a viable business. They were up and down the country with catalogues designed by the king of flyer designs Adrenaline Corporation, flying outside venues, stocking record shops, clothes shops and rave outlets and also making themselves visible at all the big dos sporting the Inta Natty silhouette on MA1 jackets or hoodies.

Murray of Dreamscape, god rest his soul, who also capitalised on the rave gear market, had sanctioned them a stall at one of his dos to help them out, a big gesture and proved what a top lad he was. They had all the right connections because Danny B, the self-appointed spokesperson and designer for the brand, talked his way into record shops and did interviews with magazines and a French TV channel and got advertising space with independents all over the country, including an interview special with Terry 'Turbo' Stone's Scene magazine. He was invited down to the old Wilton Arms to get the word on the infamous Inta Natty Crew. There was also an insightful interview with

Knowledge magazine and I remembered reading it thinking yeah, this is it, I can see them pushing on against all the odds.

The label was popping up everywhere on the backs of people who were into it and also certain deejays they had comp'd were out and about wearing the gear as well. They also had the logo unofficially endorsed by black showjumper Oliver Skeet and were kitting out Earl Brown from UB40 in the gear. So although they were creating the demand, a lot of the retail side is based on sale or return. For many of the rave promoters this fits in well for them as they tie it all in with tickets and mix tapes for their events, but for Inta Natty, this was like dead money as they needed to shell out to stock the shops. That would have been OK if the mail order side was able to supplement the cash flow, but instead they had to do a lot of juggling around to keep afloat and to keep up with the competition.

Looking back at it, people would have been under the impression that they were doing relatively well and for what they were up against they put up a mammoth fight, because at the time the word on the street and on dance floors was INTA with Grooverider, eventually even remixing his Inta Warriors anthem with yours truly on the vocals, which absolutely had Roast and a few other events he dropped it at going nuts.

I remember nudging Pete after seeing the response and without even a word he knew this thing of ours could have been and should have been huge. Over the years he would always stress the disappointment he was feeling being stuck with this clothing business losing money while at the same time watching 'Brand Grooverider' expanding globally. Funnily enough, at the time it didn't make much difference, but they did notice an unusual influx of orders that came in for the weeks preceding Grooverider dropping the anthem. Unfortunately it was the classic case of too little, too late.

A bold move to try and market the brand at a giant clothes fair, ironically called Interseason in Islington, proved a mountain too high as they also now incorporate a sister label they had started called "Ain't yer babe", an idea inspired by Danny's then girlfriend at the time,

Sarah, and her pals from Oxford, Nikki, Trisha, Jane, Sarah Jayne and the rest of them, who we aptly named the Oxford babes. This was for a good reason, as we were on a few occasions in the clubs with them, all firmed up in their little dresses and long boots wining their waist and having dudes (including us) drooling all over the lot of them.

I visited the boys at the show where they had a wicked stand with cool backdrops, hoping this was the opportunity that would launch it to the big time, but as with most ideas without a solid business plan and with the capital Pete had poured into the business now haemorrhaging, it left them in a precarious position. When the manufacturer they were using were not able to fulfil the commitments that the boys had made to the handful of buyers that were interested and cheques from Inta Natty accounts bouncing, their prospects of continuing as a going concern were seriously dented.

In May 1996, after long and painful considerations and no less than 24 months after being formed, the Cease of Partnership for the Inta Natty corporation was signed as Pete cut his losses and returned to telecoms in the employment of a local company in Croydon but I know for a fact that if he knew then what he knows now, we might have been on par with Metalheadz as an example brand and drum and bass institution. Pete in all fairness concludes this as a hard and expensive lesson learned but he has recovered from the financial and psychological strain of the whole episode.

The Inta Natty name has never really died as far as the drum and bass family were concerned, as DJ Bailey was heavily built up by myself and Danny during this time, which included introducing him and getting him on the books at Groove connection and also in with the Metalheadz family. Many positives resulted from the project as Bailey still represents with his Inta Beats. I'm really gutted that it's a far cry from the world domination conversations we had back then, but me and DJ Bailey continued to represent and we were still showing force in clubs along with Inch, Face and Killa.

Pete still occasionally came to events as the scene took another swerve deeper into drum and bass, but he was concentrating on the bars and drinking clubs in Croydon now and going on the lash with work colleagues. We still spoke but not on a regular basis like we used to because during that time, I was busy as my MC career became relentless and when he was busy fighting the tide with the Inta Natty business I felt a bit distanced by him. He confesses that the stress of the business and its pending failure at the time almost had him on the brink of depression.

What also didn't help Pete and the Inta Natty cause was the involvement of the comedy outfit British Transport Police. After a certain incident in September 1995 concerning a shit cunt useless waste of space of a certain wannabe drug dealer called Leon, the Inta Natty name was dragged through the mud because of this lying big lip cunt as everyone and his cat including me, Danny, Pete, Reggie and a few others got nicked over some bullshit. This prick owed a debt to me of over £4000. He had seen Pete and approached him in Voodoo Magic one night and had Pete a little confused, as he was selling him some sob story when Pete interrupted to explain to him, "I don't know what arrangements you've made with him but you know he's in prison yeah? Then that money his mrs is gonna need to pay the bills, you do understand that? So you shouldn't really be reeling this off to me because it's none of my business, just make sure you sort her out."

Leon then promised that he would drop the money to Helen that week and that he was back on top of things, then conveniently, he disappeared for a couple of weeks leaving me fuming. When he was spotted by a couple of my pals and politely asked for the money, the word now getting to him that me and Reggie were going to cave his fucking head in, he started a sequence of events by ringing his mum and saying that he had been snatched and holed up by some bad men until she paid a ransom or some bollocks. This triggered off an investigation by BTP after they collared him at East Croydon train station making more calls to his mother, who by this time had called the Old Bill, who by then had the usual processes in place to track the calls... (you could not make this up!)

To save his bacon he put some bollocks in their ears so they ended up accusing Inta Natty of being an international crime syndicate responsible for kidnapping, money laundering, drugs trafficking and, wait for it, here's the best part... links to Combat 18. Let me explain how retarded these so-called law enforcement officers are, because the links to the extreme right wing organisation Combat 18 was whispered to them by our even more retarded Football Intelligence Officer down at Crystal Palace, who just happened to see Reggie and me with a fella called Charlie (a main Combat 18 face) together in a pub, a Random meeting as far as I was concerned, one weekend in 1992 when I remember being introduced to him and being told later exactly who he was.

"He never called me a nigger so who gives a fuck?" was my response and as far as I remember he just looked like any other football lad and wasn't exactly sieg heiling off the place neither. Also, if I remember rightly, that meeting was about some business, and where money is involved the only colour that matters is green, so with this, plus Reggie having Combat 84 tattoo on his arm, a skinhead oi band from his Skinhead days when he was a spotty teenager in the early 80s, the leading officer, a DCI Spunkmouth, using an exceptional investigative knowhow that would put CSI to shame, put 2 and 2 together and came up with 23. So in he goes with search and arrest warrants firmed up and armed with a bulging erection.

The gavvers first go through the doors of some associates of mine, two lads Puggs and Jacko over in South Norwood, looking for Reggie. Again bear in mind Jacko was another black lad. They are still not letting up on the Combat 18 links, and I'm told it all got very heated when they were face down on the floor. Puggs offered to the officer in charge, "Cunt, how the fuck can this be anything to do with Combat 18 with black people on the firm? Who are you, fucking Sherlock?" This comment saw them hoisted off to Croydon nick because of the supply of personal class A on them, which did not help the cause I thought. Meanwhile, I was in the middle of a 12-month prison sentence on a moody drug possession with intent charge at the time when they came through my door at 6 am only to find my terrified Helen and two cats in the house as they showed her the arrest sheet and search warrant.

"Er, he's in Bedford nick!" She told them scornfully "since July! Don't you lot check your computers?"

It was laughable that this main investigating officer was some Welsh sheep-shagging prick whose real name I can't quite recall (although his teeth and breath were unforgettable) so I'm just referring to him for the sake of the book as Detective Chief Inspector Spunkmouth. It seemed at the time, he had an absolute rock solid hard on for us as he pursued this criminal investigation into an organisation that he believed was worse than La Cosa Nostra itself and probably believed that with the whole organisation locked up he would make superintendent and have his gold card approval to the masonic group of the Arse Ticklers and Ring Lickers Society. As far as this cunt was concerned we were all a bunch of gangsters doing a bunch of gangster shit. They must have thought they'd hit the jackpot when they nicked Danny after having him under surveillance coming back from a smoking weekend in Amsterdam with his girlfriend and were probably hoping for a suitcase filled with weed and cocaine when they pulled him up at Harwich, only to find dirty laundry.

There was one incident, a totally innocent encounter when Bailey, Inch and HiJak were in East Croydon for a bit of lunch and went into a bakery that Otis, a friend of theirs, was working in. Now here is the nonsense, apparently this big-lipped tosser Leon worked in the same bakery as Otis. Otis isn't even wise to any information regarding the case, but Leon pisses his pants thinking they were sent there to silence him, so now BTP take it upon themselves to add to the endless list of trumped-up charges one of intimidating the witness and conspiracy to pervert the course of justice on us.

I mean fuck me, they only went into the shop for a Cornish pasty and some apple turnovers, but because Bailey wore an Inta gilet and hat and Inch had on an Inta MA2 jacket, again, this totally 2 bob outfit that call themselves a police department took all kinds of measures to insure this grass cunt was in protective custody as if he was some kind of Black Henry Hill (Goodfellas) or something... more like fucking Benny Hill. Seriously, Keystone Cops ain't got shit on these wankers. I even knew someone, a mate of a mate, whose old man was a top copper up north and even he couldn't believe it and at the time he didn't even think BTP had the powers to conduct any 'Organised Crime' enquiry.

As time went on it began to dawn on me and Reggie that although this cunt should have been severely hurt for the dough he owed, the thought of the fallout of everyone else being dragged into it wasn't fair. The truth is, this prick just wanted to get out of paying up. At the end of the day a debt is a debt, it's all OK giving it the big one that you're some 'bad bwoy' hood rat and you want to serve up, fine, but come on, business is business and just because he was a useless cunt that allowed himself to get robbed by another crew of hood rats, Whose fucking problem is that? So instead, this prick just wanted to bring everyone and the world down and used the British Transport Police to help him do it. We even heard his mum hated this cunt, so what does that tell you?

This dragged on over the Xmas of 1995 and throughout 1996 as Pete, with the stress of an ailing business and a business partner now losing the plot because of these charges hanging over them to contend with, was forced into a dead end. Pete's mobile phone having been seized, business was even more affected and pretty much put paid to the whole Inta Natty Clothing operation because all his contacts had the number and for sales enquiries and information was that number as well, but these wankers refused to return it, saying it was evidence - evidence for what? It was an absolute joke. Our solicitors even demanded that all the evidence was presented at an old-style committal hearing so we could discredit the witness and stop wasting all this time. This was set for July 1996 at Croydon magistrates and all our legal reps were confident this would not go to trial as they each in turn ripped this poor excuse of a drug dealer to pieces.

Well it seems that as clueless as this prick was, Your Worship thought this was still an interesting enough case to go to Crown as he slammed down his hammer. Who the fuck was this cunting magistrate anyway? Oh yeah, he's another clueless cunt that wants to rid society of this terrible gang that have absolutely no interest in troubling little boys like he does. The only result that week was the acquittal of Jacko and one other lad who had all been embroiled in it just because they were seen talking to him on CCTV at East Croydon station as all our legal team looked on bewildered. Me and Reggie ended up having to have a real think about all this, how could we be just sitting back watching this go on.

I spoke to Pete on his birthday in September about the whole situation. At the time I was extremely busy on the circuit again after my release from prison following 3 months of incarceration, speaking of which according to DCI Spunkchops I'm supposed to be part of this 'dangerous mafia group' awaiting trial, yet I'm free to fly in and out of the country at will for most of that year, so work that one out. So having not really seen Pete that much, we shared a few beers for his birthday with the rest of the crew, but I was put on a proper downer when it seemed that my best mate was resigned to doing bird as a result of a miscarriage of justice.

Because of the way it was dragging out, the bad vibes had spooked his solicitor after the committal hearing, and he was now advising worst case scenario was 7 years' jail for the false imprisonment and a couple for the conspiracy. Pete even told his boss at work the whole story, and fair play to her she supported him and said she would stand as character witness if needed. So picture the scene as Reggie, a man of many connections always looking for an angle, called in a few favours because someone seriously needed to talk to this prick - who was the only one, for some bizarre reason, that the British judicial system seemed to be listening to, as luck would have it. it didn't take much, as I learned years later that two giant black lumps delivered a message to his nearest and dearest to lean on him to understand the implications if he couldn't come to his senses.

When the case finally collapsed 15 months from when the first doors went in, funnily enough by this time all the related charges had got whittled down to just 2 as it transpired, which were false imprisonment and demanding money with menaces. When the big lip grass cunt Leon, their star witness, suddenly realised he had a memory lapse and didn't want to go through with it any more it was a huge relief. We took great pleasure in blowing kisses to Old Spunky and his merry men as they looked on fuming when the judge said at Wallington crown court, "no case to answer, you are all free to go".

I remember going to the other DI in the case (some ginger cunt) and telling him when I saw him outside puffing aggressively on a Rothmans, "You should stick to checking train tickets, inspector."

Ironically it was funny to hear that a couple years after this, when Pete was working in the City and on his way home from work, he saw the prick at Thornton Heath train station doing exactly that, and Pete had great pleasure in dropping him a snide comment saying, "I see you've moved up in the world, onwards and upwards eh?"

Soon after the case, we decided to get our own back on the Chief Investigating Officer of British Transport Police's organised crime division by putting his life through a bit of misery after his bollocks with us. I mean granted, me and Reggie are no angels but them cunts were actually finding it amusing following us around and pestering everyone at every opportunity, even popping up in a supermarket whilst Pete was helping his mother with her shopping to harass him. So with Reggie's printing connection, we knocked up over 5000 business cards and went out flying until there wasn't a toilet, rest room, phone box or park bench in the whole of Hampstead Heath, Soho and Brighton's gay community that wasn't plastered with bum-boy calling cards with his home, work and mobile number on it.

So Cheers DCI Spunkmouth, we hope them sleepless nights with the crank calls you received didn't cause you too much aggravation, but knowing him I bet he was on blind dates every night because of them so no need to thank us either.

CHAPTER 16

IT'S COMPLICATED

In relation to the Inta Natty chapter I wanted to highlight a few more incidents in my life that were happening around this time. My popularity as an MC saw me working my bollocks off during 1994 and 1995, there was no rest for the wicked. I could hardly complain though, the bills were getting paid and my trusted business partner and brother in arms, Reggie Anderson, also had me running some big parcels of weed from some local gangsters for the extra pocket money.

OK, OK - because I'm a greedy prick and I love the wheeling and the dealing. All told, I'm near on back on par with Brighton days, almost true in the sense of the amount of parcels being moved, and in the sense of the complete retardedness of some of the people I'm laying it off on, summed up with the likes of the silly nig-nog, sambo cunt Leon, who I have just told you about. But unorganised as I am, I was doing really well with legit and illegit graft, I wasn't having to crack heads so much again or continually scream at people down the phone like before.

Since the autumn of 1993 until around mid-94, Bang Club was a night I was running in the old Ziggy's club in Streatham on a Thursday night. It was break even for the most part, but we had many great nights down there to start off the weekend. The line-up of DJs would see the usual main faces like Kenny Ken, Grooverider & Fabio plus Randall, Andy C, Frost, Bailey, Cool & Deadly and MC GQ headline some nights with me getting the small but intimate crowd jumping.

"HOW YA MEAAN … INTA… NATTY MC DAT AH ME, MY AIM IS TO MOVE YA BODY, SO RUN COME FALLAH ME, ROCKIN WID DA FLUX MC – INTA… NATTY MC" I am screaming out over the microphone getting the crowd all ready.

Although midweek, we would often have a full crew out, all the usual suspects Inta Natty/The Family, Under 5s, Boo Yahs all the wives, girlfriends and mistresses were out having it in this old school dungeon type venue. It's where Pete Nice (thinks he's nice) turns up one night with his blast from the past as he introduced me to his toe curler Katrina again, after so long.

"Here we go again" I remember thinking.

Having not so long ago seen his wayward and chaotic behaviour in Ibiza, it seemed as though he was putting himself in harm's way again. I joked with him, asking him if he was going to be dusting off his Luther Vandross collection anytime soon, a term Killa started using after our old pal TJB, when he was pining over a broken relationship, was adjudged to have been curled up indoors in his bedroom, crying and playing soppy Luther Vandross ballads.

Pete nods at me with a wink, but he's not in there for long and seeing her looking that good, after pushing out 2 dustbins and him looking like the cat who had just got the cream, I would have been out of there sharpish and all to be fair and it gave the desired effect I think he was looking for by bringing her there. All the other girls clock him leaving and are wondering who the new face was and I was repeatedly explaining that she was just someone on a break from a humdrum marriage and just wanted a bit of nookie with me best pal, nothing to worry about ladies, plenty to go around.

I also have my own issues as well, having started a parallel lifestyle to that with Helen when I started seeing a young American girl called Sherry. Even though life was getting more hectic and complicated I was still having fun and after Bang club on many occasions, for those who were not on a 9 to 5 or bunking the Friday off, like myself, Face, Paul Juice, Mendez, Nifty, Danny B, Tracy, Charlotte, Caroline and Lisa, we would all end up back at the Wilton, which was now called the Muddy Waters and under new management. This seemed a more lad friendly environment, with lock ins and lunchtime strippers. The landlord, Big Dave, was a degenerate cokehead like the rest of us, so we'd be in there sharing a few lines of Charlie and having a few after hours beverages until most normal folks were clocking in for work. It wasn't uncommon back then to have an action-packed weekend and it was non-stop, whether on the road with Grooverider, weekly indulgence in AWOL with the crew and with Big Dave along with some of the strippers in tow, or fulfilling work obligations at Lazerdrome.

The atmosphere in this place was always bang on when the Jungle scene in the UK becomes the genre rocking most clubs. It wasn't to everyone's taste mind you, people were complaining of it being too dark and representing the wrong type of clientele. In my opinion, yes, some clubs you could class as moody but the only shots being fired were people giving the imaginary gun salute and throwing up lighters, although thinking back, there was one particular really dark moment that I do recall, namely one event, one Saturday night in 1995.

It was at a Jungle-Splash, Clash of Roast Fever do, or whatever it was called, in Birmingham. I do remember that we had just left and were heading back down the M1 with Grooverider, Pete Nice, Paul and Inch to head back to Telepathy at the Wax Club, which was a shithole of a venue in East London but had a really vibey crowd, while in the dance, a couple hours later Mickey Finn turned up to do his set. It wasn't unusual to bump into different DJs as they zig-zag and criss-crossed the main events.

We had just seen him in the car park of the Aston Villa leisure centre before we left Birmingham and we were open mouthed at the news he had delivered to us. He said he was about to enter the building when… "This firm…" (we later learned it was Moss Side) "rushed the door." Apparently this masked and hooded up mob, armed with shooters, were there with the intention to do the place over. On stage the MC can only see what looks like fighting going on and with concerns about the fracas spoiling the night announces for the 'pussy holes' not to distress the vibe and to act like adults. Well you would. If you were paid as an MC/crowd controller you're there to make announcements, but it was unclear to them on stage the seriousness of it all. Staff were held up for the cloakroom money and people were taxed at gunpoint of jewellery and money as two balaclava'd Moss-siders headed for the main stage. Jumping up one of the men brandishes a weapon, takes aim and pulls the trigger...

Now me, I would have exited my arsehole but luckily, the Lord Jesus, Allah, Jah Rasta Fari, Jehovah and Harry Krishna were all with that lucky MC that night as the gun had jammed. The frustrated villains proceeded to pistol whip him and give him a right old shoeing, leaving him with severe injuries before they all as quick as they came in fucked off back up the M6 to Manchester. Lucky to still be alive, he fully recovered, but the ordeal would have had anyone fucked up for a while even as street tough as he was.

Thankfully he came back from that personal nightmare. He still represents the scene and is highly regarded as a pioneer and one of the original rave MCs. Now I'm not sure what was in the water with Manchester boys in the mid-90s, because I also remember them fucking up a Voodoo magic night the previous year with the same MO but without the artillery this time. They still spoilt everyone's Christmas when they robbed the cloakroom and unsuspecting E'd up punters and gave the security a pain in the anus all evening. I should have set my sister Sonia on them because she was pissed with the 'Lickle bomba clarts' that evening, describing them as a negro version of termites.

On a better note though, there were only a minority of occasions when any trouble of note was witnessed or heard about during the Jungle days as most of them passed without incident. Everyone was just out to bruck out and have a wicked time. At the time many of the tunes could have been straight from a reggae dancehall. Artists like Bujo Banton dropped his homophobe anthem *Boom Bye Bye*, Capeleton and Top cat amongst others also had their vocals sampled to the up-tempo jungle rhythms, but one reggae artist almost caused anarchy in the UK when he was quoted in Face magazine saying that he 'bigged up' and ran jungle.

I have to say, I was in hysterics listening to some of the Jungle MCs on stage at the Astoria during another Roast do hollering out General Levy to the junglist massive, saying that he was nothing more than a fake and bandwagon jumper. They even had a dig at the media and the press about all the negative views the scene was getting. To this day, there are people on both sides who debate whether what General Levy and M Beats did with 'Incredible' had any relation to any advance into the mainstream, because there were many artists and producers at the time who told the main labels of the likes of Sony and EMI to go fuck themselves, when they came looking and signed with independents anyway.

Shy FX comes to mind. He dropped the biggest anthem that year with his classic *Original Nuttah* with UK Apache. So as far as Levy is concerned, hate him or love him, *Incredible,* in my opinion, did well to represent the scene to the mainstream but as far as representing and expanding its popularity, as far as I'm concerned Shut Up and Dance, featuring Unity sounds Deamon and Flinty aka Ragga Twins (Deh bout) and The Rebel MC got there first back in 1992, especially with *Wickedest Sound* in most people's view, so misquoted or not, dance was nice whether he was 'deh pon de bill' or not.

Although he apologised for causing the controversy, it seemed to set a precedent. I heard there were a lot of deliberations and meetings by leaders of the dark and lighter side of the music regarding the scene and how many reggae artists were jumping on the jungle bandwagon. This somewhat unwelcome influx led to protests by one prominent DJ walking out of an event mid-set, where Saxon Sound's Tippa Irie was MC'ing. It was nothing personal, just people worked hard to develop the scene into a serious art and felt it was disrespecting the DNA of it all.

One evening the full Inta Natty Crew was crammed into the Kiss 100 FM studios for the Grooverider show and decided for a laugh to segment the scene by describing the genre Grooverider was playing that evening as not jungle but 'Hard Step'(yes that was ours) over the airwaves and were surprised how the scene cottoned on to it and then saw it morphed into different spectrums to get away from the Jungle tag that you even see today like dub-step for example. Again, I'm pointing out how Grooverider's influence was huge around that time and poor Pete Nice banging his head on the table, gutted at the lost opportunity with Inta Natty.

1995 was a really exceptionally busy period for me, not only working top UK promotions like Terry Turbo's One Nation, plus Slammin Vinyl, Moondance, AWOL and Innovation. I also travelled regularly to Germany, Russia, the USA, New Zealand and Japan. I was having a blinding time with the main players, including Grooverider, Fabio, Randall, GQ, Andy C and Jumping Jack Frost. I had many a good trip with that bad boy DJ as well. We had a very interesting trip to Northern Ireland, ending up deep in the heart of IRA territory with Danny B and a couple of local girls. It was funny hearing the cabbie on the way back advising us that we must have been absolutely crackers venturing into that neighbourhood, which I couldn't understand to be fair. I had been to Kilburn many a time without any grief so why the big deal? I did wonder why he was racing away at 100 miles an hour after we got into the taxi though. But hey, as Del Boy Trotter would say, "he who dares" and all that.

Anyway, on many of the trips we were experiencing the proper rock and roll lifestyle. We were VIP'd everywhere we went, lots of fanny about and plenty of drugs for those participating, until the fun was temporarily cut short when I landed myself in prison.

Like I said, it had been a couple of years since Brighton and the huge amount of narcotics being pushed around the south coast. It was literally put your feet up time as far as villainy was concerned, although you could consider a few parcels of weed here and there. It was still a far cry from the drug-fuelled anarchy of the previous years. My professional music career was into overdrive at this point, while Pete was busy with Inta Natty, and only occasionally he would be on the road with me, if my schedule fitted in with his.

More often than not, I had to rely on others. The bulk of the driving was left in the capable hands of Inch and Helen, who got me from Lazerdrome to Que Club in Birmingham for Micky Lynas's Dance trance, finishing off at Roller Express in Edmonton or Milton Keynes with Murrays Dreamscape.

It was here on New Year's Eve in 1994 when I was caught picking up a stray bag that I'd stumbled across on the dance floor. Holding it up, I was thinking "Touch!" as I inspected the packet and discovered the 4 wraps and a dozen tablets, but before I could even scratch my bollocks, one of the security team was on me and I was amazed at the strength of this chap as I tried my best to evade his grasp. It was too late, he had already radioed and 4 of the pricks were on me now and holding me by a corridor. From seeing this fella on previous occasions, I could tell that this particular security bloke never liked me by the way he used to screw me out.

I was quite gutted, because at the time (after getting these daggers from him) I was thinking that if I had nothing to do with the music scene, I should have waited for the cunt to leave work and have him served up. Anyhow, Murray tried to intervene after being notified of the incident. He explained that I was employed by him as one of the entertainers. Well, he was then told, in no uncertain terms, that if he had knowingly supported drug distribution in the establishment he might lose his licence.

"So I guess that's me fucked then?"

As I've tried to explain, the bag of goodies wasn't mine to begin with, but I was wasting my breath, because the police were on the scene now.

"At least let me have a sniff for me troubles" I asked, which fell on deaf ears. They led me out in handcuffs, in front of the whole world to see, and Helen and Inch rushed outside just as the door slammed shut on me. I could hear one of them replying to Helen as she queried "What the fuck?"

"Arrested for possession with intent to supply, madam" came the smug reply and now I was cursing out loud the half-breed cunt that caught me.

I was starting to think that maybe it was him that set this all up, but I don't think he was that clever in truth, just a lucky cunt that night. I also remembered the way he was looking on and telling the officers he could give a statement any time they need him to and sticking his tongue right up their jacksies. "MERRY FUCKING XMAS WANKER - FUCKING CUNT!"

I was released the following night. It was New Year's Day and I was greeted by one of Dreamscape's lighting people who Murray had sent down to deliver my wages. I have to hold 'nuff respect to Murray, it really saved my bacon. I spent the wages on cab fare back to the manor, thanks to gavvers confiscating my cash, which is now submitted as evidence unless I provided some paperwork.

Just to explain, so people don't think I'm being a bitch about all this, yes I did used to serve up and even on that night I did have a few bits of Percy in my possession, but I let my guard down to be honest, looking through the bag of goodies I had found in full view. I should have gone back stage or a little bit out of site. Fuck knows what I was thinking, so it was more down to complacency, or stupidity, after all, with my track record of course I should have been more aware.

Having been nicked that night Helen knew the drill and she raced home that morning with Inch to clean out my flat of any incriminating evidence ready for the impending raid that is standard police procedure, so the parcel of Es, the bagged-up grams of Charlie and the nine bar of puff sitting indoors was long gone when I was spun, but I still couldn't believe how I'd landed myself in this shit. The fact that I'd sold an untold amount worth of Es and shit over the years whilst we smashed it in Brighton may have some of you reading it and thinking, if you can't do the time, don't do the crime. Well bollocks to that, if Old Bill had turned me over back then, I could live with that, but I get nicked finding some clumsy cunt's work on a dance floor - that's just typical Flux luck that is, and it didn't end there.

The court case was set for mid-June 1995 at Luton Crown Court. True to his word the grass doorman gave his evidence. I was flabbergasted that with a straight face he told everyone that he saw me about to serve up a punter and that I was doing it all night. I swear this cunt just had it in for me because he couldn't have my Helen, who by now had told me that he had tried to chat her up on previous occasions, but I could hardly base my defence on that information could I? He was impressing the judge though, who by now, already had me in his bad books because I had arrived late. "Just apologise for being late, it was traffic, we left in good time" Pete told me, which was the truth, but me being me, I thought I would spin it a bit and tell them that we broke down and had to call the AA and ended up having to find another motor. Well you could tell straight away, the Right Honourable Justice Little-Boy Nonce Case had it in for me and instructed the clerk to check with the AA.

"Fucking marvellous" I sighed to myself.

I was remanded in custody for contempt and it's good night from me. I clocked Reggie and Pete mouthing "You dozy cunt" as I'm led away down the stairs.

The rest of the week didn't improve. The prosecution convinced the jury beyond reasonable doubt and on Friday, when the Judge asked the foreman of the jury, after deliberation, "How do you find the defendant?" the reply that came from my trainspotting, Antiques Roadshow watching peers was, "WE THE JURY, FIND THE DEFENDANT CARL RODNEY THOMAS... GUILTY."

Now don't get me wrong, I'm not saying all judges are nonce cases, but they all seem to have that nonce case look about them in my opinion, especially this one, and I'm sure this nonce of a judge loved every minute, looking down his nose at me as though disgusted at the sight of my face and probably thinking to himself, "I bet he fucks women, the disgusting animal."

He sentenced me to 12 months, which is not much in fairness. I think the cunt would have given me more if he had his own way, but I guess he gave me a squeeze because he was probably having young choirboys over his drum for tea that afternoon so he was in a good mood.

It was still an inconvenience because it would harm my ability to fulfil my event bookings, which were stacked to the rafters. I was fucking gutted. I made the first few calls to Helen, Sherry, Pete and my sister Alison as I came to terms with it all. There is always the fear and apprehension of dealing with factors out of your control and this was a cunt of a situation to deal with. All that I have done, the violence for the trade, the tear-ups at football, shifting parcels and escaping any serious nickings other than a few offensive weapon and violent disorder raps, and I get locked up for this. My main worry was, would I be able to pick it back up after a year and get the same level of bookings and wages I was commanding? I was at the peak of my career and was having it large, but now I was languishing at Her Majesty's Pleasure.

That was such a low point for me. It topped off the last couple of years when my life became so off key and complicated. Although I only did 3 months, it gave me too much time to reflect. The bird itself was quite a doddle in all fairness, but when the brain is going 100 miles an hour thinking about your career amongst other things, the last thing you need is being confined to a 6ft x 8ft cell, and it just about summed up my year.

I tell you how fucked up things were. On a personal level the work was pretty much carrying me through but on the rare occasion I wasn't working, as far as Helen was concerned, I was working, where, in reality, I would - with bags all packed - sneak round to my "second wife's" house over in East London. The old saying that a leopard never changes his spots may have you all thinking specifically applies to me. But it wasn't anything I planned when I met Sherry. Every so often, as Jedi as I have tried to remain, Darth Vader and the Sith turned me and had me venturing into the dark side.

It was AWOL at Paradise Club when I first clocked her, late on in 1993. Like with most birds that I had a thing for in my past years of

Wolverining in the clubs, I always enjoyed watching how a girl flexed, and wow, Sherry was sexy as fuck when she was dancing. She had that kind of 'come and fuck me hard look' about her, which I can't describe, although at the time I was hesitant, in case I was mistaken and she was actually thinking "Who the fuck you looking at ya mug?" When I eventually plucked the courage and caved into my predatory ways and began to speak to her, I realised she was an American girl from Texas. We had a fun time after the ice was broken to say the least. As we laughed and joked I was lyricsing them knickers off for sure. We had also both necked pills, feeling the rush and feeling the blinders Kenny Ken, Ray Keith and Randall were throwing down that night, and if I don't mind saying so, I was desperate for a bit of a throw down myself with this newly-introduced Sherman tank.

By end of the night, I was getting the impression I had lost my touch at the time. We were all gathered on stage having a joke with Groove, Juice, Kenny Ken and everyone. I signalled for Sherry to come over so I could clock her digits, but she kind of spurned me, with that stoosh looking you up and down like you was a piece of shit look that she does. Fuck she was sexy, but I thought that was that, the chance was gone, without a kiss goodbye or nothing.

Lucky for me though, when we finally decided to leave the building, she was there outside handing out flyers for the Morning After club she was promoting at the time and I pursued my interest further. Lyrics again, I was on good form and had my objective concluded on mutual terms. "I ring you soon, yeah?" it was one of them click your heel moments. I walked back to the car with Grooverider and Pete Nice and chatted non-stop about her on the way home. It pretty much started there, in between our discussions about the music business. It went from booty calls and toe-curling sex to a full-on romance. Both of our careers were intertwined with the scene so there was plenty of excuses to contact her. We also had so much in common, did I mention she was great in bed?

Speaking to Pete soon after, I remember him warning me not to fuck about behind Helen's back. He was looking out for her because they were close. "I'm telling you Fluxie, don't do it" he would lecture.

Also because he knows I don't do one night stands and that I have a tendency to drag things out longer than they should and a year down the line he was smugly reminding me, "I fucking told you didn't I?" Pete is funny like that, because ever since I have known him, he always had a way of sounding more like my dad than a mate at times, but he was right. It was ridiculous in the end the way I was carrying on. I had my girlfriend and I had my other girlfriend and as the time went on, going out was as tricky as you like. For example, if we were all out at AWOL or Voodoo Magic, I'd stay on stage or in the DJ booth, knowing the two of them were in the dance. I'd even plead with Pete to stay with Helen in the garage room with her or upstairs, saying "Take her anywhere" just so I could have a bit of respite and talk to Sherry for a bit.

Sometimes I'd even be offish with Sherry, so I wouldn't have to speak to her at all, just in case I got caught out. There wasn't a strategy, it was improvisation on a massive scale, which led to a series of lies that would mutate into more lies. In the end I didn't know whether I was coming or going. By year two, I was in love with them both. I explained this to Pete, many times, but he failed to get his head around it and he was getting the hump with me always having to cover me, saying "Take Helen home for me Pete", "Go with Helen to the VIP and buy her drinks for me Pete". "Stay in the Garage Room with Helen all night for me Pete" and on and on and on and on it went.

I'm sure we had a few heated words at the time. I was starting to get the impression it was becoming a chore for him and he was getting bored with it all... apart from of course, the time we hooked up for an old school combo and went on a double date, when he began dating Sherry's best friend Paris, which he still believes was me trying to pacify him a bit by introducing and whispering to him that she fancied him. Yeah righto Pete! As if he needed any encouragement back then.

Maybe subconsciously it could have been the case, and in all honesty, I must have been a real deceptive character to be able to play two women like that over the years, when I was seeing them both. Even more so, it was the fact that I was getting away with it, even when it was starting to be obvious to everyone around us what was going on. In the end this went on for almost 5 years and to complicate my life just a teenie weenie little bit extra, Germany became my next port of call.

Vera was a blonde 'fit ting' from Heidelberg. Here we have another example of me being unable to suppress my predatory ways. I flew over with Grooverider to rock MS connection in Mannheim, as D&B/Jungle crossover was going global. This time Grooverider was the instigator, clocking the 2 fit sorts dancing in front of us and tempting out the Inta Natty way - I came, I saw, I conquered.

While he was into his set, he gave me that look, a command that I knew, the one telling me to rack 'em up for a bit of fun later. Lucky for me, I got top picks, chatting away to sow the seeds so to speak. The pair of them spoke very good English, there were no lost in translation moments happening here, it was game on. However, Grooverider and myself were left gutted after learning that we had a bit of confusion with our departure times. There was little time left for anything else other than a smile and a hello for him and a cheeky kiss with Vera and the promise to call and link up on my next visit a fortnight later.

Pete the lecturer was left shaking his head within a few months. What should have been a one night stand spiralled into another full blown relationship and before you know it, I have myself a 3rd wife and Germany who becomes my sanctuary when the tension over juggling all three begins to take its toll.

Now I'm not looking for any self-pity here or justification for being a cheating fucker, because there are always solutions to a problem and mine was to just choose one and make my life simple. Pete Nice at the time was lecturing me constantly, "Choose one and finish with the madness." But it's never as simple as that with me, because drugs were always the answer to everything when my head was under a bit of pressure. Unfortunately, this time it would eventually come in the form of heroin and although it was a slow process, it did not take long before I was hooked like Zammo.

CHAPTER 17

GOING UNDERGROUND

Before you all think I got to the Zammo stage of heroin by the 12th day of Christmas, you have to realise that it would still take at least another couple of years before I actually hit skid row. Life still went on and when I wasn't sloping off into renditions of Lou Reed's *Perfect Day* to justify the drugs or the cast from Grange Hill *Just say no* ringing in my head, I was still teaming up with all the boys on some weekends to go clubbing.

The garage rave scene since around mid to late 1996 had gradually began holding our attention, the boys loving this scene because it was wall-to-wall fanny at most places. Pete was giving me joke when I introduced a mate of Helen and Tina's called Natasha after giving him the low down a couple of weeks back.

"You got to meet this gyal" I said. I was explaining to him the voluptuous and sturdy set build on the girl in her knee-length boots, the type that he's began to get obsessive about.

"Bangers, arse and thighs, in that order mate, I thought of you as soon as I see her at Twice as Nice," I continued.

"Set me up then" he requested back laughing.

We have had many conversations like that over the years and it's times like these I missed not having him around all the time as he's back on the 9 to 5 after the Inta Natty episode, in fact the Family, as we once were, was never the same again, as we became even more splintered. TJB had disappeared off the face of the earth after losing his marbles. We all used to think that he was on the verge to be fair, when he used to act out the Carl Galton character I explained earlier in the book, but with the weed and suspicions of steroid abuse, we wasn't too surprised, as unsympathetic that may sound, but he was still our boy and we all had shown our concern about him when we heard the news.

Following some kind of hostage situation at his mum's house, police were called and he was sectioned for a few weeks. When we visited him he seemed in a place of self-pity in my opinion, but was still in a way trying to be this controlling character, like we were his boys, kind of in the sense that he had sent for us to discuss business or something. However, he did seem to have made some good progress after and he was even back with us for a while. He was also helping Pete at times, knocking on shop doors trying to claw the Inta Natty business out of dire straits, but that was a few months ago and no one has seen or heard from the prick ever since, even to this day.

As I was saying, me and the boys were starting to see less and less of each other, other than the odd nights out. I was enjoying success overseas, touring the USA with Grooverider and DJ Phantasy, Japan with Fabio & Andy C, Australia, New Zealand with Bailey, Europe with Kemistry & Storm and the Metalheadz Family. Most of the stars of drum and bass at the time were eating very, very well, the top boys ploughing money on studio equipment, plush apartments and into top motors like top marque BMW convertibles and Porsches.

Goldie was well out in front after his success with his Timeless album and his Metalheadz label leading the way, throwing out many club bangers at the time. Andy C, who is one of the coolest people you could ever meet and his label RAM records, were also establishing themselves as premier league (but his team West Ham are still shit.) Photek I remember also pulling up at Blue Note in a crisp new red Ferrari one Sunday night.

The reason for the success can be credited to people like Goldie, Dillinger, Lemon D, Roni Size and Ed Rush and countless artists that were bringing a high level standard of music to the fore, which elevated the scene. That I believe was the golden era for the music with the type of tunes that would make you screw your face up they were that nasty. You just had to look at Goldie, Grooverider and Fabio's faces when a nasty tune was dropped which typified that, and I mean that in a good way.

Blue Note was at the forefront of places to hear the more upfront intelligent sounds that would see people come from all over the world to squeeze into the tiny venue. Cleveland Wattkis hosted the mic down there and his smooth vocals riding over these jazz funk type break beats like Adam F's Metropolis and Circles classics was pure class. Although success was not exclusive to the stars and celebrities of Jungle, they were not alone because when the circuit was split in two, the British bass lead influence created two monsters, Drum and Bass and UK Garage.

When Sunday came, it was usually a who's who turnout, when everyone dressed up in Versace and D&G and the champagne flowed at Twice as Nice at the Coliseum in Vauxhall. This had become Helen's favourite place, especially with her best pal Tina, all Gucci'd up and popping off to the garage beat. Tina was also now in a relationship with DJ Pied Piper, who from out of nowhere is headline DJ at many UK garage events. It is a change up from what the boys and I have been used to, we even joke about coming full circle and having to wear shoes again to go out.

We brushed shoulders with Premier League footballers like Sol Campbell, Emile Hesky & Rio Ferdinand to name a few, even the main Jungle and Drum and bass faces attend, and people like Frost and Grooverider have the opportunity to model off their fur coats. You might have a hard time getting your head around this, but there are a few heavy hitters dropping this pimp/player style and the women seem to love it. Here also, like how jungle was tagged due to the ethnic majority crowd at some events, people are hesitant, claiming some events felt a little bit hostile.

Maybe the gangsterish look on some people's faces may have given off a negative vibe party experience, and admittedly, there were many naughty crews attending from many of the 'Ends' around London but due to the quality of the music, obviously, many of these badmen must have left all the beefing and weaponry outside because there weren't many incidents I had witnessed going to any UK garage events at the time. Violence did tar the scene during the latter years, but it was largely attributed to followers of UK Garage's prominent Rap crews, because from an outside view, the (loutish) behaviour of the So Solid Crew on stage at the Brit awards in 2001, and people getting shot at some of their gigs, you can begin to understand the apprehension towards the scene and its clientele, influencing club owners and event organisers to swerve away from promoters of that genre which pretty much killed off UKG. But the earlier days were much more enjoyable and incident free in my opinion.

On the handful of occasions that he did attend, Pete would be slightly wasted on champagne and a bit of toot, as it feels to him as though it's compulsory when going to these events and he jokes about how he got stares and glances over sunglasses rims when he'd ordered 2 Budweisers and a couple of ciders at the bar. Later on, after complying to UK garage's drinking etiquette, he was now acknowledging Freddy again, a main face I mentioned earlier in the book. He's responding to Pete Nice but probably thinking what the fuck he was going on about, as he tried to engage him into conversations about way back when. "Come me bredrin" I interject, to save Freddy from him when it looked like he was starting to jar him.

"He's top boy, he used to be a top geezer back in the day, one of your own" he slurs,

"Yeah I know Pete" I reply, half dragging him away.

Helen was nine times out of ten in the same state too and I leave the two of them together to prop the bar up and discuss world peace or whatever the fuck they would talk about when they were pissed with me thinking, "Fucking one and the same the pair of them."

I repeat it as I point them out to Killa, setting him off with laughter. We remind ourselves of the absolute state he'd got into on his last birthday at Thunder and Joy in Raw Club the previous year, when he had spent most of the night vomiting in the toilets. This was after a full on and maybe excessive, booze, cocaine and stripper session in the Muddy Waters, courtesy of Big Dave the landlord. By the time we reached the club he was looking the worse for wear. My sister Alison in the end played mum, looked after him and got him home, but he was properly mullered at the time.

This seemed to surprise most of the people we knew, who were asking me all night if he was all right. He was all right, but it was at a time when Inta Natty was going down the pan and our pending OC trial probably had Pete hitting the liquor more regularly. Thinking back now, TJB was also in a similar situation when he took over a printing business that eventually collapsed. That may also had contributed to him being slung into a strait-jacket and in hindsight it has me thinking that Pete could have been tipping that way as well.

More recently it was only these nights and the odd night out at Blue Note, Goldie's award-winning Sunday night sessions, where the 4 of us were really out together. As we hit our early 30s, we are not as light hearted or as tolerant as we once were. Pete now on many occasions would always comment, sounding like Danny Glover's character *Sergeant Murtaugh* in *Lethal Weapon*, about how he feels too old for this bollocks. For him it seemed as though the garage scene in particular, was all about people showing off the champagne life style with many, including himself, on lemonade money.

What may also have been more the case, was the impression of too much hard work with the girls on the scene for him, especially when he considered that lemonade money didn't go very far when you want to impress a lady dressed head to toe in Chanel or Versace, so apart from a lady he took a shine to from a few years back, who he had met at our pal Gerald's Sunday afternoon sessions 'Mums The Word' in the Frog and Nightgown on the Old Kent Road, it was pretty much slim pickings.

No doubt he was probably drawn to this one because she had similarities to Katrina, with her dark curly hair and sexy eyes. It seemed he would be having conversations and a joke with her and would hang onto her every word, you would have thought her shit stank of roses. He would also obsess about her to me, how they had good conversation and she made him laugh. Yeah, OK... he forgets that I know him too well; it was more like the firm breasts and banging arse on it that he was interested in. It was also quite clear that she was into him as well, but she was the ex-wife of a very large door person that we knew. I had real difficulties persuading him to think again given the volatility of the said door person, in fact I think I remember my words were more like, "ARE YOU FUCKING CRAZY YOU CUNT OR WHAT?"

Moreover, he would possibly have an easier time in bomb disposal than he would even considering asking her out. Which on my advice, reluctantly for him, he never did. So other than her and Natasha, who he hooked up with a few times, he could not really get into the birds on the scene. Most of them, or at least the few others he did try to fly into, were only interested in whether he could maintain a steady flow of bubbly. I'm not trying to say he'd become the Grinch or anything like that, I think he was just fed up with trying to give off an image for them.

Helen, bless her, was even trying her best impersonation of Cilla Black. It was as though she was eager for him to settle down and find the happiness he was desperate for as well. In fairness, the club scene after so long mixing in that circle of VIP and the "do you know such and such?" and the "I'm on the guest list" brigade, really jarred him. In the end he stopped going out on the scene altogether and was more often than not drinking out locally in Croydon with work pals.

It's funny as I talk about going full circle and wearing shoes to go out in again, because whilst he was working for this Croydon Cable Company, organising installs for engineers, I hadn't seen him for a few months, but I ended up sorting him and a few of his new pals tickets for an Innovation dance at Camden Palace. Pete was on the phone to me the next day saying, "If I had had a bag of 100 Es last night I would have cleaned up easy."

He laughed as he explained how he was the only black guy out of the 15 strong group of lads and girls he went with and yet had people coming up to him all night asking for Es. I guess people's perception never change of a big black guy with dreads. We spent a few hours catching up, the phone now being passed back and forth between me and Helen as we both missed not having him around so much. Helen was hogging the phone trying to get all the juicy gossip about the new love of his life, which funnily, he was playing down, which was a little unusual for him after all the years I'd known him.

We did meet on a few occasions after, when we had a couple nights out at Twice as Nice and Aquarium with him and this girl from his work called Leigh, a really pretty, tall, leggy brunette with a wicked bottom. Red jeans and a wicked bottom is what I remembered about her. Helen and I remember noticing at the time him having that love-sick puppy dog look on his boat race again that confirmed the opposite from the conversations we were having around that time, because he would just shrug his shoulders saying she was a young 'ting' and they were just having a bit of fun.

I was thinking he was gearing up to start getting out and about again with me for a brief moment, but in the end, after the short affair with her, he said he only came out because the girl wanted to go there and still had the despise for the scene as before.

Me on the other hand, going out was now even more so part of my job networking, paying close attention to UK Garage MCs as this Garage scene is blowing up and I'm wondering whether there was room for a crossover. Listening, as the top MCs carved up a nice little niche for themselves, to the likes of PSG, Creed and Sparks MC. MC Sparks, whose real name is Sean, was a face I knew from the 80s hanging out in Croydon. A very funny guy and I had a lot of time for him, we would always have a good crack over a few glasses of Bolli whenever I saw him at these events.

This period also saw me hanging with Premiership footballer and Crystal Palace winger Bruce Dyer as we get involved in the garage scene, now blowing up. Terry Turbo from One Nation was now getting involved and Garage Nation is sold out and ram packed. This also saw two pals of mine, Peter and Dave, promote another top billing garage do, aptly named La Cosa Nostra. These parties are packed to the rafters with plenty of bling on show, rude boys in dark glasses and hugging champagne buckets and the girls looking all gangster.

With Pete giving much of the scene a miss and Face and Killa doing their own thing, I'm teamed up with Gerald, Paul Henry, Cedric, Kimmy, Tara, Malcolm (who was with Lyndsay Dawn Mackenzie at the time) and their little crew (all Croydon people)as we pop pills and turn up at after parties in people's houses. We mong out on tunes and take turns to mix on the decks. On my birthday in Feb 1997, I organised a champagne bash at my house with most of my new Garage crew, Face, Pete, Killa and a few Under 5s turn up. Tina, Helen and their pals including Funky Flirt and a few others are also at the gathering, as Pete once again, gets ruined on champers and brandy and is yakking up in my front garden.

We were all pissing ourselves laughing as Killa cusses him, calling him a weak heart as he wipes the bile away from his lips and glares at us with them sorry eyes he has when he is in this condition. An image that even today has me cracking up thinking about it, because it's very rare to ever see him in that state nowadays as he stays away from mixing alcohol and usually sticks to lagers. Although the next few years we remained friends, by the turn of the new millennium we became more and more distant as he socialised with new pals and I became overwhelmed with work on the Drum and Bass scene and fell deeper and deeper into addiction.

CHAPTER 18

FROM HERO TO HEROIN

I suppose after reading all this, it would be fair to say that many would class me as a person with an addictive nature, because drugs were a thing that some people can take and leave at any given time. Pete for example could go on benders for days on end where he'd be offered a crack pipe when a session was in full swing and would say NO or he would be somewhere on YAYO and booze and would more often than not at some given point would say, "That's it, I'm done in now." Me on the other hand, I would suck that pipe and carry on sniffing gear until my heartbeat was showing through my shirt.

When it came to me and the drugs, it was usually always social. As much as I smoked, popped or snorted, it was always social but would make most people see it as no wonder I fell into this precarious trap and caught a disease so vile it infected everyone around me. So why did I do it? The truth is... because I could.

There were times when a few of us used to hit the cherry during the days when we were awash with money. On the way back from raving, completing a bit of business or returning from football, any excuse, stop off and buy a bone. We even went through a spate at one point when a few of us regulars like me, Mendez, Blocker, Nifty, Jay and Inch would just have it around us all the time, not that we needed it, just that we could. In hindsight, yes, of course, we could have put our money to better use than lining the pockets of the esteemed people of the Brixton Frontline, but money was never an issue for us back then and hitting the pipe and jumping on a bit of fanny was just a way of life, like having a spliff to relax. OK granted, later on, a few people I knew got into a bit of trouble, clucking and acting like degenerates because of the cherry, but as far as I was concerned it was always recreational.

As I was saying, Brixton Frontline was a regular stop off for us, that even during the summer of 92, it led us into having one lady character over there as our crack rep who got to know us by name in the end, such was the amount of trade we was giving her. Which also reminds me of the time, when we were novices to the crack market, a funny little episode came about. It seemed like the lads over there for a period had changed their strategy when they decided on selling moody gear as rock. One night after Rage, having purchased a bit from a fake Jamaican over there, we were mighty pissed off to get back to the manor to see the wraps all filled with Polo mint.

We were all back at Nifty's gaff, screwing, but I don't know why we were all just sat there, we weren't mugs and people who ripped us off or tried back then were usually served up. So off we went. Half an hour later, we'd set a trap for one of these thieving cunts when we flashed him a wad of cash, which probably had him thinking he'd be ending his night early, I make him right.

"Show us the goods son" Blocker enquired.

"Open it up let us see" Nifty and I were repeatedly demanding, using this as a tactic, the three of us all speaking at the same time and walking off as if unfazed and uninterested in allowing him our business, which lured him away from the other hustlers on the block.

We were all soon dashing through a playground after gassing and knocking the cunt out and taking his money and his goods. That was payback for ripping us off the mug, have a night off, the two bob cunt. We have a good old laugh about it, especially the getaway car, a 2 door BMW and how we fumbled our way back into the motor after doing the geezer and Inch wheel spinning which seemed to keep the car motionless with us screaming for him to get us the fuck out of there, which still has me chuckling to this day and wondering what the hell we were thinking back then.

So, going back to the topic, it was probably around 1997 when it really all started, as I said before, and without sounding like I'm repeating myself, the last few years had had a drain on me like you could not believe. Along with that short stint in prison which was a huge strain, constantly worrying about my career, the British Transport Police up my arse with their organised crime investigation and court case, all these things had been contributing to my natty becoming dishevelled and eventually falling out. Then all the lying and deceit, I couldn't remember one lie from the next but it was becoming second nature.

What you have to understand, I was 4 days with Helen, 3 days with Sherry and vice versa, then Vera come onto the scene and having to sneak off to spend hours on the phone or trips to go see her in Germany or the two of us plotted up in seedy hotels in Croydon. In between this was the MC work, the partying, then there were the 24-hour cocaine and booze binges. I literally had no relaxation time for myself, and now as I think about it all, it was kind of ironic in a way, as my head spun out of control, that it would be Reggie, although a man I would die for, who was becoming the epitome of bad luck and would ultimately be the indirect source of my own down fall.

The heroin, a 9 bar which was unsellable because silly bollocks stamps on it with brick dust, for what reason I do not know, was left pugged up for weeks before insomnia helped me locate it during the early hours. It had been totally forgotten about for weeks, and one afternoon, as weak as I was, I thought it was a good idea to roll myself a spliff with a little dab of it. After taking a deep inhale of this heroin dashed spliff for the first time, everything went away and I no longer had problems sleeping. I always had the curiosity for heroin, John Travolta made it look sexy in Pulp Fiction behind the wheel of a big American Chevrolet with Bullwinkle playing in the background. All I remember is a numbing feeling and my eyelids feeling like 10 tons of weight and that was pretty much it, no cool music playing and no Yank motors.

When I slapped myself out of my haze, I realised it was 4 am and

Helen wasn't home yet. Then I realised, I'm not with her on Thursdays, she is Monday to Wednesday. I'd better ring Sherry and make up some sorry arse excuse. This gets worse over the next few months, as I shut myself off and steadily empty the parcel, taking the 'Fuck it, if no one else wants it' stance and I'm constantly engaged in showdown talks as they both begin to recognise the change in me.

"You used to be more lively, now all you want to do is sit indoors with the curtains drawn smoking that awful smelling crap" Helen would constantly niggle me, about what it was that kept me so withdrawn and distant. I kept telling them it was opium and that it was helping me to relax, because I knew for a fact if they knew it was heroin-contaminated brick powder, they probably would have kicked me to the kerb. And by the way, when we were reviewing for the book, Pete like most normal people was asking the same question...

"Who the fuck, in their right mind, would participate in any form of smoking/inhaling any type of gear, if they knew it was laced with brick dust?" Which is exactly my point, who the fuck? I can't even believe it myself. Had I just walked away from it or tossed it in the trash like most normal human beings would have done, who knows where my life would have ended? Sliding doors and all that.

So here I am now, first having a spliff just for the sake of it, then wanting a spliff because I had a row, or wanted to have a good kip, or I'd stubbed my toe and before long, any excuse I'd roll myself a joint of brown or chase the fumes along tin foil. Before long I no longer needed an excuse.

After renting several flats, Helen and I were making plans to buy our own place and if I did it with one, I had to suggest it to the other as well, they were so blinded by love even I can't believe how I was getting away with it. Each suspicious question they asked was evaded with a big fat lie and I carried on.

At one point Sherry was sitting outside a block of flats I was living in. This detail I'd kept as a secret from her, my sister Alison's house was my registered address as far as she was concerned and to this day I don't know what the hell she was even doing there, I couldn't even ask. But I was looking over my shoulder and peering out the window, paranoid for weeks after that the net was closing in and she'd suss me.

As time went on, heroin was included in my everyday routine, chase and chase some more, how much have I got left? That bit will last me until later, meet the guy and buy a bit more. It did get to a point when they both seemed to give up on nagging me and ignored my drug-induced stupor. More recently, I cocktailed with a nose of Charlie and satisfied them with sex because for a while, when I was in between a heroin and a cocaine buzz, my cock was like the rod of correction, which seemed to make them overlook the bad habit.

Helen also now started enjoying nights out on the town with mates. She was in with this group of girls, all good sorts, the types who look like the old man was minted and had all the Louis Vuitton and Gucci and all that. I'd watch her dress up and looking damn fine, voluptuous and sexy as fuck, which left me in a dilemma. Sooner or later 'next man' would notice how fine she was, give her the chat and I'd be dropped like a sack of shit... but even so, I would be rushing her out the door. "Go out and enjoy yourself babe, have a good time."

I would be left alone with my new love the H, as I chased that motherfucking dragon for most of the night. The pattern was then set, and when the parcel of brick dust was gone, there was plenty local dealers for me to buy an eighth, a quarter, an ounce. I was slowly spiralling downwards. I was also good pals with these dealers, so money or lack of it was never an issue, I was always good for it. From the smoking came the chasing and following the chasing came the belt strap and the needle.

Before long Helen confided in Pete, as she felt he was the only one that might be able to talk some sense into me. However Pete didn't notice any change in me. I only saw him occasionally, so how would he know? He had smelt me smoking a spliff or 2 but I'd been really conditioned to act normally under it and even he didn't know what the fuck it was, by the smell of it. He would always just comment that it smelt like 'fucking camel shit' but that was as far as he went.

Helen was left feeling in a hopeless position when Pete suggested to her, that maybe she should just call time on us. I was none too pleased after she discussed exploring this avenue, catapulting into some ugly scenes one afternoon. She had been out the previous night and by 3 am I was already warning her of the consequences if she didn't come home. With the combination of Jack Daniels, cocaine and heroin, my response for the no show until 8 am the next day, was to explode with anger. I was paranoid that there must be someone keeping her out, the next man I'd been fearing. By the time she came home and faced the interrogation, there were bits of furniture and clothes flying about as I gave her the ultimatum that eventually made up her mind.

She was leaving me and had already accepted the advances from another fella. I knew she wanted to leave me, but I refused to let her go. My ego had been shattered and even though, as fucked up as I was, I would never ever put my hands on her or any woman for that matter, she saw the button was pushed and she knew through experience the extent of my temper. The fact that I put her under extreme intimidation was not one of my proudest moments. At one point Pete was pounding at my front door after she had made several frantic phone calls to him. I kept her against her will and there was nothing she could do. I played about with blades cutting up dresses and playing macho mind games on her.

It took me several hours before the red mist receded, more to do with the fact that I was getting withdrawals and I could no longer carry on with the bad boy stance. My priority switched from Helen to heroin, followed by a big reprimand from Pete that night. Helen gave him the blow by blow account with her final deduction that "Fluxie better fix up his shit and come correct." not in that exact terminology but she is 100% right. For her that was the final straw. I couldn't bear the thought of her with anyone else, which in the end, edged me even closer to

Sherry, who softened the blow. It was only a matter of time before she also turned to Pete Nice looking for guidance. I don't think he was sensitive to the desperate plight being felt by both my women at the time, but he does feel sorry for them, that much I do know.

During a period that spun my head like a Waltzer ride at Mitcham Fair, within the first 4 months of splitting from Helen, she now became my mistress as we tried to rekindle. She missed me and we both hadn't found the greener grass on the other side. Sherry assumed that she finally had what she wanted when I moved lock stock and barrel in with her over in Battersea. The record shop business she had at least kept my mind occupied. I still had my regular work, rendezvous with Helen and also skipping over to Germany to see Vera, so pretty much nothing had changed, except that two wives and a mistress became one wife and two mistresses, or three if you included the heroin.

Vera was a girl of such good intentions. We talked openly about my heroin addiction. Somehow she discovered the signs pretty much straight away, and then she became desperate to help me. Around the summer of 1999 she would become my Florence Nightingale because she prepped and researched all she could to help me escape the habit. I spent 2 weeks over in Germany and in hindsight, if I had been more strong-minded this could have been the place to kick the habit completely.

She nursed and supported me during 5 days of hell. I went cold turkey with cold sweats, stomach cramps and basic ill symptoms and her sweet kisses and gorgeously soft voice were a great comfort. I wanted to do this for her. I got almost to the end of the tunnel and feeling like my normal self after thinking sooner or later I would shit myself to death. I had one more week to clean up completely. This is never an easy road when the pain is unbearable to even begin to explain, weed, cocaine, even a bottle of vodka you can try to come to terms with it as a distraction, but most of the time even taking a piss is hard work when your body is telling your brain what to do.

I was also missing Helen so much and I knew she had been the source of the late night crank calls Vera had received. On the Friday morning she left for work I could see the pain in her, obviously her heart was in the right place but the magnitude of the past week must have been such a weight on her shoulders and the calls were like the nail in the coffin. That and the packet I surprisingly discovered in the lining of my coat as I set off for a brisk walk to clear my head the Friday afternoon. I knew I had put it there because it was for emergency in case I was delayed or stranded in Germany, fuck knows. But I had planted it and fucking weak as I am, it was too large a resist, so I put myself right back to square one.

It then became Sherry's problem. The prescription drug Physeptone helped me battle through a trip when she'd accompanied me to Canada to work. It would eventually make her mind up when she saw how erratic and deranged I became when I misplaced it, literally trashing the hotel room until realising I had hid it in a CD case. With hand on heart, Sherry unwittingly and unfairly, because of the cunt I was, had hold of a double edge sword if I'm honest, because in the end, not only was she coping with a junkie boyfriend, I had still been sneaking around behind her back.

After 10 months of reconciliation we were separated but never apart and it was inevitable that Helen would be back to number one. Surely now this would settle my head down, but it was too late in truth, I was a heroin addict and the only lie required is to hide it from everyone else, which I did very badly.

Vera was now extremely remorseful taking it upon herself that she had failed after promising me she would do everything within her power, but it was me that had betrayed her with my weakness. It was easier to be an addict than to live a normal life. If I was a stronger man I should have chosen her, as she was the only one that challenged my addiction. Sherry and Helen were blinded by love for me and seemed to let me carry on with it. However at one point Helen persisted time and time again, so I tried again to clean myself up by going to programmes to help addiction. The doctors prescribed me a new drug to alleviate the physical symptoms of withdrawal, called Lofexidine, which went bandy when I developed a reaction that had me convulsing into a seizure and hospitalised onto a morphine drip.

This set me back again tenfold, especially with me and Sherry, and our relationship went down like the Titanic soon after, because along with the heroin addiction, I had not left Helen as I had promised and had carried on the double life. She finally gave me my marching orders after a cry for help ended up with her being hospitalised and I wasn't around to be at her side. She would eventually find comfort in the arms of another man. Personally I was indifferent about it but at that point I'd rather someone else showed her the proper love and attention that I was incapable of. Who was I fooling at the end of the day? My actions were only setting off disaster after disaster. She was better off well away from me as much as it burned me. She still cared about my wellbeing but I had become a drag on both their lives, emotionally and physically which was making her unwell and I was sorry for the distress I had caused.

Love is a very strong emotion and over the years no matter how much I fucked up, I could always talk my way back. In the end, only Helen showed how deep her love was when she said yes and by March 2001 we were ready to tie the knot.

The day of the wedding was pretty much a whirlwind and we were both chuffed at the turnout of friends and loved ones. It was a beautiful day. The boys, Pete Nice, Face and Killa, had me up early doors for breakfast after a quite night by our standards. We were in a bar having a quiet drink before turning in and unpacking our stuff in our rooms. It was probably at the time, the only occasion I had had real long conversations about life with them for quite a long while. It was in stark contrast to the same conversations from 10 years ago, as everyone was changing, and discussions on marriage, love and children were now replacing conversations about sex, drugs and violence and the 'fuck that shit' attitude of never settling down.

Later, me and Pete stayed up until the early hours and laughed and joked about past exploits, and Pete confided in me on many issues, opening up and confessing he was totally fixated on sharing innermost secrets. For the most part I feel he was using this as an avenue to open me up to him about my addiction and renounce Satan. If I was paranoid I could have easily mistaken it as my last rites, like in some gangster movies, before he plunged a knife in me while I was asleep or induced me to an overdose to put everyone out of their misery. Looking back, if I'm honest with myself, I was reliant on my poison and deluded enough that I felt I was in enough control to continue, even if it meant losing my best friend, because apart from that night, as far as I was concerned, I had already lost him.

I was relieved when he finally fell asleep so I could sneak out of the room with my feelgood kit and use a communal toilet down the hallway to take a hit and nod off. He was commenting in the morning, that every time he woke up for a piss, I wasn't in my bed and nowhere to be seen. I gave him some bollocks and he didn't pry any further, but he did not seem to believe me anyway.

After we dressed, we were back in the boozer to watch the football, and I sank a couple of brandies to calm my nerves. The ceremony in the Grand Hotel in Brighton was not an extravagant or an over the top occasion by all accounts, it was intimate with all my family and close friends attending. Reggie, who had missed out on my stag night a couple of weeks earlier, summoned me to the gents and on the window sill had lined up the biggest line of cocaine you could imagine to calm my nerves.

"Cunt, this would send Daniella Westbrook to rehab... you sure?" I said giggling.

"Shut up ya poof, get it down ya son" Reggie said laughing. Not that I needed encouragement as I woofed the line of high grade pure-o up both nostrils and felt on top of the world. The wedding went well by all accounts and Helen was looking beautiful as ever in my eyes. My mum was worried how much weight she had lost over the last couple of years but her curves were there to see in that lovely wedding dress as she was crowned Mrs Helen Thomas. As we kissed to an eruption of cheers from the boys standing beside me and applause from my family, with the big line of Charlie inside me I swear I heard my mother wailing about her losing her little boy.

"Little boy?" I'm thinking, "I'm 35 years old, leave it out."

Nevertheless, that was not her real concern. By this time people were wising to me on the brown but today no one was thinking about that, especially my best man Pete Nice, who at the wedding sitdown delivered a speech that almost had me in tears. He had the room in a fit of laughter with a watered-down version of our past shenanigans, throwing in a bit of comedy, mostly at my expense. Hearing him say to the entire room of guests how he saw me and loved me as his brother and his best pal in the world that he could ever ask for had me choked, because he has never actually said it to me before, let alone to a room full of people. It was a beautiful, emotional, well-delivered speech but it also had me guilty at the same time as I drift off into my own world. I was thinking of the wrongs I had done and what I had put Helen and the family through. I considered rehab and maybe I should stand up and confess to everyone here and now. A cry for help maybe... but who the fuck is brave enough to confess shit like that on a beautiful day like this? Not me. I continued to put up the same façade I had mastered - not that it fooled anyone but hey if you have not caught me with the needle in my arm no one can prove anything, that is how deluded I was.

It's over to me now. I stand up and thank everyone for sharing this occasion with my new wife and me. The reception and the first dance introduce Mr and Mrs Carl Thomas, and we smooch to Omar's. There's nothing like this.

BA DOO BEE WEE OOOOOOH,
Sip a glass of cold champagne wine
The rug that we lie on feels divine
And there's no no no no parallel ....For we two

Ecstasy the word of the night
Ringing in our ears, we're inflight
There's no substitution
for what we have
No others can have

We joked about the time we used to play this all the time, with happy memories and relief that we had completed this gorgeous day, which pretty much was the best day this new millennium had brought us, that's for sure. I wished the day could have lasted forever as I promised to get my act together and do away with all the shit and pain I'd been dragging her through. It would have been a good way to complete my story, ending right here, with white doves and a white carriage as we rode off into the sunset and lived happily ever after.

Instead, my life became more sinister. Infidelity was insignificant compared to the other shit going on, as everything I held dear I began to lose. Life as an addict would take many an unsophisticated road. I was still carrying on with Vera even after marrying Helen. I still had a few bits of work come my way with promoters in Europe, before their patience wore thin due to no-shows and late appearances.

I still used them as my excuse to visit my German sweetheart but it wasn't long until she had had enough of me after our three and half year relationship and the constant crank calls from Helen trying to catch me out. Now don't get me wrong, I'm no Brad Pitt as far as looks are concerned although I do consider myself a sort (Pete is chuckling to himself) but people would wonder how the fuck could I be juggling 3 beautiful women at the same time like I did? Why did they keep coming back for more of the same shit like they did? and what the fuck did they see in me? It's understandable, I am of an intense and infectious character, I wore my heart on my sleeve and they were the centre of my world, not forgetting the chat and the charm, all three women were all in love with me until eventually, my erratic behaviour catapulted them away.

Vera's camel's back breaker was me stranding her in London for 3 days. I was supposed to link her but fell to heroin as I hung with 4 likeminded individuals that weekend. I was having a good time with this couple I knew from over Brighton way, who for the first time made me feel relaxed with my heroin addiction. I tried needles for the first time and bang I was zoned, Vera who?

A phone call to Vera a few weeks later ended up with me in nick, on the day of Tony Root's wedding in June 2001. I used a BT phone tapper to make the long distance call, of all the lines off that BT junction box, typical of me, as inconspicuous as an elephant in a yellow mankini, I had to choose the one that had the proprietor of the Clifton Arms and his well-known actor son confronting me.

This was a boozer that several Palace lads that I knew had drunk in from time to time but I was having a bad day already, and the last thing I needed were these two in my face. Lack of sleep, a big fat monkey on my back (and still no Bullwinkle), I'm fed up and desperate, pleading and rowing with Vera, I'm begging for a stay of execution as the apologies flow out of my mouth so unconvincingly, not like the lying smooth operator of the past, it's all empty promises anyway and she's having none of it and these inconsiderate cunts are interrupting now when I'm in full flow. I threatened to shoot him and his fucking dog the actor, and his real dog that they were threatening to set on me, so they had Old Bill turning up to arrest me for threatening behaviour. That was curtains for me as a fake BT engineer and as far as Vera was concerned, which was a shame really.

CHAPTER 19

GAZUMPED

After the 90s and living the life of a rock star, the old saying easy come, easy go must have been a phrase designed for me because by the end of 2001, with mortgage arrears and catastrophic bills and defaults with my regular drug dealers, I was forever it seemed on my arse and desperate to make some cash.

Through football you are always going to mix with individuals who are not adverse to a bit of criminality. After a few schemes and deals that went pear shaped I could not believe it when thinking back on it later that a drunken and drug-hazed discussion resulted in a plan to do a stick-up job, a good old fashioned blag to get some quick money.

During the drug years in Brighton we were often organising raids on rivals and mouthy dealers who loved to flash money about. Although I was not involved in many of these raids, young and eager lads looking to impress us would offer info about cash houses and hideouts. We would often offer some of our more rowdy members the chance to earn a little extra cash and Reggie, Nifty and me would often get our taste of the action and get a little drink out of it for our troubles. As I have said previously, it was a very profitable time for us. It was just unfortunate that we were so unorganised and don't have a pot to piss in to show for it, as was the case with some of my pals at football where the capers ranged from drug distribution, grand theft auto and selling moody gear.

Let's get it right, It's a real eye opener when the chips are down and prospects are grimmer than a famine in Ethiopia. Add to that a drug addiction that was driving a wedge between me and my family and an even deeper rift between me and Helen, you look at every angle possible. Reggie was not having the best of luck either and had a string of hard luck stories around this period that would have had most people going back to school to train as a nurse or a builder to earn an honest crust, because it was becoming apparent that he was not cut out for this game.

For example when he took on a 25 and a half grand parcel backed by a Pakistani firm. He done the deal for a kilo in a pub where he was all rush, rush with it, only to get it back to find it was chalk or some other moody substance. Subsequently he had to lie low as the Pakistani mob hunted him down looking for their money or to kill him. I did offer him onto the team but desperate as he was, he did not fancy a stretch for armed robbery to add to his criminal record, which was already as long as *The Da Vinci Code.*

The discussions and plans - well, I suppose you could call them plans, it was more a case of shall we or shan't we. All the time we went out our bottle would go and we would return home with our tails between our legs and our broke pockets. Although the others were not in as desperate a state as myself, these lads had a lifestyle to uphold by any means necessary and I knew sooner or later we'd have to make the decision to do a gaff over or go back to looking at long-term opportunities like launching a multi-billion dollar global internet tech company like Google. This was not going to happen.

The day finally came when we gee'd each other up and set off in the cut and shut Jaguar that we were knocking about in, acquired from another face at Palace. We all knew the plan and plotted up waiting for the armoured vehicle to arrive. At the movies whenever you see the films of strategically-planned jobs, where the team of robbers plot everything out, attention to detail is always the key. Preparation, preparation, preparation. A man called Don Logan (Sexy Beast) once said, the stopwatch is also always important, to know the response time of the Old Bill. Banks are pretty much sewn up and impregnable unless you have a time machine and can go back to the 70s and 80s. What you never see in movies is a team sitting in a motor prepared, shitting themselves and anxious for the target to arrive.

"Here we go!" We announce the vehicle approaching... what you get is the driver staying in the vehicle while the number 2 gets out and walks around to the hatch to pull the collection box out. What you hardly ever see and what we did not expect was... a car screeches up, 3 assailants jump out and are on the number 2 as he half-heartedly tries to protect the cash box.

"What the fuck?" We all say in unison.

It's like slow motion but it's over in a flash as they are back in the vehicle. It full throttles up the narrow road and past us in reverse, almost clipping wing mirrors as they look in on us, just as we look on at them bewildered, just as the occupant in the back removes his balaclava... but it isn't anyone we know.

"Quick you cunt, liven up and get after them!" my pal is screaming at the driver. But we hit the corner and like a puff of smoke they are gone. Snatched from right under our noses as we curse our luck.

"This ain't us" my pal said, as we are all now pissing ourselves with laughter. "Some fucking robbers we are, even our target gets pinched off of us." He's in full flow when he's turned his attention to his old man. "As for you, you cunt... call yourself a getaway driver? Fucking driving Miss Daisy."

The four of us in the car are rocking with laughter. We throw everything out and conclude that armed robbery is not the way forward for us and we should try and think of something a little less ambitious.

Looking back it was funny but somewhat unbelievable to actually plan to do a job like that, to turn up at least a dozen times and bottle it at the last minute, then to finally get the bollocks to go through with it only to see a gang of professionals nick it from right under our noses. In truth I think it was a bit of fate really, a blessing in balaclavas, because reading the papers weeks later, the perpetrators were all rounded up by Sweeney Todd and birded off on a long one.

Everything happens for a reason. Explaining it to a pal of ours in the pub soon after, we were appreciative of the bit of legit work that came our way from him. The fella, I believe, wanted to protect us from doing anything else as stupid and audacious as that. It did not stop him from falling about with tears of laughter and ripping the piss out of us at the turnout of events. An event he found so comical he gave us the tag Brinks Mat for a few weeks whenever he saw us. We stick to what we know and move a few bits and pieces for the desperately-needed dough we was after.

So let this be a lesson to all you kids reading this, crime does not pay, stay in school, read your books and make money legitimately!

It did not last long; it never does, especially now. By the time I got the money together to pay the mortgage, the gas bill, the car bills, fucking vet bills and add to that the junk not only to get me high but required to keep me well and functioning, I was back to square one. With final notices on my doormat I was forever now cap in hand begging and borrowing. I remember being on the phone to Pete with another hard luck story, but I was desperate and he's all I've got at times like this.

Pete wasn't about much around this time as he spent a lot more time drinking in the City. He had also hooked up with a bird he worked with from Essex and spent his weekends going to restaurants or staying indoors watching porno with her, so between her and Robbie and the other lads at football I began to see less and less of him, though he was still contactable.

"Please, Peter... I pay you back, I promise... can you lend us a couple hundred?"

Pete reminds me that he was with Robbie and a few other heads from Football, Nifty 50 and a main Yid face as well, in Croydon on the booze and here's me on the phone scrounging when a full boot off was in full flow. That's how fucked up I was, because as I learned later, one of the Nifty 50 lads made a call and had called it on, confident of the 20-strong firm he was out drinking with that sunny afternoon on FA Cup Final day.

When they arrived, this rival mob cannot even remember what I was told about the other mob, it was an ongoing feud, we all learned. Even the lads that were there were surprised to see this small contingent of geezers with gardening tools, pick axe handles and large knives descend onto Bar Coast, with weapons drawn and thrust towards the few lads stood by the doorway. Saturday shoppers were soon ducking out of the way when glasses, ash trays and stools flew out of the pub doors and the rival mob was chased and backed off up the road. I called Pete two or three times after constantly losing the connection and never even enquired about the ruck taking place in the middle of George Street.

"All you were interested in was getting your hands on money" Pete said angrily when he turned up an hour later with the dough. In truth, it wasn't long ago that whenever violence was on the menu I would have been up there like a shot, but the details were all going over my head, according to Pete, who had tried to explain what was going on at the time.

"Glad my wellbeing is still important to you" he said sarcastically, which totally escapes me again. He turns around mid-sentence and jumps into a brand spanking new Mercedes driven by fuck knows who and I'm already concentrating on calling my man for my fix. This pattern was commonplace and when everyone's patience ran out, more to the point, Pete's patience, I was in dire straits.

My last MC work of any substance and chance to earn a good packet was a fiasco in Australia in 2000. In hindsight it would have been a bad idea even to board a plane to Paris, let alone a 24-hour trip to Australia. I flatly refused that I would even participate at first but DJ Storm persuaded me. I had worked with her loads since around 1995, with her and her partner Kemistry (Rest In Peace Angel) who we had lost to that freak road accident when she was killed by a dislodged cat's eye near Southampton. Jane (Storm) was a lovely girl and good laugh and let's not forget, a very good DJ. She was very persuasive and also good on the old pep talk too, and that made my mind up. In summary, it was a week's worth of drama, played out on planes and hotel rooms due to my mismanagement of medicine. I pondered on my prescribed methadone substitute Physeptone for the 2-week tour, which included New Zealand, but I knew it would never be enough to last the whole fortnight.

Day 2 of the tour it was all good. The gigs went well and I was coping, but I knew when it's all gone I'd be fucked. I considered that maybe just for once I might try and fight it, maybe drop a sleeping tablet when I could or something to knock me out for the rest of the week and ration myself to just help me function, because by now heroin is only used for maintenance. The buzz days were long gone at this point.

What I failed to realise, having already tried to rid my body of this poison previously with the 5 days I had spent with Vera, is how painful an addiction can be when you do not induce your body to a substance it can no longer do without. The knots in my belly began to kick in somewhere over fucked-if-I-know. By the time we were mid-flight to Melbourne a loud splurge of vomit splattered the sick bag that consumed half of my face. It felt as though the end of the world was coming and I was going to die. I will never forget the shock on Bailey's face by the time the air stewards were shouting out, "IS THERE A DOCTOR IN THE HOUSE?" just like the movie *Airplane,* but there was no Leslie Neilson and this was as far off from comedy as you could get. Doctor number 2 glumly came to the realisation that it was not food poisoning, going by the rapid rate at which I was deteriorating. It had me paranoid that he might realise I was just a cold turkey heroin junkie gagging for a fix. I was ashamed because sympathy from the other passengers nearby would quickly turn to contempt. Bailey had been moved a few rows back and I was riddled with guilt for the poor sod, but the fact of the matter is, things would get a lot worse.

Sweat was pouring out of me, and I would start getting into a blind panic as I wasn't interested in working any more and wished to fuck I had stayed at home. I just want the pain to stop. If I could ease it to get me through the next gig, get my wages and score more I will be sweet. However you cannot just subtly go to the concierge of a plush hotel and ask him to score you a bag of H.

Mild relief was at hand when I was taken off the plane assisted by medics, who gave me the substitute medicine to tide me over, which straightened me out. Next stop Adelaide.

"Please I need heroin right now, find someone please, please" My demeanour was all dishevelled and I was looking like the fucking Grim Reaper of Oz by the end of the week. It was a fucking nightmare to be honest. Now I had nothing left, how the fuck was I going to complete this tour? A question answered rather promptly after the final embarrassment and nail in the proverbial coffin – I was sent packing back to England. I involved the promoter and people close to him, one in particular a fully-recovered and rehabilitated heroin addict, because of the state I was in, and she had to return to that dark world to help score me some poison. By the end of it I was in tears because of the guilt. Dignity and pride fucked off out the window completely as I smiled myself off to Noddy land looking like a bad extra from *Trainspotting*. The secret was definitely out now, as the drum and bass grapevine is a busy one.

Pete got a blow-by-blow account from a worried Bailey who had already phoned home to deliver him the news that his best mate had just had the audacity to come all the way to Australia all inclusive only to call in sick with a heroin addiction. It was one of the lowest points in my life with everyone asking, "What's this I keep hearing about you in Australia?"

My answer was always to say that it wasn't as bad as people were making out and that I was just sick for a few days. I saw Bailey a few weeks later and blatantly lied, telling him how sorry I was for putting him through all that and that I was sorting myself out, going to clean myself up. It was all bollocks.

I still tried to function back on English soil with about £2.50 to my name and a £100 a day habit. An old school friend offered me a bit of work painting and decorating, but although as hard as I tried to convince people I was all right I was far from it. I mean I was so bad I could fuck up a cup of coffee, let alone a window sill. The harsh fact now was, rumours on the D&B scene of me being a junky got worse and worse as arguments broke out between people close to me who tried to stand by me and the people who wanted to turn their backs. True to form though, when bad luck decides to pay me a visit, it usually has a long run up before striking me right bang in the nuts.

One night I was working in Fabric as the meagre morsels of work came my way. Actually let me correct that, when I say meagre, around this period, I was still pretty much busy working at raves like Desire, Helter Skelter, Metalheadz, World Dance and a few others, but the wages are gone so quick I might as well have been on my arse. Anyhow, it was near on the end of the night and we were getting ready to leave, and there was a bundle of coats behind the DJ section. In the dark Helen scrambled through the pile. Please note that this was in front of everyone, she wasn't tucking it into a head bag like she was shoplifting for Tachini gear as some of my mates did back in the day.

So sifting through to find hers and a pal of mine's coat she walked out with 2 coats but accidentally took one that didn't belong to her, my pal or me either, but she bundled what she believed were our coats into the boot of the car. We did not even realise the conundrum of woe until we got home. There were phone calls and messages the next day and a visit by my neighbour which was when we discovered that I was in possession of a coat that needed to be returned.

Now do not get me wrong, it comes with the territory and when it comes to hearing about people becoming a victim of drug addiction, there is usually only one reaction, because people are people. If it was Pete Nice or Inch for example, people would have said "Oh, it's Pete, it's a mistake, I'll catch him later to get it back." But because it was me, by the time the rumour mill had finished its deliberation, the unanimous consensus was that Flux the skaghead had nicked an £800 Gucci coat.

And the owner of the Gucci coat was? Not naming names, but he was the brother of one of the main MCs on the circuit, who was ready to do everything in his powers to get the coat back. This would come via a mutual associate, but the Scene had already played judge, jury and executioner. Helen didn't help, as after getting fed up with the threatening phone calls, she was giving it Charlie big potatoes down the phone threatening to burn the coat and all sorts, when I was trying to reason with them. As time went on, I learned that there were certain people fuelling the fire so to speak, which also didn't help.

When it was finally arranged that I could return the coat to its rightful owner, I tried explaining this unfortunate misunderstanding to our neighbour and the lease holder of the flat that me and Helen had bought. This fella was not averse to the current affairs of the underworld, having had many conversations with him when me and Helen first moved in. He gave the impression that he was fully connected and he was also a close pal with the coat's owner.

Unluckily for me, he couldn't give a fuck what I had to say. He did kindly note that I was lucky to have the privilege of keeping my two kneecaps for stealing this expensive coat from one of his people. Because as you well know by now, when you are struggling a bit to make ends meet, which includes payments under contractual agreement with leaseholders who turn out to be the coat owner's best pal, whose version would I expect him to believe?

There were also other contributing factors, not to do with me, but another person associated with me. There were some minor disagreements going on at the time, 'keep away from my wife' kind of incidents that seemed to trigger an unreasonable response towards me. When the people concerned switched and set out to end my name and respect on the scene, I was an easy target and so the seed was sown. From what I was hearing at one point he was declaring all-out war, and words of anger from the coat owner's inner circle, had me swerving certain places because I was certain my life was being threatened.

One time, I missed a message from the promoters of a do I was scheduled to work and on the night, the surprised faces were all quizzing me why I've turned up after they've left me messages. They suggested that I leave immediately, which I did after getting my wages, especially after the daggers I was getting in there from old Gucci coat and his crew. Believe me it was totally escalated, there was plenty gun talk going on I was told and even promoters threatened about getting their dance ruined if I was on the bill as well.

All this as a result of me having an addiction, in a scene that is rife and goes hand in hand with drugs, let's have it right. OK I'm not bigging up or promoting drug abuse by any means, but the hypocrisy of some people turning their noses up at me, you'd have thought these were Mother Theresa's or Catholic altar boys for fuck sake. You take away a joint or bit of nose candy away and see how cranky some of these fuckers get, then tell me if it's not the same thing.

It was starting to get to a point when I was considering falling back into that wartime state I was constantly in during the days down in Brighton, what would anyone else have done? It's them or me now and when I'm backed into a corner, I'm going all in, what the fuck have I got to lose.

I explained all that was going on to good people of mine who I had done bits and pieces for over the years. This was after Reggie had got word to them and had been going on at me for weeks to stick the boot in first. Despite all my troubles, for these guys, because of my history with them and favours and scores I had settled for them over time, they were ready and willing to help me out, to make the problem go away so to speak, by promising they could make it look like random racial attacks.

At the time I pondered over it for a while and I would have been happy to take them up on their offer but knowing my luck, if some poor cunt got hit by a bus at that time and I was on the same street, I probably would have got the blame for it, either that or some other poor cunt taking a battering due to mistaken identity. I'd be better off and have more pleasure sorting it out myself.

Luckily for me, the whole saga was ended mutually as stakeholders of the drum and bass scene wanted an end to it because an assassination of an MC, me in particular, at an event is bad for business in anyone's book and I think crucially discovering that the coat was genuinely picked up by mistake when my pal's own coat eventually turned up.

Even though things quietened down, it was all water under the bridge now, but at the time, this incident, compounded with turning up for gigs late all the time, a few no-shows and the fiasco in Australia, had already sown the seeds of doubt. From then on, as far as many of the personnel on the scene were concerned, people I was not so long ago having a laugh and a joke with were entertaining the fact that not only is MC Flux an unreliable skaghead cunt, he is now an unreliable, THIEVING skaghead cunt.

CHAPTER 20

ENFORCER

I have to admit, violence was something that throughout the years had been more or less part and parcel of whatever I was involved with and as you may have already read, it always gave me a weird sense of enjoyment. But it wasn't always one way, and on a few occasions I found myself getting severely served up. For example in 1980, I was knocking about with a few skinheads and rude boys, all schoolmates. Back then everyone was into that two-tone scene that came about when bands like Madness, the Specials and the Beat came to prominence. During this time, there were loads of parties we would go to, and sometimes 15 to 20 of us would jump on buses to parties we were invited to.

One occasion I was seeing a girl from over Coulsdon way, who I had met at a party the previous week and she had invited me and my mates to a party at one of her mates. We all moon-stomped to Selector's *On my radio* and *Too much too young* by the Specials and after a couple of bring your own cans of Hofmeister later, the party had ended. After offering to walk her home, I got the kiss and fumble of her tits over her Harrington jacket, remembering that as a schoolboy, this was classed as a right result back then as I so rudely mentioned in the first chapter. My teenage urges satisfied, I walked humbly to the bus stop, as most of my mates would have been long gone on their way back to Croydon by then, and waited for the 190 to take me home, not realising the 7 strong crew tailing me as I scanned the bus schedule.

"What are you doing around here nigger?" came a menacing voice from behind me and now I'm thinking, "Fuck sake."

I turn around and realise my predicament. From what I recall the gang surrounding me were in Fred Perry polo shirts, braces and 12 hole-Doc Marten boots. I was dressed in my Crombie coat and stay press trousers, surely they would see I was one of them? Foolishly I threw what I could at the one doing all the talking, but was soon in a ball being kicked to fuck as they rained a world of pain on my black arse and insulted me with every blow... "BLACK CUNT!" and "HAVE SOME OF THIS YOU MONKEY!" as the voices fade away.

It was the last thing I heard for the next few days. I was lying in a hospital bed for two weeks, looking like I had been run over by a tram filled with hippos that got off and done a dance on my face. Mates of mine over the years still believe that this beating is the reason I am such an airhead and have the memory of a goldfish, which I think is bollocks by the way. I have to admit though, it was the worst shoeing I had taken in my life even to this day and the reason for the mind set in me after that, that if I'm outnumbered like that again, I'm evening up the odds by any means necessary or I'm tooling up, which is not a point to be proud of for any of you young readers out there.

Admittedly I have had many scraps over the years and been lectured by many pals about my ability to detonate at the slightest provocation, whether involved with football or drug rivals or just simply down to road rage - work that one out, I don't even drive. Again I'm reminded of a time we were going to Rage during its heyday. I was with Pete Nice, TJB and Inch when we had an altercation with some prick who cut us up, then looking like he wanted it, got out of his vehicle at a set of traffic lights. Jumping out with a baseball bat I stung the geezer big time in the ribs, only to find out when his passenger jumped out that the geezer just wanted to inform us that our brake lights wasn't working. I did apologise in the end but this is an example of how easy I used to flare up.

So throughout the years I have been always at hand to help any pals that were in a bit of aggro or a sister's boyfriend needed a slap, and I was usually first number on the speed dial button. It was no surprise, receiving a call from a fella I knew who was at the top of the tree at the time doing narcotics distribution, This fella was an old Nifty 50 head that I knew from football who I had done plenty of ecstasy business with in the past. I was asked if I could help in recovering some debt.

In fact, the request came second hand. The fella on the phone was another Nifty 50 face asking me to back him up as he said he could always rely on me to do a decent job when it was time to pay someone a visit. I was on my arse at this time, which was mid-2006. My addiction had taken over my life and after a few jobs where I had become too unreliable, either turning up late for dos or not turning up at all in some cases, when I would fill my veins with poison and black out. It was inevitable the MC bookings would severely dry up, so the chance to earn a few bob was not something I could turn down.

The job turned out to be a piece of piss in the end but I was sternly instructed that I was allowed to show a bit of steel to put the frighteners on but they were persistent in letting me know that they wouldn't be comfortable unless I promised that I would use it in an orderly manner, being a loose cannon and all that.

"You are a cranky cunt, ain't having you tooled up with a chiv and doing a murder stretch, we collect the money slap him about and that's it" My boss had instructed.

After a bit of breakfast in a local greasy spoon in Croydon, we discussed at length the pattern of events and the pending plan of action to resolve the matter, a meeting which went well and our objective set out. Arriving at the designated address, I stood back as the other two approached the door. I was told this fella had sat on a safe house that was used to stash big parcels of gear and the place was utilised as the count house which, surprisingly, was identified and robbed, with the main fella facing a huge loss. In this game you develop a sixth sense that make you aware of when someone is trying to get one over on you, hence the visit to this unfortunate individual.

I'm now introduced to the geezer as my two pals stand back asking the questions.

"Where's the gear and the money?"

"I swear I don't know, I had nothing to do with it" was the feedback.

This alone to me is admission enough. I introduce him to cheaters justice and the 'Casino Hammer' which if you don't know is something I picked up from that scene in the movie *Casino* where Bobby D playing Sam Rothstein asks "You can have the money and the hammer or walk out of here with nothing, which one will it be?"

A very useful way to get the truth out of people. The fella would eventually cough up the majority of the dough over the next few days and fully squared up by the end of the week, and I earned myself a lifeline to pay bills and stuff like that. It was only ever enough to last me a couple of weeks and it wasn't exactly a cure for my addictive personality, which was probably half the idea as I was available for more enforcement work over the next few months.

Unfortunately, I was instructed to put away the casino hammer, my bosses were saying it was a bit too strong, but overall they were happy with my work. Although losing the weight due to the skag I was still strong enough to cause damage with my fists, but I do feel because of my predicament I was taken advantage of a little bit as I was only paid enough to keep me interested in more work. But hey, it was a few hours' work and beggars can't be choosers. My options at the time were limited, so hanging fellas out of windows and chasing some through housing estates with meat cleavers became a norm for a couple of months as the main fella paid visits to people who had taken the piss, which had me thinking, if I was more efficient like this during my time in Brighton and had paid more attention to detail I could have been sunning myself with the wife in Majorca on a big boat instead of freezing my cock off all day looking for these pricks that owed money.

I saw Pete during this time, which was first time in months possibly since the Watford playoff match back in May (2006) when the main fella, my boss, had a birthday party over in the Red Lion pub in Shooters Hill. Pete had been living over on this manor for some time now, after settling down and shacking up with a girl from Greenwich. It was only on a handful of occasions, mainly football, when I would really see him over the past 7 years. In fairness he was in a serious relationship now, having hit his 40s and mortgaged up, so I could hardly blame him. Seeing me, I could see the disappointment in his face as I walked into the pub.

Don't get me wrong, he still held me dear to his heart truth be told, they all did, but I knew he was hearing all this stuff about me and the heroin. Even though he wasn't about much with most of our mates, he still pretty much was in contact with loads of people, many worried about my appearance or telling him about incidents going on around me, all the rumours from the scene, arguments with other MCs, promoters docking my pay because of my time-keeping and work drying up because of it. After evading the inevitable for as long as I possibly could, the flat was eventually repossessed and all my belongings transported to temporary accommodation in black bin liners. That was the day of my wedding anniversary.

Speaking of which, my story with Helen ends here. It's horrible, even disgusting when I think back about what I put her through and I am truly sorry from the bottom of my heart for how things turned out for us after shattering our marital dreams. What a heart of gold that woman was. In her eyes I could never do no wrong, and she lost many friends to stand by her man. If you read this Helen, I'm happy for you now though babe, even though I've said it in person to you and we have both conquered our demons, you are one truly remarkable woman and I'm sorry, for what it's worth, for everything.

As I was saying, it was the incident that finally brought it home to him back in 2000 following the little trip to Australia with Bailey that was the lowest point for me as far as Pete was concerned. He now had a live independent witness and ever since then I knew deep down he was totally different towards me. For the most part Pete had always given me the benefit of the doubt, despite what my other mates like Face and Killa, Inch and everyone else thought, but after 2003 onwards it seemed, harsh as it may seem, he had run out of patience with me.

I was lying to convince people I was straight, especially Pete, he's my best pal, but you don't have to be a scientist to know people on heroin are on a different planet and if it was obvious the sky was blue, I'd tell you it was red. Even though he gave me umpteen opportunities to come clean with him, I just couldn't burden him, other than using him as a source of income for me whenever I was in dire straits. All he got was hard luck stories and empty promises that he would get the score back next week or the tenner back when I got paid. It was probably the reason why he would rather swerve me than have to put his hand in his pocket every time I saw him.

Pete Nice is what he is though, and still, as long as I was able to show I was functioning, he would just treat me as normal. He was becoming more relaxed around me the more beverages we all consumed, although it seemed a strange choice for all us CPFC fans and hooligans to be drinking on our bitter rivals Charlton's manor. The main fella's business partners were from over this way so we treated the place like it was one of ours anyway.

The main fella promises me the possibility of more work, although I was already aware that with a busy few months of retribution and recovery, there wouldn't be much need for my further services anyway. Whilst in front of Pete, Robbie and a few other pals on the table, some of the events of the past few months were revealed as the booze and sniff took over with stories of past boot offs at Palace and me and the casino hammer, which is the topic everyone was waxing lyrical about, saying what a top negotiating tool it was.

I could see Pete's look of despair, although there was also slight admiration. He muttered "cranky cunt" out loud with a wry smile, as I looked on embarrassed from the appraisals. As expected, more work never came my way, following that. Like I said it only takes a few cracked ribs and fingers and the odd Chelsea smile to restore the status quo, but it seemed the main fella was witnessing that I was a little too out of control and would become more of a hindrance than a solution, as they were sure I would end up topping someone.

During this period, hard as it is to recall, no one was buying the fact that I was OK, because I know, when there were days I was desperate, I didn't give a fuck who knew. I came through the 80s and the 90s high on life, but the millennium years I was going through days high, but lifeless. I even took the 9 to 5 route for the first time in around 15 years and attempted to hold down a few 'normal' jobs during this period, but they were all disasters.

Trying to recollect and process incidents and things going on in my life around this time has been extremely difficult. The fact that I was getting myself into so many scrapes and scraps, from having had so many touches through unlimited avenues during my early years, earning money in unethical ways and putting the hurt on people, was starting to make me believe that this period in time, as I crashed and burned in a heroin-induced stupor, I was being punished for past actions. But surely that could not be the case, because my downfall had all been self-inflicted. It was as though I had hit some kind of self-destruct button and my whole life came crashing down around me.

Only the permanent cycle of heroin had me forgetting everything, thinking "Fuck my life" and then pondering after, on the come down, how this would all end, and I wasn't alone. Discussions in my own family were running on the same topic and funnily enough, Pete believes it was probably around this period he was resigned to the fact I was an addict and half expected a phone call to say I had died of an overdose. He tells me this as he jokes about Mr Kirk's Nightmare.

"Mr Nice, do you have a pal called Flux, MC Flux?"

"Yeeaaahsss."

"I'm sorry Mr Nice - your pal is dead."

But all joking aside, by 2007 I had lost contact with all the boys on a one-to-one level and our relationship was more or less non-existent.

Killa and Face were about now and again at drum and bass events, but pretty much just avoided me. Pete was away from the manor and was starting a new family with his wife Ashley, who was pregnant at the time. I heard the news from Inch and was quite distressed at the fact that after all we'd been through, I should have been with him celebrating and wasn't, but I can understand why and I had to accept it. Much as I tried to deny it, everyone knew and I know now Pete, Face & Killa were all getting bits of info back off people who had seen me looking fucked.

Even worse was the night when I tuned up at Face's house around midnight one evening with claret everywhere having had all my teeth smashed out of my head after I was blindsided by some cunt with a knuckle duster. Now the story around this at the time was that the security guard from Lidl had caught me thieving and given me a slap, which is bollocks, because security people employed by legitimate businesses do not go about knocking people's teeth out for shoplifting. It was my own fault, to be fair, I was usually ready for confrontation, but the telephone conversation at the time must have been of high importance because we were in the process of repossession and my marriage on the brink of divorce.

All I remember was being on the phone to Helen at the time and giving this hench of an Afro Caribbean male a glance, with that "who the fuck is this cunt looking at?" stare. I had not paid him much attention after that and was literally just putting my mobile into my jacket pocket when all of a sudden I felt like I'd collided with a bus and soon after I saw stars and then darkness. Now I have had many a punch to the face in my time but the force and sharpness of the blow makes me believe that either he had a baseball bat, which would be pretty unlikely because a nigger Babe Ruth I definitely would have clocked onto, or he had an iron fist, and by the evidence of the damage left and the loss of half my pearly whites, I'm 100% it was the latter.

It took me a while to come to and the dizzy and confused state I was in it's a miracle that I made it to Face's house at all. Not at any point did any cunt even stop to inspect my wellbeing, which was beginning to give me the impression that the passion and humanity in the people of Croydon was not quite second to none. I even remember a group of teenagers casually stepping over my outstretched legs as I wrestled myself up with the assistance of a brick wall before heading off like a newborn baby wildebeest in the general direction of mayday hospital, stopping at Face's house, who helped get me cleaned up before fucking me off to A&E.

So it seemed that I was losing more friends than a rat informer in a mafia setup, but one person I couldn't seem to shake off was my good pal and infamous sociopath, Reggie Anderson. He had been in and out of prison so many times since the mid-90s. His longest was the six-year stretch for 20 grand's worth of cocaine and heroin rap that saw armed police acting on information obtained by some 'fucking grass' or another. They came crashing through his 1st floor flat SAS style, resulting in his incarceration. This was a culmination of always wanting to play catch up and get his empire back, because up to this day he claims me as the sole destroyer of it, like it was me that encouraged him to threaten civilian bar owners with guns and chivs, like it was me telling him to drive the car into a shop window after trying to out run the police, eh eh?

Truth is, we both lived life on the edge, but our luck was as bad as Tottenham Hotspurs' push for 4th place in the premiership and not just bad luck, some of the worst luck you could ever perceive when it comes to earning a bit of poke to get back on our feet. So after a few shorter terms in prison for a variety of offences, he had got himself wrapped up in some deal to move some gear, something I wouldn't have had the luxury of, because my line of credit had run thin and people would not be entrusting me with anything valuable to hold or try to pass on.

Being hoodwinked by some people who sold him a kilo of Persil had left Reggie desperately in need of some income, and it was one of these situations where life gets as precarious as a stack of dominoes lined up on the hard shoulder of the M25, where the slightest meander

264

has everything going horizontal. Reggie ended up with not only an anonymous but tasty Pakistani firm looking to kill him but now, following a subsequent deal, another firm was after him when the promise to deliver some parcels of sniff went awry because the shipment got back and wouldn't wash because it was pharmaceutical grade and useless. So this little firm was now on his case wanting their money.

The day I got the call from him, he said he was bang in trouble and could I meet him in the Wilton. At the time I was a little confused because he mentioned "bang in trouble" and "these fellas want their money", but I didn't have a pot to piss in, so my only assumption was that he had unfriendly people with him and the request was for me to come heavy. I had had one of these calls from him before, during our time in Brighton, which ended up with me and Nifty chasing off these black fellas out of a pub in Lewes who had tried to muscle him out of his money because he was being a flash cunt, as he was. If I remember, I'm sure these guys were Usain Bolt's relations because I've never seen niggers run so fast.

So here I am, making my way to the Wilton. I remember it was a hot day in July and I was sweating my bollocks off in the 3 quarter length Burberry coat. By the time I got there I had to sit round the corner for a couple of minutes in the shade to cool off. I wasn't in good shape and I needed a bit of composure to complete this mission, so I get him up on the blower as he panics, "Where the fuck are you?"

"I'm here" I said and asked him, "how many they got?"

"Two grand" was his response. Not an intricate code, but I understood.

So this is the situation now, these fellas want their money, so here they are, one is the brains and one obviously the muscle, so if the money isn't forthcoming, Reggie is going for a drive. Now we're at the Thomas A Farley, formerly the Wilton Arms, formerly the Muddy Waters. Its heyday is long gone and on a Wednesday afternoon, it's a ghost town, just a few grandads having a read with a pint of ale, so if Reggie has to go, he's going, and no one is going to stop them.

I enter the pub and take up a seat next to Reggie and opposite the wannabe Don Ciccio Montana of Sicily and his meathead bodyguard (probably nicknamed Knuckles). In fact he wasn't that big when you stood up close to him, and even smaller when they realised what I had brought for them. I educate them, I sit down and show them the end of the huge Magnum Desert Eagle. This tool was a heavy fucker and I was hoping that there wouldn't be the need to pull back on that trigger. The mood immediately changes and Reggie is now in high spirits, after the initial shock, when I'm putting it on the geezers, who are in total meltdown now.

"See this you cunt? This is what I'm talking about. What the fuck you saying now?"

"Whoa, whoa, whoa, leave it out mate, we just came for our money, what's this all about?" the shorter of the two guys said, with his hands up in the air. They were no longer acting like big time gangsters and Reggie used this opportunity, after a few days of bullying from this firm, to set an example.

"You cunts trying to take me for a mug, fuck your money" he says. We then explain that these things happen in business and sometimes you have to take a hit from time to time.

"Do yourselves a favour and fuck off back to toy town" I said, as they backed out of the doorway. Fuck knows how they got away so quick after. We followed them outside but they were in their motor screeching off like Formula 1.

Reggie's dropped me back home and we had a few beers and a few lines reminiscing on days gone by. Our day got even better when I received a bit of poke from the fella I was holding the artillery for, I didn't let on that it had been moved from the place he had asked me to pug it up for him as a favour for a couple of grams of gear and an extra monkey. It later transpired that after a tip off, his drum was raided by Old Bill a couple of days later which had him thankful that I was able to help him hide that bit of tool for him. That's probably the only stroke of luck I've been blessed with for the last 5 or so years.

It was kind of ironic, as I became unreliable with things that could earn me a decent wedge and supplement my escalating habit, that I gained nothing from the game other than a rush on par with my first heroin buzz. It was the only time when people could really rely on me and that was the exposure to violence, which would continue, as the group I used to get involved with in rows at football started to get out and about again and were calling for Black Rodney, the game cunt, who was always up for a row.

CHAPTER 21

DIRTY 30

We decided before writing the book that we would divide up my involvement with the Palace firms into a couple of sections, and no it wasn't just because it's Palace, like I know how a lot of cherubs will be giving it large that Palace couldn't fill up a pub, let alone a book. The main reason was because this wasn't going to follow the same template as the ones about super firms talking about who had the biggest cock (no disrespect) but mainly because unlike some of the other books about football hooligans, surprisingly, being a football thug for me was not a 24-7 365 days a year job, and there was, believe it or not, other shit to do like shag birds, go raving, become an international music entertainer, become addicted to drugs and fuck up a criminal empire.

Due to the entertainment business I hadn't gone down there with a mob for a while, but I had started going to a few games between 1995 and 98, compliments of Bruce Dyer, who I'd become friends with after sorting out a few guest lists for him for Jungle raves when he first came to London. Any ticket request was just a phone call to him to get comped for any home game at Selhurst Park, and as the UK garage scene took off I became friends with a few players alongside Bruce, like Leon Mackenzie from Palace and Sean Newton and Richard Rufus from Charlton. I even had Bruce and Richard play at an event I was promoting with Sherry at the time, as they tried to boost their pastime profile as DJs on the circuit.

So at Palace my only last known boot off was the fun we had a

Neasden in 1996. A relatively quiet spell had the hooligan network coming down and enjoying a few hours unchallenged, confirming that Selhurst Park was a family club. As the internet expanded and hooligan forums became the new communication tool (for the Old Bill also) I was surprised to hear that rumours were rife that no one ever saw any opposition from Crystal Palace ever, with many Charlton keyboard warriors leading the bullshit.

By 1999 Pete was hanging out with a few mates on a regular basis, Robbie, Rangers Paul, Jack the biscuit, Hammers, Boycie, Jermaine, Ginger, Martin, Lee and a few others, lads he'd known through working in telecoms. With a bit more dough in his pocket now he's working in the City, his weekends were often involving meeting up with these boys and getting out on the lash early doors, and on a few Saturday afternoons they would attend the games at Palace, including the odd away game.

Let's make no mistake, although ready to stand up if required, and there was the odd skirmishes and standoffs with other like-minded individuals, they were not classing themselves as 'Palace's firm' by any stretch of the imagination. Their main intention was the booze and the sniff and giving the stewards a bit of grief from time to time with their drunken behaviour, all in the name of lads on the lash. However it was this lot that organised the trip to a midweek cup match away to Liverpool in early 2000, when I was surprised to get the call from Pete asking if I wanted to come. I hadn't seen him for nearly six months at that point, but I had spoken to him quite regularly when he rang me up and of course he would mention to me the stuff going on. I was often trying to tell him to write on these football forums and educate some of the pricks on there, but Pete explained the cyber hoolies were having none of it, Palarse were shit and that was that.

We set off the Tuesday morning 18 handed, piled into a minibus plus the aptly named Hoolibus, which was a Mercedes Viano people carrier that Hammers, who was a salesman at Croydon Mercedes, accosted from his work.

The booze and class A-filled journey saw us land in Liverpool early afternoon. We stopped off at our digs to drop our luggage off and then we got on the booze. I sneaked off at every opportunity to get a blast of H to keep me going. Earlier at service station piss stops, all the lads were taking group photos and I was missing on every occasion, getting on the nod.

Pete, Robbie and the boys played pool and Pete impressed them all with stories of me getting involved in past shenanigans. These Palace lads were a few years younger than Pete and me and were saying that many of them used to be in awe of the legendary 'Spider', the name they used to call me during the early nineties when they used to see me going nuts at Palace and having it with different firms. Also Pete reminds them all about the 'legend' being even noticed by Millwall lads when Kevin from the Blue, who he worked with at BT, pulled him up one day with the knowledge that he knew many Palace lads, and quizzed him, "who's the black fella with the spider hair cut like your'n, wearing a red Burberry mac down the Palace on Saturday?" He declared that I was a marked man following that game against them in Oct 1989, where there was a lot of verbal between the segregated fans and me offering up any of them to have it with me, as you do. It was kind of weird listening to Pete telling these stories the way he was as if in a strange way he was proud of me. At least there was something he could be proud of given my recent track record.

We headed off to the Arkles pub later on and everyone consumed more liquor. I bump into some old Nifty 50 faces and caught up on old times. Some were also impressed that lads were organising and getting out and about at least. It was a blinding turnout from us despite the result on the pitch that night and inadvertently set the scene for us getting things back together when a few weeks later we all travelled to Watford with more or less the same boys, including Face and Killa. As we travelled up, a couple of the main Nifty lads, including Frankie, were getting everyone prepped that if we stuck together with what we had, we could still have a bit of fun as a proper firm. We landed on a Watford pub 20 handed and confronted the lads in there, but these were times when police were getting a tighter stranglehold on mobs having it in town centres as only verbals and introductions saying 'we're here' took place before we were surrounded by officers demanding that we leave.

I remember also vividly some strange Watford dude with piercings and weird clobber bowling into a pub we were sat in after getting all sarky. "What 'ave we here? Palace has a firm?"

He was about to be duly knocked out before a couple of Old Bill manhandled him out the door, so he must have been known to them as he continued stalking us for the rest of the day. Without really getting into much toe to toe action that day, it set the tone and slowly we were getting together and becoming a decent mob again.

The following season again in Watford we were more or less the same number wise, although a few dropped out who were only interested in boozing rather than scrapping on a Saturday afternoon, a good thing no doubt as even 20 handed with everyone standing and backing up his mate we would do all right. The 4 of us, Frankie me and a couple of others, took it upon ourselves to organise everyone, rallying the troops so to speak.

Landing in Watford it took a couple of minutes from disembarking off the train and entering the first boozer to have Watford lads chased out of the pub after being attacked by us. Again not a lot to write home about, but as the season went on we were getting together and having it with different pockets of mobs here and there as we begin to travel together. We even had a late recruitment drive at the beginning of the 2001/02 season which by 2003 included the introduction of some game youth lads as well, like Smiler, Young Dan, the Carter brothers and the Twins, so under the guidance of Frankie and the Old Niftys we began to turn the tables on certain mobs.

Stockport County 2000

That season Palace were in dire straits leading to a last day of the season relegation battle against Stockport County. We'd been getting things more organised recently and organised a team of boys to travel up via coach to Edgely Park. Reggie had just been released after a 6-year sentence for narcotics and was giving it the old "I'm behaving myself today" bollocks. We gathered at the Crescent Arms for the early doors meet. Pete, Robbie, Dom and a few other lads had been regular at Palace that season and as I said it started out more for the beer and a laugh than getting into any hooligan activity.

The organising of pubs to meet and away games saw us getting lads together, influencing some old Nifty 50 heads to get out and about again, putting the word about at every opportunity of where to drink and stations to meet and when to all bowl down together to the game. That season saw a nice turnout at home against Norwich after payback was planned when some Palace were bullied at the away game by Norwich NHS or whatever the fuck they were called. After we fronted a mob of nervous young casuals to get something going after the game, the Selhurst Park fixture saw nothing more than a few handbags as Palace attacked a few Norwich and caused the gavvers a few headaches that day. Nothing major but it was showing that we were getting our act together and letting some of these trappy cunts know if they wanted it.

We also had a few young Millwall NTO chaps down with us that Pete and Robbie had got friendly with while holidaying in Faliraki. Just to make things clear, they were only down to have a few beers with them, they were not teaming up with Millwall for Norwich. Anyway other than the cat and mouse with police not a lot really happened that day.

The day we left for Stockport we had some good heads on the packed coach and beer, cocaine and the banter flowed. It was a mixture of game lads, seasoned hooligans and lads coming along for the crack, hoping Palace would avoid relegation, with Frankie offering to set fire to the burger stall and roll it down the terrace if we got relegated. We landed in Stockport and were plot up in a boozer before heading to the game. Nothing exciting to write home about, we were getting the odd reports of sightings of Stockport boys but all avenues were more or less false alarms. Many unconditioned heads now started to complain of cigarette and beer-induced fatigue as we jogged, fast walked and sprinted after all the false reports we were getting, until finally, after getting collared by Old Bill, we headed for the game.

In the ground there were many more of the old boys all over the place, many old Nifty 50 faces, and it was a while before I went round shaking hands and saying hello as the game went on. I was in one area where a few of the Palace lads were talking to Stockport lads they knew from following England, but I wasn't having none of that bollocks and I was sounding them out asking where their boys are, with the Palace boys looking at me quizzically about my attitude. "Fuck 'em, it's what where here for innit?"

I was wasting my time. They all sat silently as if I wasn't even there and were relieved when I finally fucked off to see Pete and the others, just as Dougie Freedman scored and triggered off a pitch invasion.

After we celebrated with the players we realised by sheer coincidence we had 15 old school Whitehorse and South Croydon squaring off with Stockport fans on the centre circle after the home fans took offence to the liberty we had taken on their pitch. More verbals and the offer "You want it?" and the usual bollocks ensued but it was as though everyone realised at the same time we were possibly being captured by Sky Sports cameras. After getting a few "outside... see us outside" requests, we returned to the old school terracing of the away end.

Our safety in the championship was secured with the 1 nil win and we were all in a good mood heading back to the coaches. Dom got a call from the England Palace lads saying Stockport were right behind us and when we turn around they were bouncing up and down on the other side of the road, all sounding like your typical Coronation Street resident. "Come on Palace, you fuckin' coon mob" (they were also calling us a Paki firm all over the internet that evening).

We weren't sure of their numbers at first but me, Dom, Pete, Rob, Frankie and a few more led a charge into them which had them backed off as police straight away waded in and Stockport were back bouncing again as the police turned their batons on us. One of our lads recognised one of the Stockport group as a BNP lad from Oldham, some fat cunt whose name I can't remember, it was clear now though that it was a combined mob of Stockport and Oldham and fair play, they were no more than 15-20 handed breaking away from the gavvers and tried to make some kind of effort at us. We were happy to send 'em back with a few slaps as some minor skirmishes had the already organised GMP swinging batons and using horses to separate the two groups.

Without thinking, as was my fucked-up state of mind at the time, I drew out a carpenter's knife and took a swipe to within a cunt's hair of this BNP prick's boat. Pete is witnessing this and is frozen as he sees the Old Bill on horseback arrive to intervene just as I lash out, missing fat boy by a very slim margin. If I had connected I was bang to rights, but by a miracle the handbags are dispersed and we are all cattle marched back onto our coach. Most of us were chuckling at the hilarious site of one of ours getting put on his arse by a galloping police horse during the scuffle. Pete described the blade incident as time standing still and gave me a good old ear bashing about it as we take our seats on the coach.

"Where'd the steel come from? You're fucking mad you cunt, that was you gone if you connected, what the fuck you playing at?"

Like I explained previously, our relationship was strained at that point and had been for a couple of years after he discovered or at least was suspicious about my drug habits, which were at an all-time high (or low depending on what side of the fence you were standing on), but later during the journey back we did still manage to share a few jokes about old times.

Grimsby Town 2001 & 2002

We planned this trip as another piss up and opportunity to get the newly-formed Dirty 30 active. I recall the name came about one Saturday, I think it was a week after a Fulham game when about 25 or

30 of us were trying to get at a contingent of Fulham lads but were battened off by Old Bill. We were joking about afterwards that we weren't quite Nifty 50 again and needed a name. I think it was left at SE25 Casuals at the time. We decided against the 50 because it was what it was and the good old days were well behind us, but I was out the following week with Robbie and Frankie and a couple other boys in Croydon for a quiet beer.

We were discussing some nasty incidents we had been involved with recently like the tear-up at Victoria against a few Chelsea that got lairy, along with a raid on a pub nearby as a result of an ongoing beef with some of our lads and a local mob which saw the aftermath leaving many of our rivals injured by metal bars, bar stools and CS gas. The Dirty 30 name was bandied about and in the end that was what we went along with and also with the reasoning that we would have to go in dirty to get our reputation back and change the perception of some cheeky cunts running their mouths off on the internet.

So any ways, the main lads called an early morning meet at Kings Cross where we were optimistic about the 40-odd heads that turned up to make the long trip to Cleethorpes, but as was with Palace during this period, we ended up with 15 of us leaving the ground after 15 minutes and 2-0 down to go on the piss, hotly pursued by the Old Bill. We eventually slipped their surveillance by nipping out of the back door of the pub and onto a moody-looking housing estate where we found an out of the way boozer, with every intention of just having a beer. It was a few hours before we emerged and made our way back towards the station to make our way home, tracked this time by a couple of Grimsby lads, but we paid them no attention.

As we crossed a main road, the police we'd given the slip to earlier were out of their vans and advising that if we didn't leave Grimsby immediately we would all end up in nick. We never gave them any lip or any aggro, we had had a bit of a skinful anyway. A couple of the lads had engaged them and joked with the Old Bill by asking how they had managed to lose 2 darkies in Grimsby, referring to me and Pete with the notion of us being the only back people in the town ever.

Immediately after this, around 40 Grimsby lads emptied a pub they were in and made a beeline for our small although tight crew. I traded blows with a couple and the Old Bill sprang into action. A combination of police truncheons and us up against it due to the numbers offered a bit of resistance. The Grimsby lads in all honesty were outnumbering our 15 plus the 8 or so gavvers when they attacked. We showed them the whites of our eyes but we could have come unstuck if Grimsby had taken more initiative.

Other than a few slaps dished out by either side it was over relatively quickly, with more police reinforcements as shoppers looked on. I remember a man and his wife getting a bit lippy towards me and Pete, as though they were outraged that 2 niggers had taken liberties bowling about on their manor like this.

We were eventually fucked off on the train while police continued to wade into a handful of Grimsby who continued to attack but ended up getting themselves and nicked after hurling racial insults to me and Pete. They were on the phone to our main lad as well later saying we took a liberty, but would not have it that there was only 15 of us.

We made the return trip the following season. This time again we set off 40 handed as we now had 20 youth on the firm, now tried and tested during a busy season as the Dirty 30 became more visible on the hooligan network. Calls were made to their lads and they were ready in Cleethorpes to welcome us for some payback. Unfortunately the train broke down, which delayed us, but the delay gave us an advantage as CBP (Cleethorpes Beach Patrol) called us as we waited on our stricken train and believed we were bullshitting and weren't coming at all.

We hadn't a choice now, and we were determined to get to Grimsby even more. When the train eventually continued the journey we again assured our Grimsby contact that we were coming. It must have dawned quickly on one of our newly recruited lads, Afghan Joe, that we might have a welcoming committee on arrival, because when we arrived at Doncaster or some other distant northern station he had all of a sudden developed a belly ache and jumped off the train, to a bellowing laugh from Killa as we all took the piss out of him about his severe meltdown after he had seemed up for it all day.

We finally landed in Grimsby at 3.30, with the youth having emptied the buffet of crockery and cutlery. With no gavvers to meet us we marched from the station through the city centre. We approached a pub with a few boys sitting outside and without even the confirmation they were their lads or not, they saw us and quickly scattered into the pub, setting the youth into action as cups, saucers, knives and forks peppered the boozer and we pursued the fleeing group into and through the pub. Before I knew it I was out the other side on my own, which had me worried to begin with before the door flew open as the rest of our lads exited.

Having made our announcement and with no sign of the CBP, we bowled out of the city centre and plotted up in a pub out of the way as calls went to and fro with reports that it wasn't their main boys that the youth had rained Virgin trains cutlery on. One of the CBP lads said in the Hooligan A-Z book that most of the lads were pissed off with waiting for us and had already gone to the game and struggled to get numbers to come and meet us. He also said he was in a small reconnaissance group of 3 who took a drive down to take a glimpse and confirmed us in People's Park with bottles and big sticks, as they jokingly called it 'On', sending the Dirty 30 youth in pursuit as they ran back to their car and sped off.

The residents must have thought it was a bizarre sight to see a bunch of cockneys congregated in their local park. It wasn't long before police vans came screeching up, truncheons at the ready as weapons were tossed into bushes. It was funny when one of ours shouted out, "all sit down and pretend we are having a picnic" to a chorus of laughter.

We were rounded up and section 60'd and it seems there were a couple of Old Bill who recognised me and Pete as part of the small group here last year, which we denied of course, with our witty pal piping up about us 'black boys' all looking the same. There was another attempt by a small group of CBP to attack us again by the train station, with a couple getting nicked as again the monkey and coon abuse was directed at us. Later the Grimsby lads were on the phone to us, only this time holding their hands up and having to say fair play at our efforts to get it on with them.

Walsall 2003

During a full on active season we were regularly getting 25-35 heads organised for most games. There were also the funny little incidents that would always provide us with plenty of banter with Frankie and other main lads ruining whoever was unfortunate enough to be the source of their amusement. Afghan Joe was the regular victim, not just for his Grimsby meltdown, when he had to find a hospital because he had a dickey tummy, but also the hilarious incident when we had mobbed up for Cardiff. We were bowling down together through a few back streets, Afghan Joe wasn't looking where he was going and got run over by a car. It wasn't a serious accident, the car was only doing 5 miles an hour, but he had 45 lads roaring with laughter after Killa had screamed out with laughter at the poor fucker as he dusted himself off after falling flat on his face. I don't think he turned out for any more games with us after that.

Nothing happened with Cardiff in the end. I went to meet them early doors in the Wetherspoon's opposite Thornton Heath train station. I was a little bit fucked going in there, probably half cut as well on the heroin. They were good as gold the Soul crew that were there, they provided me with the number and said get your boys ready then ring us. That's one confident mob, he didn't bat an eyelid to be fair, he knew the game. The Old Bill from London and Wales or Heddlu, however the fuck you pronounce it, turned up and began section 60ing everyone and with our spotter clocking me, he was fishing and asking what we were organising. The Soul Crew fella piped up saying we were mates and I had popped in for a quick drink.

I'm not sure what happened after that. I met my lot in Crystal Palace later, 40 of us began our march to try and meet Cardiff's mob. Someone decided that we take a silly back street tour so we could come out of one of the side roads off Thornton Heath High Street to surprise them. The Afghan Joe incident on the way down was all the entertainment we could manage because the Old Bill were all over us as soon as we popped our heads out of the side road and that was pretty much game over, Cardiff probably left with notion that we've got no firm.

The Walsall game was another early meet in Beckenham and this time the youth members organised a coach that we filled with 30-35 good heads, a mixture of us older heads including me, Pete Nice, Frankie, Robbie, Ashford Andy, Biggin Hill Joe, a couple old Nifty 50 faces and the youth. It was the usual turnout, beer, some class A and a bit of banter travelling up to the Midlands and everyone was in good spirits as the news came through on the radio of the England rugby team beating the Aussies for the Rugby World Cup. Not that I gave a fuck about it, fucking can't stand the sport, but at least the bugle is good and is small consolation for me and suppressing my need for the devil that is well hold of me at this point in time now that I am a full blown junkie.

We landed in Walsall just a little before opening time and entered the first boozer and settled in. The youth were up to their usual chestnut, ringing other youth mobs they had met at England games, when a fella walked in after calling one of our lads, a connection I wasn't even aware of. He was a Chelsea geezer living in Walsall who was also getting calls from Walsall's mob to inform us they were coming. We weren't convinced that they even had anything and continued our boozing when before we know it a small group of around 20 lads arrived calling it on. "Come on Palace you cockney cunts, we're here."

Saucy little fuckers, not sure they knew our numbers. In fairness we were more or less on the 30 mark as the pub emptied and we were backing them off up the road through a churchyard and into a market place. During the graveyard skirmish I did notice a couple of large clumps of masonry land beside us but it wasn't until one of the boys with us that day, fuck knows who he was, Tomb raider we later called him, because he was seen launching something which I realised was a Tomb headstone, which was a bit uncalled for, I thought.

I remember thinking at the time that duppy (a Jamaican term for ghost) would probably haunt that cunt for the rest of his life. The Walsall lads were chucking back as good as they got as well, so duppy would be on their case too I hoped. Other than a few slaps there wasn't much hand to hand combat going on, they weren't running as such but after the customary roar and missile throwing we had pretty much fucked them off and then had to make a move as sirens surrounded us.

A few of us walked back to the pub as I had stupidly had left my coat in there and after the little skirmish began to feel the winter chill. I was confronted by an angry landlord at the pub door who threatened to confiscate my coat. I duly educated him that a few smashed chairs and pool cues was better than a fire burning down his establishment before pushing past him to retrieve it. After getting a cab to Walsall station we had to call from another pub as the cry baby landlord refused to clue us in on any numbers for local cab firms.

We regrouped with the others, who then had us all in stitches on the train as we headed off to Birmingham when they said that after we had run the Walsall lot and jibbed away after hearing the sirens, four of us were surrounded by gavvers and then proceeded in giving the PCs the impression that they had just been terrorised by a group of Walsall hooligans. The sympathetic police officers fell for the tale, surprised but duly incensed that these poor innocent Crystal Palace football supporters who had made the effort to come to Walsall should have to be subjected to such horrendous violence. Our lads played up on it further and offered up the notion now that they had had enough and wanted to go home, so the police generously gave them a lift to the train station. As they rode shotgun and in the back of the police vehicle, the officers roundly apologized all the way for the behaviour of their locals and told them that Walsall was generally a peaceful town, before wishing our lads a fond farewell. So if anyone should ever want to take a trip for a lovely day out in Walsall and wants the services of a decent cab company in Walsall - ask the Old Bill.

As for the coach, well 35 set off on it, but only 9 returned home on it as the rest of us had a quite drink in Birmingham before setting off home to London on the train.

Leicester City 2004

Derby County was our opponent that weekend and after dragging my arse all dishevelled out of bed after the 50th call on my mobile from various Dirty 30, I reluctantly headed toward East Croydon for the meet. I was impressed with the collection of 50 plus heads pottering about as I was greeted with sarcastic comments about the state I was in. "I was fucking working last night, I've only had 2 hours sleep" was my angered response with the added aggression for them to stop the piss taking name of Sommy I've repeatedly told them to quash these past few weeks. Sommy is an abbreviation of Somalian - my comical football friends seems to think I looked Somalian.

During that season we had been pretty busy and gaining possibly a few reluctant words of respect in Hooligan Cyberworld. We had a few good results as well as the usual conflicting versions of skirmishes involving us, QPR for example at Kensington Olympia after Young Billy give their youth spotters a slap. We charged at an even number of QPR down a side road, where later they were giving all sorts of excuses and versions of the event that they had us on the run and we were out of order for slapping one of their main boys' little brother, hey they don't call us dirty for nothing and it's not like we all ganged up on the kid - our Billy was only 17 himself.

Anyway more to the point, Old bill had sprung out from out of nowhere after the roar had gone up and started to set a few suspicious heads into overdrive because old habits die hard with some of the old

281

Nifty 50, when they began to tie up a few incidents of Old Bill sussing out our meets and sniffer dogs turning up at our boozers.

Our suspicions were bang on when it became known that the youth lad we called Fat Lee who lived down the south coast was exposed as the rat. Frankie was onto this fat fuck and asked to borrow the lad's phone the following week and discovered a contact list that read like the A-Z of Hooligan Youth firms, no personal numbers just hooligan mobs and the worst thing is, after the game we were waiting back at the boozer for Fat Lee hoping he had not been spooked by Frankie borrowing his phone. Another youth called Lee returned with disturbing news and told us that during the game Old Bill had collared Fat Lee under the guise that he was in the wrong seat and in the wrong section and abruptly whisked out of Selhurst Park into a police van and away. He has never been seen again.

Good riddance, the grassing fat cunt, because as all the events came to light it made sense now why he was such a busy fucker, ringing people out of the blue and trying to organise drug drop offs at games and stuff like that, constantly asking what firms we were going to have it with, just busy stuff. It also came to light when we were trying to work out why he flipped. It was one of the youth that explained that they had attacked the Jolly Sailor on Norwood high street with Norwich in it, with CCTV all over the gaff and Fat Lee nicked for affray and violent disorder. That was caught on candid camera, he was fucked and decided to try and save his bacon, the fucking wrong'un.

Anyway, as I said, it was a very busy season with all sorts of shit happening and the visit to Derby County that season was no exception. The local cuntstabulary decided that they would be treating us like Nazis treated Jews during the Holocaust, overseen by our Football Intelligence Officer Elmer Fudd. I can't use his real name in case of libel (cunt, fat cunt, wears women's undies). He looked on with a smirk as we were jostled about and marched round to the ground, only to get there and them tell us that we wasn't getting into the game without tickets. So they were marching us back to the station and enjoying their day fucking us about, then they slung us on the first train to London.

Undeterred, we decided to stop off in Leicester to get on the bevvy. I slipped myself away to grab a sneaky toot of H and I was kind of in my usual haze listening to the young'uns with us making some crank calls to some Leicester youth they knew to wind them up that we were on their manor. I remember thinking that we were only 25 handed and knowing baby squad would be able to muster up some boys even if they didn't have a game. "Hope you young'uns are ready if they decide to call it on you know," I had warned them. "I don't want to hear anyone complaining of belly aches". Which looking back would have dawned on them quickly as Frankie came back after a bowl about to report to our other main lad, "I don't know about this mate, there's a few of them and with what we've got I ain't too sure."

There was a Walsall lad with us that day as well, who went on the bowl with Frankie and confirmed a good 40 or so naughty looking Leicester boys were about in one of the bars in town. In truth this wasn't Nifty 50, where we would go in without question, here we weren't 100% confident that we had the quality, this being not so long after getting embarrassed by Stoke's Naughty 40 earlier in the season, one of them bad days at the office when facing up to a quality mob, and many of the youth had back-pedalled. We pretty much had had to have it on our toes, so now after our stance of harassing Leicester over the phone, we had to follow this through, this is why we are here after all.

The next few minutes there was an influx of calls to the youth from Leicester boys with the offer, or maybe confirming whether we really did have the bollocks to come down and make a show. By the 3rd or 4th call it was time everyone knew that this was it, game on and our main lad gave his pep talk to get us all inspired.

"Fuck it, we're fuckin' here now so let's have it with 'em, come on we can do these cunts, but listen… no fucking joking about now, this is it, anyone fucking runs, win, lose or draw, I'll fucking serve them up when we get back home, so if you ain't up for this, fuck off now…"

One of the England lads was with us and fair play, he held his hand up that he wasn't up for it. "Go on then, off you go ta-la" …

Even fairer play to the youth, or maybe it was the threat of getting chopped up when they got back to the manor, they were game and seemed up for it, so we left the boozer and walked up a few yards through the main high street and spotted a gathering of bodies. There they were, baby squad, who must have been thinking this was going to be their day as we spread ourselves across the road. It seemed they had the advantage numbers wise and confirmed our arrival as they sprinted up the road to us. The hit of brown I had earlier was seeping out of me now as the adrenalin took me up another notch as the roar went up, "HERE WE GO, COME ON!"

It was going off wicked as we stood toe to toe with them as makeshift weapons' butcher signs and everything that wasn't nailed down was launched back and forth. Everyone was holding firm and going in, which surprised them and had them backed off, then they put us under a bit of pressure. I remember taking two good clumps before unleashing a bottle at one and drop-kicking another. A few of the youth were raining blows and steaming a couple of theirs to the floor. We began to get the upper hand again. I noticed a couple of bodies on the ground but they were none of ours. The baby squad were now looking at us and hesitant to keep going, we backed them off further and further up the road as we continued looking for more.

It seemed that as a result of them taking a few casualties their confidence seemed to be shot to pieces and a Buddy Holly-looking geezer from the Baby Squad was pleading with us to recover the wounded. The Young twin was shouting back at him to come and get them. We dispatched the remainder of their mob back down the way they came and gave chase on the stragglers. But pretty much everyone was on their toes now as well, after hearing the sirens in the distance, and had me clocking for the odd CCTV camera on show. That had me wondering whether having that boot off there was a big mistake.

We made it back to the station chests all puffed out as I paid dues to the twins and the other young'uns that showed their mettle. We jumped straight on a train back to London. Later we learned of some of our lads who had gone off in the same direction as the Leicester lads when the Old Bill showed up and had to hide out on building sites or in alleyways until the heat died down. Only a few of us got collared that day, including Frankie, who ended up with the right hump after he tried to shake off a few of the youth who had followed him and were clocked by the Old Bill.

It was a blinding off, with several Leicester reportedly wounded and one jooked up, we later heard. But it gave us and the off rave reviews on the ITK site, which was pretty much like hooligan News at Ten at the time. This was one of the good tear-ups that I and most lads enjoyed rather than the 300 v 300 handed jobs that only ever result in handbags. This was an evenly-matched blood and thunder scrap, the kind that usually sorts the wheat from the chaff, and the youth amongst us gave a good account of themselves.

Since we are on the topic of Youth appraisals, like I said, you have your good days and bad days, I've been there, and this lot over the last few seasons were very active making a decent name for themselves. The very top pick of the Dirty 30 youth mob included Young Dan, the Carter boys, Smiler, Lee, Billy and the twins. They were as game as anything, taking it to all-comers.

Young Dan describes it - *Two of the most memorable incidents for me was when 5 of us youth lot bumped into Cardiff that season (2006) under the bridge near Selhurst station. They were in an Old Bill escort. We was going to the Selhurst Arms while the game was on. Bumping into The Soul Crew, they broke out of their escort to get to us, we had it with them for about a minute or so, smashed them all over the gaff, which in fairness, was an even number of mainly youngsters like us. I remember us running up the road after, singing D D D 30. It was a good little tear up, they were game lads though, fair play to them.*

Another little story with the youth lot, again about 15 of us was in the Cambridge Arms the afternoon we were playing Millwall at home (2003). One of their youth lads was calling it on all day with us. We were not sure what to do because we didn't have the numbers and it was Millwall after all. The game was well under way, we were still gathered in the pub, they called us and said they were at Selhurst train station. Obliged to meet them, we said "fuck it let's go!" En route there was a skip, so we all got tooled up. The adrenalin was well kicking in, added to the apprehension of not knowing how many Millwall there were. As we turned the corner to the station, there they all were, spread out all over the road an even number, all shouting 'come on!' We ran at them, they fucking shat themselves as we went at them full pelt. A few of them ran on to the platform and others jumped on to the tracks to get away from us, shitting themselves.

Two pretty good results in my book.

Just to finish off the row with the Baby Squad. Later on after Frankie was slung out of Leicester by their constabulary, he arrived back in London and got lashed up, then got thrown out of the Flying Scotsman after turning on a couple of drinkers in there who were Gooners, who Frankie actually knew if I remember rightly. They were saying "but you know us." He took exception to them giving it muggy Palace and taking the piss. He switched and wanted to fight the world by now and launched a stool onto the optics after starting on the Gooners. Frankie was in cranky mode also for some unknown reason, and he turned on one of our other lads in a taxi, which resulted in the kid jumping out of it while moving. This apparently had Robbie in bits with laughter at Frankie going into his usual liquored up psycho mode on the fella, which Frankie reports he was only joking about.

Brighton and Hove Albion

Our first encounter for years with them was October 2002 when we beat them 5-0 at home. It was pretty much everyone and his dog out that day. We had an Early meet and was holed up in Crystal Palace by 10.30 with a good turnout of 120 lads but Old Bill was on us pretty much all the way within the hour with sniffer dogs and riot shields and everyone section 60d with a few of ours carted off for possession of class A, especially those that didn't use Pete's dreadlocks to hide their stash in like everyone else did. It was tied up in a ponytail and always went undetected during the searches. I think we had joked at the time that he must have had about half a kilo tucked up in there at one point that day.

We also heard reports that Brighton were mobbed up in Clapham Junction so you knew straight away it was heading for a disappointing day as they and us are jostled in escorts before the game, where a few give the usual verbal but no one is making much effort to get out. After the game was the best opportunity to get it on as we have 70 lads gathered in Bensham Manor Road which if we were lucky we could bowl all the way down and come out bang on top of Thornton heath Station and hopefully into Brighton.

Unfortunately for us, Brighton were escorted to Norwood junction instead as we got the call but it was too late to try and head them off as had to come full circle. I remember Face leading a charge as rumours passed down the line that they were here, but we just ran into busy shoppers minding their own business before finally being headed off by riot police at the junction of Whitehorse Road and Thornton Heath high street. That was pretty much game over, with only the odd skirmishes against small pockets of fans in the surrounding areas. The police had done a pretty good job that day and had averted some major disorder.

Fair play to Brighton about an hour after the game they were off their train and through the police lines to confront the few Palace about at East Croydon after the majority of our mob were trapped in a pub surrounded by Old Bill further down the road, so there wasn't much we could do about it. You heard them on the internet chuffed at their little attempt, but it was nothing to get excited about - but they can have that one if they want.

The following season or maybe the same, they were up against Wimbledon but early doors they were making crank calls to one of our main lads saying they were here and taking the piss on our manor. Our lad put in a few calls but couldn't get nothing together early enough to get at them before the game. I got the call when I was out and about with Inch and seeing them by the ground I was out of the car fronting them with a concealed cosh. I got all abuse from them before I was pushed back by Old Bill.

We eventually got 20 to 30 lads together in the Selhurst Arms and took a walk up just before the final whistle and lay in wait inside the park gates just adjacent to South Norwood Library. Just before that we had a little skirmish when some of their barmys decided they wanted to have a little pop. They knew we were Palace but we offered them politely to fuck off with a few flying kicks. Lying in wait, we saw a group of Burberry and Stone Island clad boys bowling up the road and jumped out on them, tooled up with pieces of fence and bottles. A few of them bounced up and down, before realising their pals had left them. We chased a few of them up the road as another group at the Clock Tower realised what was going on and turned in our direction. They did fuck all when fronted with a few slaps dished out.

I was still pretty much on my own chasing some Brighton pricks all the way past Selhurst Station. This is another incident which is usually the topic of Frankie and the other boys' humour when they take the piss, calling me Yifter the Shifter, saying I must have thought I was an Ethiopian marathon runner after continuing to give chase. What I didn't realise as I gave chase after Brighton melts was that all the others had been grabbed by gavvers because they were 'known risk supporters' and a few got nicked. I don't know what the fuck Old Bill would have had to arrest them for because I don't know what the charge is for chasing people, but fuck all else happened and it wasn't surprising to hear them silly cunts with the old chestnut

"That wasn't our main mob!"

Funny that! How come previously they were making crank calls and giving the big one about being on the manor taking the piss, but when we got our numbers together and tried to call to meet them after the game, radio silence is all we heard? 15 lads bouncing up and down

288

dressed in hooligan clobber is fair game in my eyes so they can carry on with their bitching on the internet and boy did they bitch. Don't get me wrong, there are some good lads over there and I have plenty of time for people like Paul C, who by all accounts said fairs fair whenever they've been turned over by us, like the Crescent Arms incident.

In 2004 Brighton lads landed on the manor and into the Crescent Arms un-detected with a good turnout of 40 game lads and shortly after their arrival a battle ensued against 20 odd Palace who were in the Duke of Cambridge pub opposite. It was a good battle where Brighton had the upper hand. Our boys had to put on a strong rear guard action. When we got the call we were already on the move from the Saints and Sinners Pub in Mayday Road where our main lads had organised us to meet in.

We made a bit of a schoolboy error by mobbing up in central Croydon initially, but were discovered relatively quickly. We disappeared for a couple of hours and regrouped in the Saints to keep as low a profile as possible until Brighton were mobbed up and ready, so with a good 70 heads plotted away we began making our move. The phone was going off a few times to Frankie and a couple Youth at the time because Brighton were putting the lads at the Cambridge under a severe bit of pressure and all the time I was hearing "We're coming" and "hold them there were right on ya."

It was funny, I was driving Frankie mad all the way down when he told us Brighton were here and I thought he was leading us all on a wind up. I was fucked and we were marching like Romans what seemed like 50 miles from Mayday Road to the bottom of Pawsons Road.

One of our lads Mickey, said it was a sight for sore eyes just as they were getting done to see us bouncing across the road sending Brighton lads scattering and clambering over each other trying to get back into the Crescent as a baying mob, a mixture of main Dirty 30 and Dirty 30 Youth attack them viciously, bottles and street objects where picked up and launched into the retreating Brighton, leaving casualties on the pavement and the rest trapped, some hiding under tables in the pub as others were fighting for their lives defending the door, trying to hold the Palace lads at bay.

The mob out of the Duke, held their hands up and admitted that Brighton were on the verge of a result until we showed up, like the cavalry with trumpets blaring, then smashed them where I was also trumped by Frankie getting hold of their top nose, Beaky, and I was half on the floor with laughter as I watched Frankie having him by the scruff of the neck giving him a few slaps and him trying to squirm away. Cunt couldn't sort out his footing and got trapped in the doorway where him and a Christopher Biggins lookalike took a fair old clumping with Frankie caught the Beak plum on that gigantic hooter of his.

What was also good about that day was hearing how gutted the current Football Intelligence Officer, aka Elmer Fudd, was. He foolishly had 3 of our other main boys under surveillance, having foiled our plans in central Croydon earlier, only to hear the news over his radio that Palace hooligans had just caused major disorder on his patch. Whilst he's shuffling his cock and wasting his time watching them having a quiet drink in Anerley our lads had already received the blow-by-blow account and were now teasing him as his jaw drops and he turns red on hearing the news.

"Ha-ha, it's all over you fat cunt" our lad laughs out as the police van he's in springs into action and fucks off up the road.

That was a good turn out that day. Brighton, left gutted that they'd got turned over, got things together after the game, but police were all over it now. Frankie even got nicked head butting a Brighton lad that fronted him. But we still managed another result when 25 South Croydon and old Nifty 50 attacked another mob of Brighton in South Norwood. I also have to mention as well, Brighton's main boy, the Christopher Biggins lookalike, had a terrible day that day, especially after he met the left hook of one of our lads called Sniper after he was racially abused him. The poor fucker, he was all over the local paper the following week after having to receive hospital treatment after a bit of roadside first aid. He was sparked out cold and reportedly given mouth to mouth by a heroic Palace supporter who was on the scene at the time.

So that was pretty much our day in anyone's book, but in fairness to Brighton credit where credit is due and all that, they had decent numbers out but not enough when it mattered because we had bare quality out that day.

Luton Town

It got personal with Luton, which indirectly culminated in some close ties with Tottenham being severed after the fallout. It all started after a pre-season friendly in 2003. A few of us made the trip, a few old heads but mainly youth who were playing up all day, including getting the local Asian community upset as the pub got surrounded with some beards that had to get moved on by OB after they mistook us for EDL. We bowled about with not much offered by Luton, who in all fairness probably were not expecting anything from us that day, but some fresh young Luton pup fronted us at one point as we walked back after the game and took a slap off one of the youth. Surprisingly this little slap on this turd, for whatever reason, initiated a catalogue of crank calls to one of our main lads who wasn't even in Luton that day, and this was going on for a few months and over a couple of seasons.

One day the main Tottenham face from the Danny Dyer show brought this lad onto the manor drinking in boozers in and around Crystal Palace, which pissed off a few of the boys to say the least. He did apologise in the end about it saying it was inconsiderate. A sitdown was called with Frankie and other Nifty boys, where they had said it would be the same as us flaunting Chelsea or Arsenal in front of him, but he still tried to defend the kid, saying he wasn't the one making the threatening calls. That set the tone because our lads were certain he was aware that this Luton fella had crank called one of ours on a few occasions, threatening to burn his house down with his kids in it and all that. It got very personal, so bringing this cunt onto the manor was unforgivable.

I remember even one cup game we was at home to Doncaster and had stayed in the pub when suspiciously this Luton Youth bod and 2 others diverted from their match at Charlton and landed on us. I say it was suspicious because there were only a few of us left in the pub at the time, so did he get a heads up, or was he just a total loon intent on vengeance?

Announcing their intentions, they were duly attacked, as Frankie introduced him to a Budweiser bottle and a kick up the arse. I remember banging one in the face just as another Palace lad said good night to him with a bar stool and left him ironed out on the pavement. The 3rd and final one had already crossed the road. He had seen enough, as gavvers turn up we've also had it away as the landlord was up in arms about his furniture getting damaged.

We couldn't believe the kahunas on this cunt coming down to us in such a way, but it was good because they started off an enjoyable night in the end as we later mobbed up to meet that night's opponents Doncaster, who surprisingly later on were put in the Albion by the Old Bill, who must have known we would be looking to plot back in there after the game. We had all bowled up asking Donny lads to have a walk up the road, but they refused, so the ensuing battle outside the pub saw missiles from the boozer and a few slaps dished out where later they were reporting on ITK or one of them sites about some spade waving a blade about as if he was Zorro. It made me chuckle when I heard that.

After the handbags under the glaring cameras viewing that section of South Norwood High Street we pretty much all split up, some of us paranoid that our local Old Bill had set the whole thing up and hiding in back gardens until the heat wore off. Me and Pete stopped further up the road and tried our best to just look like a couple of bredrins hanging out on a street corner, which must have worked, as the Old Bill looked right at us and carried on. It must have been the way Pete had fashioned his jeans and dreadlocks after hiding his baseball cap and Stone Island badge to make himself look as ragamuffin as possible. We had a good old laugh about it, relieved that we had bamboozled them.

When the Palace Luton fixture came up in 2005 entering the Albion after the game 12-15 or so Luton who also had some Yids with them apparently, were in there. Frankie had fronted them as this Luton Youth prick is here again, mentioning our main lad by name with the intention of doing him something making it known he was tooled up as well. Anyway one of them, he was Tottenham I'm sure I was told, was giving it proper big potatoes and totally disrespecting the gaff, calling us Palace mugs and saying we're out of our league that there were main faces here, top Luton MIGs or some bollocks. Sometimes a reputation can stop people dead in their tracks and melt, I suppose he thought he's a top Yid face and usually has a crowd intimidated with his presence. I was having none of this shit don't give a fuck who he was. "WHO THE FUCK IS THIS CUNT?" I've questioned as I'm looking around wondering who would have the answer to this quiz "FUCKING COMING IN HERE GIVING ALL THAT TALK. CUNT FUCK YOU!"

He was right in my face at this point, swinging and smacking me plum on the jaw. Anyway, that was it, I've put it on this cunt and the whole pub just went up. We ended up chasing them off down the Portland road and I remember after Frankie went for one of the main Luton boys with a bar stool, some of the Youth smashing him quite severely just outside the pub door and the ones on their toes not even looking back for this poor bastard. Now I don't know what was said on the internet re the incident, but it was played down a little and even reports that Luton had this big mob down that took the piss all day long. That may have been the case but certainly not in the Albion that day. I don't need to say no more. The 'real' main Tottenham lad was on the phone making enquiries with Frankie and giving a version of the events that was reported back to him which was totally different from ours. That's part of the game, though we're always the underdogs, which is fine, but I know with all our game lads on top form, MIGs, Yids, whoever, we can have a row.

Personally despite everything I've always been in awe of the Yids, seeing them up close on a few occasions, a top mob and one of the best in the 90s that I had seen. Now by no means am I playing the race card here, but just like with the Zulus, I love it when I see a mob with black lads going in, it makes me proud, black power and all that.

Also knowing main lads like the Desire boys, who I would have a laugh and a joke with when working for them at their promotions, always teasing them that I was going to bring a firm over and have it with them, all light-hearted stuff, but all this other stuff had nothing to do with me anyway in that sense. I respected the fact that there was a connection with them from years ago and they still are sweet with certain names over there I believe, but as time went on there have been other accusations and counter accusations of incidents which I was told were documented in the Massive Attack book. I had heard a different version of events. It's at a point now where all sides have just washed their hands of each other, but seeing that the fella concerned isn't an author the fact he got done with a glass from behind was what they were mostly upset about and it probably could have been squashed. That's just my personal opinion.

Not long after being released from prison in 2010 I saw the Yid author at a do. It felt at the time that he was a little hostile towards me when I said hello (told me to fuck off), I don't really know why and this was before I learned of the bad blood that had been brewing for a while. After I left the gaff he later turned on some Palace youth who were out in this bar I was at in Herne hill that night. Him and some of his pals attacked them and hospitalised one, which I think was a bit of a dig to prove a point or to send a message to the Palace lads he had fallen out with.

Charlton Athletic

I fucking hate these cunts, I already mentioned about the Charlton incident at the Goat house in Penge, and there have been one or two incidents mainly during the 80s when we were ground sharing when we have got it on and have been evenly matched as far as any tear-ups I had been involved with, but you wouldn't have thought it when you listen to half of them pikey cunts. Now in recent seasons at theirs, like in 2007, we had a decent sized mob descend undetected in Lewisham and put the word out that we were 'about' and where to meet them, only to be confronted with "Why are you in Lewisham?"

To lose the Old Bill you retard... and then hearing bollocks about we should be coming to them, so with no proper instructions to meet them anywhere sensible other than "come to them" we left and made our way over but found it unbelievable that they still have some of their people run their gums to all that would listen to them on forums. What else could we do, as we have now had to leave Lewisham 100 handed to get to Charlton only to get wrapped up by gavvers, and the fact one of ours who is local went on drive-bys to find that lot had already reported back earlier that they were already wrapped up themselves by Old Bill in some boozer in Woolwich. Then they are all over the forums slating us and in the same breath claim that they had Millwall out with them.

By all accounts they did make a good attempt late on after the game. We were already marched back to Lewisham when we were put in a pub and surrounded by Old Bill. I'd left the main escort and gone into the Yard food shop when I see 15 odd Charlton bounce across the road. Just as I step out of the shop I'm suddenly set upon by them & with a few other Palace lads, and we end up scrapping as Old Bill are all over it in a flash. So as well as losing my beef patty I'm now on the pavement in cuffs thanks to silly bollocks rushing me in close proximity of the Old Bill, who had already squashed the chance of any disorder by surrounding the pub the main Palace contingent were in, so nice one lads, your timing impeccable and you owe me £1.70 for my patty.

I do also remember early doors one season around 87 when they did come down with a very impressive firm. There were reports that there was a very good lot mobbed up in the Port Manor pub, but I was still in bed when it happened because much as I love a row, I'd still take a bunk up over violence any day of the week, so I can only go by the reports off my pals when I met them later that day, who admittedly confessed to a poor show from us that day. They do also like to claim a particular victory when, fair play to them, one pre-season friendly in 2002 they bought a good mob down, about 40 or so, and caught out a few Palace who had little out that could be classed as a mob and left a few wounded in the Wetherspoons on South Norwood high street that day. Like I said we had fuck all out and underestimated them, but it all counts as a result I suppose.

Just to make it clear, I'm not trying to say Charlton are a shit mob or anything like that, because most sensible lads know that pretty much anyone can have their day of glory and in my humble opinion, it doesn't have to be a scene from Braveheart to class as a good row, but it gets up my nose when all you hear is them carry on as though... what was it some cunt said in some book or another? "chasing shadows" or some bollocks, as if all they do is turn up, run us and take the piss at every opportunity and we never want to have it with them. It seems at times as though they consider themselves the runt of the family compared to their neighbouring Millwall counterparts (from Kent) and always trying to prove a point. Fuck knows why because Millwall class them same league as us, so fuck knows why the clueless cunts among them give it Charlie big potatoes and go on like they are London's number one firm.

In regards to the Sydenham incident in 2007, I hold my hands up to the fact that many were out of order that day, including myself, although I never slapped anyone on the actual train, other than grimace and threaten the odd shirt. Others acted like raving lunatics, but that's neither here nor there and I admit my state of mind was fucked at that period in time, but please don't buy into British Transport Police's media spin that women, children & old age pensioners were attacked and a one-legged man got battered with his own prosthetics, because they are talking cack. I have history with BTP and they love to put a spin on things, as with the botched Inta Natty investigation I mentioned earlier in the book.

Admittedly we took a liberty on clueless Charlton fans who unfortunately, got lairy and got slapped. If I'm on a train and see a mob on the platform, the last thing I'm going to do is give it the big'un out the window, especially if I'm just an innocent scarfer as they so sweetly put it. You wouldn't do it would you?

They were on the train, maybe not their main boys which was bad planning on our part. The call came in from what I heard that they were on that train, but banging on windows giving all the wanker sign and all that bollocks. As the doors opened they foolishly had the front to call it on just as more Palace had entered the platform and got done. They knew they were fucked and clambered over Joe public to get away. It's no wonder it seemed as though some mindless thugs were on the rampage on a well organised "pincer movement" as the BTP described it. It resulted in 16 of us, including myself, serving time.

Fucking pincer movement? I thought it was more crouching Charlton, flying kung fu kicks. I guess with the way it all ended up you can add whatever spin you like, as a small minority of, tanked up on booze and gear, were bang out of order and got over excited on the odd Charlton when little resistance was offered, but the description of the incident is way off. And let's get it right, bad as it may seem, it doesn't take much for Joe Public and the media to scream outrage about hooligans. Charlton should know. Singing insulting songs on a train about a black kid getting murdered in Eltham would also get the BTP on your case looking to lock people up, so let's not get on any high horses here.

Facebook Firms

Since the sentencing, Palace as a mob were still at it on a few occasions, Dirty 30 including the few Nifty 50 faces and some of the Younger lot still got a little bit of action, and Arsenal away during

2013/14 season saw a small contingent take on Gooners outside one of their main boozers before being well outnumbered and told by the Gooners to fuck off back to Penge.

There is also the new 'men in black' that suddenly appeared down here calling themselves the Ultras. Although many might argue that these lads are not part of any hooligan group but kind of act out a pro-Italian style approach with the big flags, masked-out faces and flares they have been, I've been told, involved in bits and pieces with rival groups.

The younger casuals also are still having the odd skirmish against some of the usual suspects and the Old Bill CCTV captured images of Palace lads away against Peterborough and Brighton at Kings Cross causing violent disorder, awarding profile cases for the Met and Transport Old Bill, resulting in a few young Palace serving some bird and match banning orders. Nowadays, for me, apart from the odd phone call I get for meets for a beer before games, I've pretty much knocked it all on the head. The good old days are dead and gone, although the great atmosphere down at Palace is second to none at the moment so I'll happily continue to venture down there to support the Eagles.

As far as the violence is concerned, with all the posturing and posing, general Old Bill overkill and silly sentences, It just isn't worth the effort any more. It will never be the same again, but we may still always turn out for the main ones like Grimsby, Leicester and Stockport County, seeing that there's no joy with them other lot that are supposed to be our main rivals any more. So after this, maybe you will get the usual clueless divs and the never been active wannabes still running their mouths over the internet regarding Palace. When I look at Facebook and the other social media and see the profile of some of these supposedly 'ITK' individuals it does make me chuckle a little bit. I will tend to leave them to it though, there's no point responding anyway.

As far as I am concerned CCTV and lads posing just for the sake of Facebook likes is not what I'm into. The days when we were facing good mobs ready to get into a good old dingdong in groups of 20-30 is not fashionable enough to get the old SI badge ripped off or the Adidas Gazelles to get ruined in claret. It is not for most of the 'hide behind the 150 lads in a police' wrapper type hooligan, so I might as well just end it here.

Just one more thing, I thought it only fair to add the BTP and media version of the Sydenham events, just so nobody thinks I'm taking a biased opinion, but more importantly, to reiterate for any of those who have any reservations that the Old Bill and media never lie.

EPILOGUE

So there you have it. I'm going to bring my story to an end here, although the adventure still continues. My outlook and perspective have totally changed since being sentenced for 3 years and 2 months by Judge Stephen Robbins, which in a twisted sort of way, was probably the best thing that could have happened to me. December 5th 2008 was the start of my long road back, and one particular gentleman I should be thankful for crossing paths with. No, not the fat cunt Officer Elmer Fudd that reigned us all in.

No, luckily for me, there are some honest and decent people within the prison and legal system that helped me recover, especially a prison officer by the name of William Barnet. His coaching and belief in me set me in good stead. I'm really appreciative of the hard work, commitment and discipline at the Therapeutic Community at Channing Wood and the many words of wisdom that influenced the way I am today. "Look around you, Carl, " he would say. "Something got you here but I know, and you know yourself, you are not like everyone else in here." It's not rocket science and nothing comes without hard work.

It was seeking attention that got me here. From a very young age I always wanted to be at the centre of it all, whether it be the attention from the women in my life, or with my pals showing off and always being loud and the joker, sticking the boot in at football and showing the rest of the lads that I was one of their own.

HMP Channings Wood prison in Devon also helped me get away from the institutionalised inmates and the open access to whatever high you required at Wandsworth and Bristol and made me realise I had to change my perspective and habits unless I wanted to be eaten up by this prison system like the rest of these cats. One particular prick in there from Nottingham was wanting to test me as soon as I stepped foot inside Bristol. Prison is no easy ride and in my case it is another story in itself, but who needs another prison story? It's a shit place to be and should be avoided at all cost. I had my fair share of confrontations and intimidation that pushed me to the edge during my time in both. William Barnet and Channings Wood prison saved me and helped me to reach the other side, it probably saved my life too.

Since my release and rehabilitation I have had a lot to be thankful for. I still have the love of my friends and family, which I treasure more than the fact that I could and should have had more reward. I still love the music and feel proud to have been one of the foundations of a prominent underground movement that has brought success to many individuals that I hold dear.

I miss the days when everything was so raw and untainted I guess, but I don't want to sound bitter that I've not gained any great financial benefit from it. It's rather how a few continue to judge me on past mistakes, which I guess I have to take stock and come to terms with. I have proud and fond memories of the way things were, when it was all fresh. That includes the clubbing experience, because I don't care what has come after, there is no better feeling I get than when I glimmer back on seeing the lights and atmosphere during the acid house party days. I would love to just go back and experience that feeling just one more time.

As Frank Sinatra sang, "regrets, I've had a few", but all in all I can't complain. I should really be counting my blessings. I feel lucky to be alive to have one more crack at it to bring some good to the world and end on a high (not literally).

Looking at my life through the years in these chapters, I've tried to be the best at what I was, what I wanted to be and what I wanted to do. Some may say I'm nothing but a drug dealing skaghead thug - fair enough, it took a 2nd prison sentence for me to look at myself and ask myself, who am I, and who are my actions affecting most? My journey to be cleansed of my addiction was a lengthy process, but I've reached the end.

My first letter to my pals was to Pete. I felt I had let him down badly. He would never say it to me but I know I did. He was like my brother during the late 80s. We were inseparable and I miss the days when we were out on the prowl hunting women and cracking jokes with each other and the rest of the boys in the clubs, the happy times at acid house parties before the darker times at football and with my pharmaceuticals business. There were so many laughs along the way when the funniest things would be the most silliest things to other grown adults, and even small children for that matter.

A pack of dogs were chasing a solitary cat, that was what Pete, Inch, Nifty and me witnessed as we drove during the early hours down Purley way. Dogs chasing a cat, what's funny about that? But to us it was a funniest thing in world to witness and we still piss ourselves about it to this day. My point is, there are times with your boys that you catch a joke, but it's only yourselves that would get it and it's the silly little things like that that I miss the most.

Everyone is grown up now. We have all come through difficult times at some point and I still share a few laughs and a beer with many of them today. Face and Killa will always be family, we still crack the same old jokes and have the same old arguments. Most are settled down with children. Nifty has a lawyer wife and no longer ducks and dives, less Harry the Axe, more Larry the Lamb, and has a successful legitimate business. Pete Nice has been a real inspiration, when we compare how we used to view life as young men to how we view life now. Discussions of marriage and having children we would scoff at with a 'fuck that shit' attitude. Now when I see him and his family, I'm so happy that Pete has found a strong, loving woman like Ashley. He has himself a beautiful and successful wife, 2 beautiful children and has his hands are full with his life (and a bigger Derby) but he took all this time helping me get my thoughts on paper, how fucking cool is he?

I wrote to Pete when I was in Wandsworth and suggested that I should write a book about my life, after I was on the verge of depression with my predicament. We discussed it in letters, just maybe to have a focus on something and we have talked about it ever since my release from prison. Now, finally, here it is.

I still feel overwhelmed at the end of the day. I seem to be playing catch up now just to remain on my own 2 feet. I have a few projects on the go with a young mentor, DJ Verdict of Mastermind record label and inner-city youth worker projects in Liverpool where I now reside, which keeps me busy and out of trouble. Hopefully this is my happy ending, I think I deserve it. I now have a lot to behold for the future and a lot to reminisce about from the past. It's a past I wouldn't change for the world, except for one thing, I would have left that dirt the fuck alone. Then maybe, who knows where I would be today? It's been hectic and I've learned many lessons.

"To err is human, to forgive divine" is the saying, and I hope I have done enough to show many people I have changed even though some find it hard to remember the good I've done along the way. But what hasn't changed is that I won't bow down, so you take me as I am or shake my hand, I wish you well and stroll on. Life's too short, but it's been long and eventful. And it's been fucking mental.

THE END

GLOSSARY

Bandulu - scams

Bins - a pair of glasses, shortened from binoculars

Bit of poke - wages, earn some money

Bone - crack

Bloodclaart - Jamaican curse word

Brass – prostitute

Bruck out - let your hair down, have a good dance in a club

Butchers - butcher's hook - have a look

Chiv - knife

Chirpse – chat up a bird

Chored – shop lifted or stolen

Combo - Double date

Cory – male organ of reproduction

The dark side - tempted by the pussy

Derby – Derby Kelly - belly

Didgy - nervous/paranoid and scared

Disco biscuit – a brand of ecstasy tablet

Dorises - females

Drum - House

Duppy - Ghost

Garms (garments) – fashionable clothes

Gavvers - Pikey tongue for police

Gooners - Arsenal supporters

Going on the lam – running away to lie low

Grant Mitchell moment - being the shoulder to cry on to get a shag

Gyal – girl

Hampton (Wick) - prick

Jedi - remain monogamous, be a good boy and not be tempted

Jooked - stabbed

Hitting the cherry – using a crack pipe

Lemonade - Spade, derogatory name for black

The Manor - Your home town, where you live

Moody - fake

On the Rory - Rory McGrath/half, to crouch down out of sight

Plating – cunnilingus - licking pussy

Play a Luther Vandross - saddened by a relationship breakup

Party Like its 1999 - go on a mad one all weekend

Puff – cannabis

Quim / velvet cavity - vagina

Riderism - losing out on a girl to a famous individual

Silent journey – to travel a great distance for a bunk up

Skag – heroin

    Skank – dance to heavy music, ie dub or drum & bass;
    to rob someone

Sort - an attractive woman

Terry Waite Country - Thamesmead - Abbey Wood, SE London Area

Toe curler - girl who's great in bed

Tom (Foolery) – jewellery

Yids – Tottenham's firm/Yid Army - Tottenham fans